F[...] [...]y

Not [...] my

friends of the dedication

Brenda Collins.

VICTORIAN VISIONARIES

Brenda Colloms

VICTORIAN VISIONARIES

Constable

London

First published in Great Britain 1982
by Constable and Company Limited
10 Orange Street, London WC2H 7EG
Copyright © 1982 by Brenda Colloms
ISBN 0 09 463370 3
Set in Garamond 11pt
Printed in Great Britain
by Ebenezer Baylis & Son Ltd
The Trinity Press, Worcester, and London

To my friends at
The Working Men's College

Contents

Illustrations

Acknowledgements

In my book list I have recorded only the main authorities consulted in addition to the books, journals and pamphlets mentioned in the text or in the Chapter notes. A good deal of the material is in the library and archives of the Working Men's College and I should like to thank the library staff there, past and present, for their help.

I would also particularly like to express my gratitude to Lionel Colloms and to Gillian Hughes for their interest, advice and encouragement in reading the manuscript at various stages of production.

Introducing the Company

This is a book for the general reader which tells the story of a group of friends known in history as the Christian Socialists.[1] They worked together in a definable movement which is usually taken as starting in 1848 and ending in 1854, a view which does less than justice to the men, to their aims and to their achievements. This present account examines the early Christian Socialists in human terms as the product of relationships and interactions within a group of honest, likeable men who saw something wrong in the world they lived in and tried in various ways to set it right.

The name was given them by Frederick Denison Maurice, an Anglican clergyman who resolutely refused to be their leader. It was his hatred and mistrust of political factions and organizations which prevented the Christian Socialists from becoming much more than an influential pressure group drawing attention to social injustices and suggesting possible solutions, but none the less it was a group which represented the conscience of the age. Their activities began in 1848 when the formidable quartet of Maurice, John Ludlow, Charles Kingsley and Thomas Hughes gathered around them a number of energetic, idealistic young men who were in hearty revolt against Victorian materialism.

Except for Maurice and a later member, Edward Vansittart Neale, the Christian Socialists were all in their late twenties or early thirties, old enough to be effective and young enough to be vigorous. Their friendship and shared campaigns for social reforms became the formative experience of their lives and although after 1860 they tended to branch out in separate and individual ways, each man bore the imprint of his Christian Socialist vision until the day he died. They had hoped to build a just and satisfying society, their kind of socialism, through work, example and education, awakening the middle class to their responsibilities and the working class to their potential. Class warfare would be replaced by class reconciliation and competition by co-operation.

Coleridge and Carlyle were their background influences and a sense of social responsibility was accompanied by belief in Christianity, so that the ideas of early French Socialists were assimilated in their progressive Christianity. They pre-dated by more than thirty years the collectivist Fabian Society, an interval of time which explains why these hard-working and self-sacrificing visionaries seem to have achieved relatively little compared with the politically committed reformers of later generations. The Rev Stewart Headlam, of the second generation of Christian Socialists, shows a direct link between Maurice, whose ideas formed him, and the Fabian Society, of which he was a member for almost forty years, and on its executive committee for three.

Most of the early Christian Socialists came from Puritan stock, which was hardly a coincidence. The Puritan strain is an important feature of the English national character distinguishable before the sixteenth century, and it crops up repeatedly in the history of social reform. Happily the Christian Socialists displayed it in a pleasantly free and sympathetic manner with very little of the harshness and hypocrisy which bedevils many Puritan movements.

They were born, one might say, with a predilection for social service and several of them had also undergone a severe emotional experience, often the loss of a dearly loved relative, which they could not endure except by making a token sacrifice themselves. It manifested itself in reform campaigns carried on with such openness that the Christian Socialists became marked men denied the promotion or worldly success which their energy, intellect and conscientiousness merited. They were quite defiantly optimistic even when disillusion and depression lurked round every corner and their idealism had a strongly romantic flavour, making them the moral counterparts of the Pre-Raphaelite artists. Those two interesting aspects of Victorian creativity met briefly in the Working Men's College in the 1850s and in the next generation were splendidly united in the work and philosophy of William Morris.

To the general public the Christian Socialist movement was epitomized by Maurice and popularized by Kingsley. 'I think this will explain a good deal of Maurice,' declared Kingsley, speaking of his novel *Yeast*. Indeed, Maurice was a complex man, much given to paradox, who needed a good deal of explaining. His friend, John Sterling, said Maurice was the humblest man he had ever met, but that he had the haughtiest intellect he had ever known. His intellectual distinction was obvious from his student days at Cambridge and the secret and exclusive Apostles' Club, just started, considered him to be a founder member, helping to create its tradition of argument and academic brilliance.

Maurice believed that he was born to speak the truth to the world at large, and that in order to speak freely he needed to be free and independent. On the other hand, he also believed it was quite wrong to force his opinions on other people—after all, he might be wrong!—so he continually modified his train of thought until it became so complicated that he was frequently praised by individuals of quite opposite opinions to his own under the mistaken impression that Maurice was supporting their own prejudices and beliefs. Others complained that it was hard to fathom his meaning and that all they really wanted from him was a plain 'yes' or 'no'.

He had a magical talent for drawing out the best in people. Nobody wanted Mr Maurice to see them at less than their very best. On one occasion when he was staying at a country house a fine lady's maid, normally known for her supercilious behaviour, was discovered cleaning his boots. She explained she had never before met anyone like Maurice. He treated her so chivalrously that she felt she was a lady and she yearned to show her gratitude. She had no gift to give him so she cleaned his boots instead!

Few men or women could hope to match Maurice's appealing grace, certainly not his devoted lieutenant, Ludlow, who hid his essential kindliness behind such a stern exterior that Tom Hughes nicknamed him 'Old Gruff'. Ludlow was as religious as Maurice but much less tolerant. He was ready to impose authority upon others and did everything he could, quite unsuccessfully, to persuade Maurice to become leader of a new political party. Ludlow was born to be the man behind the desk, the prompter from the shadows, and for all his organizational gifts he was unable to step into the limelight and assume a leadership role.

Kingsley was too impulsive, too quixotic and burdened with too many family responsibilities to be a leader. Besides, he had a

Hampshire parish to take care of and the early Christian Socialists were most definitely a London-based group.

The fourth member of the quartet, stalwart, unassuming Hughes, was far too modest to go against Maurice and start a political party, although he was always ready to put his time and money at the service of the various causes.

Varied these certainly were, fitting into education or co-operation in a broad sense. Maurice was a pioneer in the field of girls' education and he helped set up in 1848 the first important girls' school, Queen's College, Harley Street. Then he and his younger followers started a night school in a slum part of Blooms-bury and followed that in 1854 with the pioneering adult educational establishment, the Working Men's College.

The Christian Socialist vision was of a believing, caring society in which the cruelties of capitalist industry could be eliminated by the creation of producer co-operatives which would teach men to work together in co-operation and brotherhood. The group of friends had been made aware of poverty through, as much as anything, Henry Mayhew's articles on London work and the London poor and they borrowed the idea of producer co-operatives from the early French socialists, with possibly a dash of Robert Owenism.

Their achievements fanned out in all directions, from the co-operative movement generally and the early trade unions, to sanitary reform, slum clearance and settlement work. Hughes had connections with the United States and Ludlow was interested in India and in Continental socialism. Frederick James Furnivall, another zealous recruit, made such a success of his activities in the Working Men's College that he sallied forth into literature, and almost single-handed founded half a dozen learned literary societies. He was a dynamic assistant in the concept and organization of the mammoth *New English Dictionary*. John Ruskin established a fine art department at the Working Men's College, helped by Dante Gabriel Rossetti, and although one could never call Ruskin a Christian Socialist in the Maurician sense, his contact with working-class students changed his social outlook and led him to the philosophies he expounded in *Unto This last* and *Fors Clavigera*. Ruskin was rich and he could afford to finance project after project, if he judged them socially worthy. Amongst these were Octavia Hill's slum housing reforms.

Another Christian Socialist of great brilliance and sensitivity was Charles Blachford Mansfield, a chemist who was hailed as a successor to Michael Faraday at the Royal Institution. He died in an accident whilst preparing benzol samples for the Paris Exhibition of 1855, but had he lived his patented processes would have made him rich and under his guidance the Working Men's College would have possessed a science department equal to its famous art department.

Most of these Christian Socialists were middle-class professional men but they had one genuine aristocrat, Lord Goderich (as Lord Ripon, he would one day be Viceroy of India), born at No 10 Downing Street. His Christian Socialism gradually wore off but his personal friendship with Hughes was a lasting one, and so was his belief in the co-operative movement. The movement had another 'swell', Cuthbert Ellison, a friend of Thackeray and of Tom Taylor, and a member also of Disraeli's 'Young England' circle. The young men earned their livelihoods in London and pursued their visions in their spare time as unpaid volunteer organizers and propagandists. Cambridge became an important secondary centre for Christian Socialist ideas because Daniel and Alexander Macmillan, the booksellers, were disciples of Maurice, and their bookshop became a centre for Christian Socialist sympathizers. When the brothers took up publishing they took most of the Christian Socialist writers on their list, a principled decision which also helped to make their business profitable as Kingsley, Hughes and Maurice all became very successful authors.

The Christian Socialists were quirky individualists, innocently convinced that time would prove their theories and their dreams correct. The visions which look so Utopian today were considered sane and practical by them. Hughes naïvely believed that you only had to exhibit the model of a good society for all decent men and women, of every class, to start building it.

While they lived, the Christian Socialists were highly controversial and subject to bitter attacks. The middle and upper class attacked them in 1849 and 1850 for co-operating with the moderate Chartists, and the militant and extremist Chartists, who were atheist and revolutionary, attacked them for the same reason. Industrialists and shopkeepers attacked them for their work with trade unionists and co-operators. Marxists attacked them on the grounds that their activities helped soften class antagonism and by their contributions to improvements in working-class life they prevented or postponed a British working-class revolution. Beatrice Potter, in her history of the co-operative movement, was so prejudiced against them that she did not give them credit for the years of effort members like Neale and Hughes put into it.

After Maurice died in 1872, followed by Kingsley in 1875, interest in the Christian Socialists revived for a new generation of thinking men and women. If Maurice did nothing else, he made it impossible for the Anglican Church to ignore social problems. An era of cheap reprints and of adult and self-education brought Christian Socialist ideals and activities to a far greater public than had been possible in the struggling days of 1849 and 1850, and indeed two of the original Christian Socialists, Ludlow and Furnivall, lived to carry their beliefs and criticisms well into the twentieth century.

The Making of Maurice

From the year of Nelson and Trafalgar, through the troubled post-war period: the first Parliamentary Reform Act of 1832, and the social reforms following it; the social and economic unrest which culminated in the 'Year of Revolutions', 1848.

The story starts with Frederick Denison Maurice who was, like Coleridge,[1] a questing spirit, and a complex man who needs to be studied in the context of his family. The Maurices, of Welsh extraction, were Puritans during the Civil War and remained so after the Restoration. Maurice's grandfather was a farmer and Presbyterian minister who sent his son, Michael Maurice, to Hoxton Academy, the famous school for Dissenters. At that time it was run by converts to Joseph Priestley's new Unitarianism who despised the old-fashioned Puritanism, and young Michael automatically imbibed the Unitarian ideas where religious faith merged into philosophical concepts. One day, honest and sincere, he informed his father that although he still planned to become a minister, he would be a Unitarian and not a Presbyterian. His outraged parent promptly disinherited him, a foreseen but none the less distressing action. It did not, of course, change Michael Maurice.

He grew up remarkably tolerant, convinced that every man had the right to believe what his heart and soul told him was true, but the word 'toleration' always irritated him, and he said it reeked of cant and hypocrisy. He was quiet, patient and hopeful, believing that given the time he could convert the whole world to Unitarianism. It is hard to see what grounds he had for that hope, since Unitarianism was frequently identified with advanced political opinions and aroused prejudice and resentment. Joseph

Priestley's house had been sacked by a reactionary mob during the 'Church and King' riots in Birmingham, to the horror of Michael Maurice.

In 1794 Priestley emigrated to Pennsylvania, and Michael Maurice moved to Yarmouth, a well-known centre for Unitarianism, where he made friends with a rich family named Hurry, also Unitarians, and before the year was out he married one of the daughters, Priscilla. The rift with his own family was more than compensated for by his new relatives, who were loving and generous. Priscilla's brother lent the newly-weds a manor house near Lowestoft where they lived in some style. Michael Maurice tutored pupils who boarded with them. Six children were born to the Maurices of whom John Frederick Denison Maurice, born in the Trafalgar year of 1805, was the only son. An orphaned niece and nephew, Anne and Edmund Hurry, joined the family, and there was the requisite number of servants. It all made a large but happy and easy-going household with a succession of guests. Maurice gained a name for himself as a man of broad sympathies and deep scholarship and he had no trouble attracting pupils. The poet Southey[2] sent his young brother to him. Leading topics of the day were discussed at length and in depth at every mealtime. It was a perfect environment for an alert, intelligent child like Frederick Maurice.

That pleasant existence endured for eleven years after which the gap between the money the pupils paid and the expense of such a large establishment could no longer be ignored. The Maurices would have to economize. Their doctor suggested moving to a warmer district because Priscilla Maurice was asthmatic and one of the girls, Emma, was very delicate. Accordingly the Maurices moved to Somerset, and Michael Maurice became Unitarian minister at Frenchay, a hamlet four miles from Bristol. Their new life was much more restricted. Young Frederick (he would grow up to be his reverent disciples' 'Prophet' and 'Master' but in the bosom of his family he was 'Fred'), was then a precocious nine-year-old who had cut his reading teeth on the Bible, and had just finished reading, with admiration and approval, Neale's *History of the Puritans*. As an adult he said it was 'heavy and undoubtedly a somewhat narrow book', but as a boy he loved it.

Michael Maurice was justifiably proud of his bright son and

expected he would become a Unitarian minister one day.

The long Napoleonic War ended, but peace brought unexpected problems to the Maurice family, and in place of national conflict the family faced domestic warfare. The Maurice daughters became bored with the cool freedom of the Unitarians and yearned for a more exciting religion, something personal, emotional, bigoted and authoritarian. The 'vital' religion of the Wesleyans was popular around Bristol and the adolescent Maurice girls found it attractive. The first to reject Unitarianism was Anne Hurry, whose brother had died, and she found no solace in Michael Maurice's faith. She was followed by the three eldest Maurice girls.

True children of their father, they had not only to abandon Michael Maurice's religion: they had to be seen to have abandoned it. To make their point, they joined the Society of Baptist Dissenters and underwent a second baptism, a startling change of faith which was communicated to their father by letter after the fact, it being one of the peculiarities of the Maurice family that although its members could, and did, discuss ideas with perfect freedom, they were quite tongue-tied over personal matters. Their father therefore had been entirely in the dark over his daughters' religious problems and their letter was a bombshell. Worse followed. In the following year, 1817, his wife also turned away from Unitarianism, informing him by letter naturally, and she even begged him to reply by letter since she found it all much too painful to discuss with him face to face.

What could the stunned husband and minister do but capitulate? Nevertheless he drew certain conclusions, one of them being that it was all his fault for having allowed his elder children such freedom of thought. That mistake would not be repeated with the younger ones, whom he would compel to attend his Unitarian chapel until in his view they had reached the age of religious discretion. In the meantime he accepted the situation, only asking the older girls not to proselytize within the family circle, a prohibition which they hotly protested was unfair. The family was united on only one point, to keep these fundamental differences hidden from young Frederick in case he was upset.

Concealment was impossible. He was highly receptive to the charged emotional atmosphere and his sister, Emma, his 'almost twin' and close confidante, knew all about the discord. From her

conduct, and that of the others, he became aware of the unhappiness and confusion in the home, once so free and happy. His
father supervised the boy's education, took him on the parish
rounds, introduced him to meetings of the Bible Society and the
Anti-Slavery campaign.

Frederick Maurice was gentle and affectionate, shuddered at
country tales of blood sports, and harboured secret ambitions to
be a Radical social reformer, like some of his father's friends. He
shrank away from any kind of sectarianism and he already knew
he would never make a Unitarian minister. He finally plucked up
courage to tell his father this, dealing the unfortunate man another blow. Michael Maurice was, however, nothing if not fair-
minded and Frederick was sent to London to be tutored for the
Bar by the son of Michael Maurice's friend, the abolitionist
Thomas Clarkson. Frederick would live with his cousin, Anne,
who had given up her flirtation with Calvinism when she married
an Anglican clergyman, the Rev Alfred Hardcastle.

The young man had never been away from home, and had
never mixed with Anglicans. At the Hardcastle home he met an
older woman, a follower of the Scottish theologian Thomas
Erskine. She was kindly and feminine, and she was there, and the
shy young man unburdened himself. The situation was commonplace, and quite innocent. She listened sympathetically to his
doubts and anxieties and lent him improving books, including
some by Erskine which Frederick devoured with growing delight.
So it was possible to repudiate a Calvinistic doctrine of election
and to follow an Erskine line of choosing a God of love! He found
it a revelation. Erskine's writings had a lasting influence and in
times of stress or depression in later life he turned to them for
strength.

He decided to go to university, preferably Cambridge, and as
his father agreed, arrangements were made, so that in 1823, a
preternaturally serious young man of eighteen, Frederick
Denison Maurice entered Trinity College. Like so many of his
kind and generation he expected too much of the university and
was quickly disappointed at the low intellectual calibre of his professors, with the exception of his classics tutor, the Rev Julius
Hare. Hare was then in his late twenties but already a world
authority on Plato and also one of England's leading German
scholars. He was a born teacher and very methodical, and when

John Sterling. From an oil painting which belonged to Caroline Fox of Falmouth. 'A more perfectly transparent soul I have never known,' wrote Thomas Carlyle

Maurice himself became a teacher he modelled himself upon Hare. Maurice made friends with another student, John Sterling, the brilliant son of a military family, and the two were soon inseparable. Sterling proudly introduced Maurice to the secret, intellectually élite 'Apostles' Club', where Maurice so quickly established an ascendancy by raising the quality of the debates and by dazzling his hearers through his gift for paradox that in no time at all the Apostles were hailing Maurice as their true founder. (In more recent years one thinks of the Apostles in connection with the famous Bloomsbury intellectuals such as Maynard Keynes, and of the inter-war period when the Club was a seed-bed for some notable Soviet sympathizers and defectors.)

Sterling was one of those tantalizing individuals who attain fame through the admiration of their friends. These insisted that, had he not died young, he would have ranked as a thinker and innovator alongside Coleridge and Carlyle. As it happened, his published work remains scrappy, so he has to be judged by the effect he had on other people, by what they said of him, and by the two starkly dissimilar biographies which Julius Hare and Thomas Carlyle wrote of him.

He admired Coleridge deeply, and visited him, passing on this admiration to Maurice. In those days Cambridge thinking was largely Benthamite. Against it Maurice and Sterling led an informal opposition. Just as Erskine had freed Maurice from a restrictive religion, so now did Coleridge and Wordsworth free him from the narrowness of Utilitarianism. Intoxicated by all these new and romantic ideas, Maurice realized he could not be happy in the constrictions of the law and agreed with Sterling that they should both pursue freelance journalism in London. This would be a precarious profession, but Maurice was not interested in making money, only in expressing his ideas about society and democracy.

Nobody doubted that young Maurice had great potential and most persons assumed that he was poised on the threshold of a dazzling career. Not a bit of it. He was deeply depressed and frustrated, having found that journalism was just as confining as any other profession. An unforeseen problem, for Maurice at least, was that a successful journalist needed to possess the knack of making friends. Sterling had it, Maurice did not. He shared the family failing when it came to personal contacts. 'I have felt a painful inability to converse even with those who loved me upon the workings of my mind,' he wrote to his father in 1829. His 'conversing' had to be managed through long letters! He lived modestly on what he earned and occupied himself writing a socially significant novel called *Eustace Conway*, sending it in sections to his mother for her to copy it in a legible hand for submission to a publisher. Sometimes Mrs Maurice had to put the manuscript on one side, for her time was taken up with caring for Emma, who was very ill.

A political crisis in Spain at that time resulted in a drop in the value of Spanish bonds in which, unfortunately, a good deal of Michael Maurice's money was invested. The family had to move to cheaper accommodation and took a small house in Southampton. Any mute hope which Frederick Maurice might have entertained that his father would make him an allowance was killed. The material misfortunes of the Maurices were compounded by fresh personal ones when Emma announced she had some time previously left the Unitarians to join the Evangelicals. Emma's unexpected change of faith affected Maurice deeply, for they were so close as siblings that anything which touched her touched him also, and he began to examine his own faith more sharply. The first result was a personal vow to live a better life; the second was to give up journalism and decide to study for the Anglican ministry. He sat down to write a letter to his father to that effect.

It was necessary to return to university to study for ordination and Julius Hare was ready to help one of his favourite pupils if Maurice chose Cambridge. That, however, appeared too comfortable for Maurice in his mood of austerity. How could he take an easy path when his adored sister lay dying? He went to Exeter Hall, Oxford, taking up residence in the bitterly cold winter of 1830. It was very different from his first days at Cambridge. He felt out of place in Oxford, being older than the average student, much lonelier and very much poorer. He went through the motions of living but in his imagination he was at his sister's bedside and he found emotional release in his letters to Emma and to his mother.

England in that year was shaken by stirring demonstrations for Parliamentary reform. The Maurices, as Whigs, supported reform but when Maurice wrote to Emma, asking her opinion on

solutions to practical problems of politics and living, she replied
that he should study the Bible. There he would find the answers
he sought, even to secular problems. He accepted her wisdom
although he had hoped for something else. The months passed
miserably and he shunned his old friends, even Sterling, who was
now the centrepiece of a lively intellectual circle. One reason was
that Maurice had no money to spare to travel to London on short
visits. He made one exception when Sterling got married to a
flamboyant, dark beauty called Susannah Barton who, like
Sterling, came of a military family. Maurice scraped together the
fare and attended the wedding.

Sterling had good news. *Eustace Conway* was to be published,
through Sterling's perseverance. Maurice would not get much
money but the book would be in print. Maurice felt pleased, but it
had come too late. He was preoccupied with his dying sister and
disappointed Sterling by his lack of enthusiasm. In the spring of
1831 Emma's condition worsened and Maurice took a term off to
sit by her bedside in Southampton. She died in July.

Although the end was inevitable, Maurice was overwhelmed
by its finality. He could not bear to return to Oxford although it
was essential if he wished to get a good-class degree. He applied to
be examined for his degree at once and then proceeded to the
ordination, which took place in January 1834, he being then
thirty years of age. He entered the Church of England at a time
when there were calls for reform, just as there were calls for
reform in other walks of life. Not long before, the Rev John Keble
had preached his famous sermon on 'National Apostasy' and the
Oxford Movement was in its infancy. It might reasonably be
expected that the Church of England would be delighted to have a
man of Maurice's immense talents. The real question was, not
would the Church have Maurice, but would Maurice have the
Church? Could he work within the structure of the Church, or indeed within any structure? He was always his own man, and once
he had decided that the root of all social evils was ignorance of
God, he saw that his mission in life was simply to teach people
about God, about the nature of God and about the kind of society
which God intended for mankind. 'Mankind' was perhaps too
broad a word: in practice Maurice tended to worry about what
kind of society God intended for England.

His first post was that of country curate, for which he was pre-

eminently ill-suited and his loyal friends pulled strings in London
to have him offered two part-time jobs, one as Professor of
Divinity at King's College, London, and the other as chaplain to
Guy's Hospital, London. The combined salaries were sufficient to
live upon, Maurice accepted the two positions gratefully, and
with his sister Priscilla accompanying him as housekeeper, he
moved to London. He continued to write articles and took a pupil,
Edward Strachey. Maurice was meticulous in preparing work for
his King's College classes, and he visited patients in the wards as
well as preaching in the hospital. Guy's opened his eyes to the
problems of working-class people and the seamy side of city life.

We have a picture of him in those days through the eyes of
young Strachey, as a shy, gentle man, much given to moods of
deep depression when he would be heard to mutter, under his
breath, that the world was out of joint, at which his sister would
jolly him along by exclaiming playfully that it was his duty then
to set it to rights! He drew comfort and strength from prayer. As
his biographer-son[3] later described it, Maurice never 'read
prayers'—he 'prayed', and with impressive sincerity and
reverence. However effective prayers might or might not be for
others, they clearly worked for Frederick Maurice. It was never
what Maurice actually did which struck people, it was what he
was.

In London he could be with his friends again, especially with
Sterling, but Maurice noticed with distress that Sterling showed
the signs of advanced tuberculosis, and what was almost worse,
he was being tempted by atheism. He had deserted Coleridge for
Carlyle, enjoying the 'old growler's' brand of pantheism, which
Maurice greatly mistrusted. It seemed all the more astonishing of
Sterling because he had become ordained and was actually Julius
Hare's curate at Herstmonceux in Sussex.

Maurice was not alone in being disturbed by Sterling's professional Anglicanism and his support of Carlyle. Mutual
acquaintances enjoyed gossiping maliciously about him and
whispered that an ordained atheist was an abomination. They
whispered because Sterling had indulgent friends, not least of
whom was Julius Hare. Unpredictably it was Maurice, Sterling's
closest friend at Cambridge, who turned openly against him. His
disappointment at Sterling, his dismay at the growing gulf
between them, awakened surprising bitterness in Maurice. Here

was his best friend opposing him on two issues which Maurice thought vital, religion and education, and whenever they met Maurice was hard, cutting and bitter. There was also an element of jealousy. Once Sterling had looked to Maurice for intellectual ideas and guidance; now he sat at Carlyle's feet.

Sterling understood his friend very well, and could see how the situation was developing, but was either too weak through illness or too sensitive to his friend's unhappiness to fight back. By 1837 Sterling was so ill that his wife sent for her sister, Anna Barton, to help her nurse him. Anna lived in Germany with her widowed mother and was delighted to have any excuse to be in London. She was a happy, extroverted young woman of twenty-three who did not get on well with her mother. She had met Maurice for a few minutes at the Sterling wedding six years earlier but had not seen him since. Now there was an opportunity for the two to become friends and Sterling watched their growing relationship with pleasure. Anna Barton's mother heard about it and made objections, which only spurred Sterling on to fresh match-making, and the couple became officially engaged during a visit to Julius Hare's home at Herstmonceux that summer.

The effect on Maurice was nothing short of miraculous. He was a man transformed. He felt, he said later, like a man who had travelled all his life under oppressive cloudy skies and suddenly came into perpetual sunshine. Never before, and indeed never again, would he experience that quality of pure elation and release. Anna Barton shared his emotion but on a less intense level. She was an intelligent girl with a bubbling sense of humour. 'Mr Carlyle has been talking for four hours in praise of silence,' was a sample of her style of talk. Everyone liked her informal, candid manner and Maurice for the first time could enjoy a close and free relationship. They were married in October 1837, Sterling managing to summon up enough strength to conduct the wedding service.

It was a successful marriage. Anna Maurice created a delightful home where guests were always welcome. She took down dictation from her husband for his articles and lectures and she translated German articles for him. He revelled in being married, and was settled and content enough to collect some letters he had written to a Quaker acquaintance to form the basis of a book entitled *The Kingdom of Christ*, whose main thesis was that only

Frederick Denison Maurice, as a young man

the Anglican Church was flexible enough to answer man's religious yearnings, for the Dissenting churches were too narrow. (Since he was writing for Protestants, he did not deal with the Roman Catholic Church.) He enjoyed writing that book and began to see that in order to be free to say everything he wanted to say, he must refuse preferment. High office would imprison and silence him.

The book sold steadily and slowly won him a following among serious men and women, clergy and lay alike. It also marked the first of the attacks upon him from different sections of the religious press. Uneasy because Maurice defied categorization, those papers first attributed to him opinions which he neither held nor expressed, and then attacked him for those so-called opinions. He was hurt and exasperated by the unfair criticisms but relied on his wife's support and sympathy and his own sense of personal mission to sustain him. It was just as well he learned to do so, for similar articles were published about him throughout his life.

Busy and fulfilled in that first year of marriage, Maurice was blissfully unaware of the troubles ahead. In 1838 Carlyle delivered some lectures which Maurice disapproved of and which Sterling admired. The Carlyle home in Cheyne Walk was a centre for the London intelligentsia and although Maurice was a frequent visitor he never felt comfortable there. He believed that Carlyle thought he was 'a sham' and he was seized with impotent fury when he saw Sterling agreeing with Carlyle. Maurice cut a lamentable figure, as well he knew, yet he could not control himself. He was sarcastic and aggressive whenever Sterling tried to be conciliatory. As he watched Sterling drift further and further from Christianity, Maurice grew cooler and cooler towards his friend. Anna Maurice did all she could to stem the frightening coldness of her husband, but without success. Maurice's whole personality appeared to have altered. He felt that Sterling's rejection of Christianity was a rejection of him personally, and such rejection was too painful to contemplate. Sterling watched Maurice's reactions and was powerless to help him. The knowledge shared by both men that Sterling's illness was terminal gave an added dimension to the profound emotional discord between them.

Death was starting to be a familiar companion to Frederick

Maurice. His sister Elizabeth died at Easter 1839. She was the only Maurice who had become an Anglican, and he had valued her support. Not long after Elizabeth's death, Anna Maurice was delivered of her first child, a still-born girl. The Maurices needed all their religious faith to bear their disappointment. Maurice's way of overcoming grief was to undertake extra work, and he gave a series of lectures upon education. To his surprise and great annoyance, Sterling wrote some articles on education taking a contrary view. Maurice assumed from the timing of their publication that they had been written as an answer to him. Was Sterling trying to insult him? The pair, whose friendship and mutual admiration had once been golden, became even more estranged and although Sterling by now was often confined to bed, Maurice neither wrote nor visited him, so hostile was he.

In June 1840 King's College offered him the additional post of Professor of English Literature and Modern History, which he accepted willingly as it would allow him to drop the journalism. He was rather surprised to learn that W. E. Gladstone had been amongst those recommending him for the post. Maurice had never taught large classes of sixteen-year-old boys but he approached them as Hare had approached Cambridge undergraduates. The boys found Maurice a change from their other teachers. Forty or fifty boys had to crowd into a small hall with not enough seats to go round, so latecomers had to stand. Maurice would lecture, would read long passages from books and would devote considerable time to the discussion of words and their derivations. He never set homework or gave tests, nor did he even inquire whether the boys read the set books. It apparently never occurred to him that some might not read them. The serious students, who seemed to be in the majority, came under his spell and took more notes for him, and did more reading, than they did for any other teacher.

His reputation as a serious man with important views began to spread. An earnest Scot who worked in a London publishing house, one Daniel Macmillan, asked Julius Hare for the name of some sympathetic Anglican minister who was prepared to talk about theology to working men. Hare gave Maurice's name, but when Maurice was informed he did not respond positively. He was engrossed with his work, and with his family. The Maurices had a son, the first of two and they were busy and happy. Anna

Maurice sometimes hinted, superstitiously, that they were too happy. Maurice tried to reassure her. 'I do not think it right to expect trials. When they are to come, God will fit us for them,' he told her. In the following year Daniel Macmillan again asked Maurice to meet working men, and again Maurice declined, although he was willing to meet Macmillan. 'We generally break-fast at nine, dine at half-past two, and drink tea at any time. If you can come at any of these hours we shall be most glad to see you,' he wrote. Macmillan presented himself very promptly and a long-lasting friendship began, soon to extend to Daniel's book-selling brother in Cambridge, Alexander Macmillan.

The trials which Anna Maurice had feared started to arrive in earnest in 1843. First old Mrs Sterling died and then, two days later, Susannah Sterling. Anna Maurice grieved for her dead sister and Maurice grieved for his bereaved friend, forgetting all his earlier and unworthy disagreements. Sterling, gravely ill, managed to take his three children to the Isle of Wight for a summer holiday. Anna Maurice went with them, much to Maurice's apprehension, for she was expecting a child in June. The birth was uneventful, luckily, and the Maurices rejoiced in their second son.

Maurice journeyed from London to the Isle of Wight as often as he could, as conscience-stricken now as he had once been haughty and bitter. There was no sacrifice he would not make for his friend Sterling. His ordinary work load was increased by the letters which came from strangers who had read his books and felt free to ask his advice on social as well as religious questions. His correspondents included laymen as well as clerics, Noncon-formists as well as Anglicans. One friend formed in this way was a young Hampshire Rector named Charles Kingsley, although in those early days neither dreamed that they would become close friends or that their association would make them national figures.

Sterling made new friends, too, during his spells of better health. He met the Fox family in the West Country, cultured and liberal Quakers with a delightful daughter called Caroline. She was attracted to Sterling, as was almost everyone, but when he hinted at marriage she had sufficient worldly sense to decline to marry a dying man with three orphaned children. It therefore fell to Anna Maurice to bear the brunt of nursing Sterling in the summer of 1844. Maurice commuted between Ventnor and London, and on each visit Sterling looked worse. He persuaded himself that his friend was returning to Christianity and by the time Sterling died in September Maurice was quite sure that his dear friend had discovered religious consolation in his last days.

The cost to Anna Maurice was the very highest. She developed tuberculosis and the disease took rapid hold. Maurice wrote in December that they hoped she would recover because only one lung was affected, but he was mistaken. Her condition deteriorated and next spring she was taken to Hastings for the sea air. 'When I look on her withered face and limbs I can scarcely dream that this measure will be blessed by her recovery,' he told a friend. He was correct. She died at Easter 1845 and was buried at Herstmonceux. The links between the Hare and Maurice families were tightened when Maurice's sister, Esther, married Julius Hare, and the motherless Maurice children remained at Herstmonceux with their Aunt Esther, where they were joined by Sterling's daughters for a while. Sterling's son, to Maurice's chagrin, was by his will placed in the charge of Francis Newman, the Comtist brother of John Henry Newman, the future Cardinal. Priscilla Maurice returned to housekeep for her brother.

An opportunity to leave Guy's Hospital came when King's College offered him the newly created post of Professor of Theology. It would be a wrench to leave Guy's, where every corner of the hospital building held memories of his dead wife, but he thought the move would be best for the children. Then he was also asked to be chaplain of Lincoln's Inn at a salary of £300 a year. That tipped the scale. The two salaries would allow him to rent a house in Queen's Square, Bloomsbury, within walking distance of both Lincoln's Inn and King's College.

Attendance at Lincoln's Inn Chapel trebled soon after Maurice took over. He had the gift of seeming to address each member of the congregation individually, on a man-to-man basis, which brought the services to life, and at least one young barrister, Thomas Hughes, felt uncomfortable if he missed morning chapel taken by the new man.

Another young lawyer, John Malcolm Forbes Ludlow, working in the busy chambers of a successful Whig barrister, held a different opinion. Ludlow was a sensitive young man who was eager to perform practical social work. He was sickened by the

vicious squalor of working-class homes in the Lincoln's Inn area
and he hoped that the new chaplain would direct the young
lawyers into district social work. He called upon Maurice, hoping
to be told something of that nature, and was received courteously,
but vaguely. It seemed as if Maurice had no thought beyond his
chapel services. 'Good but very unpractical,' said Ludlow to his
mother.

At the very best of times Maurice's brand of practicality was
different from Ludlow's and when they first met, in 1846,
Maurice was living through a minor nervous breakdown. Any
spare time was reserved for his children. He was involved in
completing a long article on education and was in no fit state to
follow what Ludlow was saying. Ludlow, of course, had no idea of
Maurice's personal circumstances and could make no allowance
for him.

Outwardly Maurice appeared in control of his life. He
supported Gladstone's candidature at Oxford in 1847; he visited
his mentor, Erskine, in Scotland; he promised Charles Kingsley
that he would write a preface to the latter's verse drama, *The
Saint's Tragedy*; he spoke in favour of admitting Jews to Parliament, a somewhat unpopular view; and he supported the nomina-
tion of Dr Hampden as bishop, which brought down upon his
head the wrath of the High Church party, thus neatly balancing
the anger of the Low Church party which he had incurred some
three years before.

Education became his chief interest, apart from his family and
his work. He helped organize a committee of King's College professors to consider ways of raising the educational standards of
governesses, and the highly practical outcome was the setting up
of Queen's College, Harley Street, in the spring of 1848. That
school was a pioneer in education for girls, and Maurice was its
chief founder.

His sermons became noted for their concern with public issues.
His friend, the Rev R. C. Trench, who had gone to Ireland to see
conditions for himself, wrote heart-rending accounts of hunger
and poverty. There was unrest all over Europe and when France
adopted the revolutionary path in February 1848, the broad
questions of belief, brotherhood and revolution were duly covered
in Maurice's Lincoln's Inn sermons.

The Paris revolution affected Ludlow more acutely than it did

Maurice because Ludlow had grown up in that city and his sisters still lived there. As soon as he heard of the overthrow of Louis Philippe, Ludlow hurried to France to see how his sisters were. After finding them quite safe, he remained there for some days, a fascinated and approving spectator of the French experience. He returned to London, brimful of enthusiasm, determined to take some action, or at the least to contact men who would. Ludlow was a solitary man who did not know any particular person likely to be sympathetic, but he noticed that Maurice's sermons suggested that the chaplain was at least interested in social issues. So Ludlow sat down to write a full and deeply felt letter. Working men in Paris, he insisted, had turned to socialism precisely because it appealed to their consciences. Socialism must be Christianized, or else it would shake Christianity to its foundations. The clear implication was that Maurice and Ludlow had a moral and religious duty to do something about it.

That letter, with its contents and its timing, was crucial to Maurice's development and future activities. It marshalled his inchoate thoughts and gave them direction and character. 'Could you spend any evening with me—the sooner the better?' he wrote on 16 March. The young man went at once, paying the first of many visits to Queen's Square. The two men spent hours talking together and then one evening there occurred a sudden moment of intense communication. 'The veil between us was parted and it dawned upon me that the new friend I had made was the greatest man I knew,' wrote Ludlow in his diary. Maurice had shared that moment of close sympathy. The young man he had been addressing formally in letters as 'My dear Sir' became overnight 'My dear Friend' and a relationship began which would change their lives.

Ludlow, the Resolute Young Man

France, 1821–1837: Right-wing influence in government, increasing in reign of Charles X. July Ordinances, 1830, leading to July Revolt. Louis Philippe invited to become a constitutional king.

England, 1837–1848: Chartists; Anti-Corn Law League; Irish potato famine; Repeal of the Corn Laws. 1848—unrest and uprisings, home and abroad.

John Malcolm Forbes Ludlow[1] was something of an outsider, a man in the shadows, dark, reserved and implacably resolute. His formidable intelligence and immense capacity for hard work would have made him successful in almost any profession but, like Maurice, he chose to dedicate himself to social justice. As a young man he was poor, chivalrously romantic and almost pathologically shy, and Charles Mansfield complained that he ought to stop mailing himself in steel because only very close friends knew the 'unfathomable depths' of his 'noble heart'. However, when that remark was made there had been so many emotional doors slammed in Ludlow's face that he wore armour deliberately for protection.

He was born in India in 1821 where his father was a colonel in the British Indian Army. That man died when his son was six months old and Mrs Ludlow returned, with her son and three daughters, to Paris where she had grown up, and rented a spacious apartment just off the Rue de Rivoli. There was a strong military tradition in the Ludlow family where the men were proud of being descendants of Cromwell's subordinate, Colonel Ludlow,[2] but it was quite a different matter with Mrs Ludlow's family. Her father was Murdoch Brown, a daredevil Indian nabob who would have gladdened Thackeray's heart, and her brother,

Frank, was a chip off the parental block. Both father and son maintained establishments with Indian ladies so Ludlow had an array of Anglo-Indian cousins.

Living in Paris, where he was a foreigner, a Protestant, a person with Indian connections and a champion from earliest boyhood of the poor and downtrodden, he could not avoid feeling he was an outsider. His earliest influence was his sister Maria, seven years his senior, who looked after him and taught him to read English. Ludlow felt much closer to her than he did to his mother. His first language was French and he attended a French school, doing well at his studies and managing to avoid most games and sport through reliance on a weak and treacherous ankle.

When the Paris revolt which toppled Charles X in 1830 took place young Ludlow had a grandstand view from the family flat. Guns echoed through the apartment as he gazed out of the window astonished and—being an officer's son—slightly contemptuous of the royal troops who flinched in the face of the Paris rabble. Was this the best army France could muster, he wondered. And would the British or Indian troops be any better? His nine-year-old ambition to become an officer like his father was severely shaken, and it was the final straw when he saw a polytechnic student appear in front of the crowd, the tricolour sash round his waist and a sword at his side. The young man lectured the crowd until it dispersed in favour of more peaceful and effective action elsewhere. Ludlow was lost in admiration for that heroic figure, and learned a lesson from him. Courage and moral principles could tame and guide a brutal, uneducated crowd. Ludlow had a model; he would be a fighter for a better world, and indeed many of his activities in the English working-class movement in subsequent years bore a striking resemblance to the actions of that polytechnic student.

The boy was happy and at ease in Paris, with Catholic as well as Protestant friends. They were all very like himself, clever, industrious and rather smug. Then, when he was about twelve, his world fell apart as his much-loved Maria confessed, amid some embarrassment, that she had fallen in love with a French colonial civil servant, one Charles Liot, and longed to marry him and accompany him to Martinique. However, if Ludlow raised any objections she would give her lover up.

It was, to say the least, a contrived and unfair situation. Maria was well aware of her young brother's idealistic nature and his masochistic leaning towards self-sacrifice. He would never deny her, of all people, the chance of happiness and he was too inexperienced to suggest that she could make a better match than Liot. Mrs Ludlow was delighted to have one daughter safely married, and soon Maria was wed and half a world away. The boy, feeling deserted, suffered in silence, confiding his sense of loss only to his diary. No one in the future ever took Maria's place; not his mother, with whom he would live until her death, nor his wife (another Maria) whom he married in middle age.

Meanwhile he immersed himself in study, passed his examinations[3] a year early and developed a taste for the opera, mooning over beautiful prima donnas. He expected to enter some profession like his school friends and was perfectly willing to take out naturalization papers when the time came. All this was knocked on the head when his mother casually remarked one day, Ludlow being about sixteen, that of course Colonel Ludlow would have wished his son to grow up in England and become an Englishman. The boy took it as a command from beyond the grave and prepared himself in a spirit of martyrdom to obey without protest, although he hated to leave the lively, cultured city of Paris for the unknown barbarity of London. Mrs Ludlow had no idea of her son's state of mind and the pair shortly removed to England, the older sisters remaining behind in Paris. The Ludlows first lodged with a gloomy, elderly relative, whose company did nothing to raise Ludlow's spirits, and then they took a small house in Cadogan Square, which in those late 1830s was on the outskirts of town with a view of distant farmlands.

John Ludlow saw himself as an exile of exiles. His diary, written in French, described his alien environment and his lack of friends. He had nothing in common with the few young Englishmen he met and was emotionally starved. He vowed to devote himself to the underprivileged and to the task of bringing the civilization of democratic France to poor benighted England. He had hoped his future might be different, but at least he could use it to improve mankind, whilst self-discipline was always good for the soul.

Those high-flown moral and religious principles were thrown to the winds when news reached England that Martinique had been devastated by an earthquake. Ludlow instantly visualized the deaths of Maria and her entire family, and he blamed God. How could He have allowed it? Ludlow remained in a mood of passionate resentment until his mother's patient resignation made him ashamed of his attitude, and he performed a complete turnaround, offering himself to God like a new religious convert. When word came from the Liots it was to say that they had all, miraculously, escaped harm. Ludlow solemnly thanked God and the calm faith he possessed at eighteen remained in large measure with him throughout his long life. (Frederick Maurice in a similar way had deepened his faith when he endured the crisis of his sister Emma's death.)

It was impossible to live for ever on an exalted pinnacle and Ludlow began to take an interest in social and political campaigns. He had a particular interest in the newly formed British India Society, of which his uncle, Frank Brown, was a leading organizer, for Brown visited the Ludlows and told them stories about atrocities committed by East India Company officials. Daniel O'Connell, the famous Irish orator, was another member of the society, as were many Liberals and Nonconformists. A stream of Indians visited the society's offices, giving evidence, and its work received a boost when the Penny Post was started in 1840. Ludlow enjoyed the feeling of being at the centre of a reform campaign. He had a similar respect for the Anti-Corn Law League and began to see how minority groups, even small ones, could influence public opinion and change laws.

In 1841, just about the time when Friedrich Engels toured Lancashire, Ludlow and his mother visited the same area. The young man's impressions were rosier than Engels', and he adopted the idea that if each factory were to be regarded as one living organism, then the workers, acting as a single collective, could compel a factory owner to improve work conditions. He wanted to see facilities like nurseries for the children of women workers. He had been reading about the *phalanstères* of Charles Fourier, the French socialist, and had come to the conclusion that collectivization would solve many of society's ills.

He was sent for a short time to an English school, and then, through the good offices of some relatives, was found a place as a pupil in the chambers of Bellenden Ker,[4] a successful Whig barrister. No question of university arose. Bellenden Ker took a liking to the young man with a Continental background, who was much smarter and quicker than the average English pupils. Much of the barrister's practice was in the field of drafting governmental legislation and Ludlow had only to learn and to work hard—second nature to him in any case—for his future to be assured.

Next year Ludlow and his mother went out to Martinique, where they were horrified to find that Charles Liot, having mishandled public accounts either through fecklessness or venality, was threatening suicide as an alternative to prison. The two Ludlows had to assist Maria, and the only thing which could help was money. Accordingly they lent Liot almost every penny they had, so that he could smooth matters over with his superiors. That was another sacrifice for Ludlow, one which he performed most willingly, but it was depressing none the less to be so poor. By the time he returned home he felt almost as suicidal as his brother-in-law had been. 'The worthlessness of life lay upon me like lead,' he confided to his diary, and one day, crossing St James's Park he actually opened the blades of his pocket knife intending to slash his wrists and end it all. Then a vision of his mother's face, contorted with grief, swam across his eyes and he folded his knife and returned meekly home. But how he yearned for some cause to live for, or better still, some person!

Heaven obliged him by providing his cousin, Maria Forbes, one year his junior. He knew her already and her Tory family with its High Church pretensions, and did not care for them or for her. Maria was dutiful, rather plain and much given to hypochondria and she had not impressed him. Yet when he paid a formal Christmas visit to the Forbes home in 1843 he saw her as if for the first time. She was not long recovered from an illness, and looked washed out, but Ludlow paid no attention to that. He looked deep into her eyes and found such purity and innocence that he fell instantly in love. Characteristically he kept his feelings to himself, for how could an impoverished young man with uncertain prospects even hint at marriage? Indeed, it took eleven years for him to find courage to speak of it to Maria, and then only because close friends, to whom he had confided his secret, urged him to do so. Not that it did him any good. Maria said she put her duty to her aged parents before her own happiness, and certainly before Ludlow's, and he must never speak of it again.

She did in fact relent but only after another thirteen years had passed, and then she promised to marry him.

Whether as the unattainable damsel of his youth or the wife-companion of maturer years, Maria Forbes served her purpose in Ludlow's life as a romantic sheet-anchor. His propensity for self-sacrifice encouraged him to obey her dictates and a low sex drive was easily sublimated in social service. From time to time he even flirted with notions of celibacy as a higher rule of life, but was rather disappointed to find that none of his friends, not even Maurice, thought much of that idea. Lack of time, money and opportunity made Ludlow celibate in practice as well as theory and his repressed sex yearnings were given expression in love poetry which was inspired by his cousin but naturally never shown to her.

Now that he had found a person to live for, he looked round for a cause, and from the day he chose Maria as his woman he was, consciously or unconsciously, ready for some challenging enterprise which would give meaning to his life. Before he could discern any suitable campaign he caught measles, and on recovering was sent to Madeira for convalescence. There he sat in the warm sunshine, reading most of the time. He skimmed through Richard Hurrell Froude's *Recollections*, disliking every word—'shallow juvenile bumptiousness'. (Many years later he met Froude's younger brother, James Anthony, through Charles Kingsley, and disliked him too.) He read several books by Coleridge and dismissed them as unsystematic. There was, however, one book which he found impressive, A. P. Stanley's biography of Dr Arnold, the late headmaster of Rugby. As Ludlow read on, he felt as if the good doctor were at his side, talking to him, putting his vague aspirations into coherent order. The life of Dr Arnold was to Ludlow what Ludlow's artless letter in 1848 would be to Maurice, and the dead headmaster seemed for a brief period to be providing a substitute father-figure for Ludlow.

Another possible father-figure, with the added advantage of being alive, was Louis Meyer, a French Lutheran pastor whom Ludlow had met in Paris. Meyer's work was socially orientated, and it led Ludlow to make contact with some Evangelical groups in England, but he found them uncongenial and narrow-minded, and mindful of Meyer's work in Paris, wondered if he could not find a similar clerical figure in London who would direct him to some useful volunteer activity. It was this idea which sent him to the Lincoln's Inn chaplain, F. D. Maurice, who was said to be a good man. Ludlow was disappointed when Maurice refused to take action which might be construed by the local clergyman as interfering with his parochial matters. If Ludlow wanted to help in social work, he should approach the parish priest, said Maurice.

Repelled by that negative attitude, Ludlow looked for somebody of his own age and found a young man called John Self, who assisted in parish visiting in the Lincoln's Inn area, was a lay scripture reader, and who organized periodical dinners for the poor. This was obviously useful work but far too ordinary to appeal to Ludlow. He was much taken at that time with a particular fantasy which involved going into politics, becoming Prime Minister, introducing great social reforms in Parliament and then renouncing everything to become a humble parish priest in the city slums. Helping John Self would not take him far on that road!

He was excited when the Corn Laws were repealed in 1846, a response to the 'awakening cry of the social spirit', he declared. Filled with admiration and respect, he composed a poem addressed to Sir Robert Peel, the Prime Minister who had placed humanity above party.

But when would Ludlow's call come?

It appeared to come early in 1848 when news reached London of the abdication of Louis Philippe and the proclamation of the French Republic. Peel commented in the Commons that revolution was what a man got when he tried to run a government without out a majority and without paying attention to the wishes of the public. Ludlow could not afford the luxury of such detachment because he and his mother were worried over the safety of his sisters, so he caught the first available boat and train into Paris after the fall of the monarchy.

He was relieved to find that his sisters were in no danger and spent the rest of his visit roaming the streets to observe history in the making. Paris was like a latter-day Athens, with arguments and debates on every street corner, dealing with the big question of how to construct a new society. Ludlow was full of pride in the city of his boyhood. Everything that was happening in Paris in that February of 1848 would be a blessing to the world, he wrote to his relative, Sir Charles Forbes: God had shown His power and

His mercy in scattering the old government to the winds in a single day. Socialist ideas, like the workshops of Louis Blanc, were being tried out, and soon the position would be reached when the fruits of the workers' labours would be returned to them.

Ludlow became increasingly euphoric as the days passed, delighted that in all the talk about a new and fairer society he heard no hint that God and Christianity must be overthrown. He called upon Louis Meyer, who shared his enthusiasm and who was preparing to embark upon an evangelizing crusade throughout France. He invited Ludlow to join him, and the young man was certainly tempted, for there seemed nothing to keep him in England, with the possible exception of Maria Forbes, who was still ignorant of his feelings for her. He did not quite see himself in the role of popular preacher, being very shy and reserved still, and had been thinking of editing a journal which would promote a Christian bias to the new social revolution in France. He put the suggestion up to Meyer, who managed to sound sympathetic, but pointed out that such a periodical would need financing. If Ludlow had no money, his best plan was to return to England to raise money there and return to France when he was confident he could run the paper. Such sound advice was highly unpalatable, and even more so as Ludlow was forced to agree and return to London.

Back home he was gloomy and frustrated, let down by the low-key political atmosphere in England as well as the chilly weather. If money were the key to revolutionary activity in France, he might as well forget the whole thing. Yet he was driven to try one last possibility, to find one last sympathetic hearer. With no other person in his circle to turn to, he returned to Maurice, the very man whom he had earlier written off as ineffectual, and wrote him a long, moving letter about the need for action.

It reached Maurice at the precise moment when he felt as much in need of direction and activity as Ludlow did. He, like Ludlow, was a lonely and exceptional man at a crossroads in his life, aware of his potential but uncertain how to use it. Ludlow's cry for help showed Maurice where his future lay.

The Band of Brothers

Our hands no man will hire,
Our skill there's none will try;
With head, throat, heart, on fire,
We see the great go by.
Of sustenance for all
The fertile earth has store;
Our wrongs for vengeance call,
We will endure no more.

Chartist verse

The more Maurice and Ludlow spoke freely together, the more Ludlow assumed they were in perfect harmony. Maurice criticized the Anglican Church as no better than atheism, and said that what was needed was to reach the masses who were turning to socialism and make them turn to God. That in fact represented the fullest extent of Maurice's aim but Ludlow did not realize that, because he was demanding radical changes in society and hoping that through the medium of working men's associations they could together establish a Christian civilization where men lived and worked together like brothers. Maurice believed that a truly Christian country would lead on to a New Testament type of communism: Ludlow believed that once England was organized along socialist lines it would automatically lead on to Christianity. It was a fundamental point of difference which Ludlow did not appreciate until after he and Maurice had collaborated for several years.

Social unrest in England in early 1848 was seen most publicly in the Chartist activity. Goaded by increasing unemployment, low wages and rising food prices, the Chartists had already begun to collect signatures for a new petition in 1847, but it was slow work because a number of former Chartists had left the movement for more promising causes like the Owenite Home Colonies or Feargus O'Connor's Land Plan or the co-operative stores in the north. But the February Revolution in Paris stimulated the Chartists as it did Ludlow, and they were amazed to see French workers doing in days what English Chartists had failed to do in years. The petition was resumed with new vigour, with some Chartists hinting that this time they meant business and that under extreme provocation there would be riots and damage to property.

At the National Convention of Chartists in London held on 4 April it was decided to present the petition to Parliament on 10 April. Nothing more was agreed, for at the convention the division between the 'physical force' Chartists and the peaceful moderates was too deep to bridge when tactics were being discussed. Arguments were bitter, exacerbated by the press, which in any case was exaggerating the situation. Shopkeepers in London boarded up their premises anticipating a day of violence and the government enrolled 150,000 special constables, among them Louis Napoleon Buonaparte and Thomas Hughes. Even Maurice applied, but was informed that clergymen were not eligible as special constables.

Ludlow disregarded the affair, convinced that the authorities were overreacting and he commented that revolts did not start like trains, keeping to timetables. He was therefore at his office desk as usual on the morning of 10 April, when a tall, stammering stranger entered and gave him a note from Maurice.

The visitor was the Rev Charles Kingsley, Rector of Eversley in Hampshire and a young friend of Maurice. Kingsley had been reading about the Chartist plans with a mixture of sympathy and apprehension and was alarmed when his friend of Cambridge days, John Parker, told him of his father's plans to protect his business premises in the Strand. John Parker senior had published Kingsley's verse drama and was a publisher for Maurice, so Kingsley felt particularly interested. As a priest Kingsley deplored violence, but as a man he could not escape the excitement and tension around him, and he decided on impulse to go to London on the day and view proceedings for himself. He certainly hoped the Chartist meeting would pass off peacefully—poor fellows, they meant well, he insisted, and he resolved to go to the meeting on Kennington Common himself in case his moderating influence in some small way might be needed.

He explained this to Ludlow, adding that he hoped Ludlow would go with him, at which the young lawyer gazed thoughtfully at him and re-read Maurice's note of introduction. Kingsley, wrote Maurice, was 'deeply in earnest and seems to be obsessed with the idea of doing something with handbills'. Maurice added that Kingsley shared Ludlow's idea about founding a socially conscious religious periodical and the two young men should try to work something out together. Maurice was housebound that day with a bad cold or else he would have joined them.

Ludlow felt he would like to know more about Kingsley, so the pair left the office and began walking towards the river, talking continuously as they found many common points of view. Ludlow's stiff reserve began to melt in the warmth of Kingsley's sincerity and impatience and he responded eagerly, speaking more easily with Kingsley than he did with Maurice because Kingsley was his own age. Indeed, Kingsley was the first man like himself whom Ludlow had met in England and he became Ludlow's first real friend.

The two young men were talking so hard that they did not notice how far they had walked until they met the first trickle of returning demonstrators, trudging home through the mournful rain. The meeting had broken up without having reached any climax, the petition had been taken in three taxi-cabs to the House of Commons, where it would meet with no better fate than had the previous petitions, and most of the Chartists felt let down. Ludlow's assessment of the situation had been vindicated, but he did not bother about that any more for he and Kingsley had other things to talk about, and together, new-found bosom companions, they hurried round to Maurice to make him as eager as they were.

The pair had several points of similarity in their background, beliefs and talents. In spite of being the clerical son of a clerical father, Kingsley was not a parson at heart, but a campaigner, a social reformer and a poet. His background was comfortable middle class, although poorer than Ludlow's, and he certainly needed now to augment his stipend by freelance writing. The Kingsleys, like the Ludlows, could boast of their military and Puritan descent, and indeed if Kingsley's father had been rich enough he would have purchased a commission and become an army officer instead of becoming a morose and disappointed Anglican clergyman. Again like Ludlow, Kingsley had foreign connections on his mother's side, only West Indian in Kingsley's case, not Indian as in Ludlow's. This meant, however, that they shared an interest in overseas and colonial problems.

Kingsley had been a very shy boy and remained a shy young man, his stammer proving it. He had grown up more at ease in the company of girls than of boys, liked reading and studying and was slightly pompous. Like Ludlow, he had suffered a family loss. In his case it was the death of his brother and close companion, Herbert, when both boys were at school, so Kingsley knew all about loneliness, although he was more fortunate than Ludlow because he met the woman he would marry quite young and had the comfort of knowing she returned his love.

There was a point of difference in their early upbringing, for whilst Ludlow was city bred, Kingsley grew up in Devon and was proud of being a Devon man. It gave him a love of science and natural history. When Ludlow was watching the 1830 revolt from the windows of his home, and admiring the polytechnic student, Kingsley was at school in Bristol, with a glimpse of mob riots and drunkenness in the streets. It left him with a revulsion against mob rule and a more negative attitude towards social disorders than Ludlow acquired. Kingsley's undisciplined imagination fed upon the jumble of ideas in Coleridge's books which Ludlow had dismissed as 'unsystematic', and sometimes his fancy soared upwards in mystical fantasies whilst at other times it plummeted in terrifying, recurrent nightmares.

Both men had been rudely taken from their happy surroundings at about the same age, Ludlow having to leave Paris for London, and Kingsley having to leave Clovelly for London. Kingsley hated living in a city, and lived a private life sustained by books and by the inner conviction that he was destined for something out of the ordinary. He went to King's College in the Strand (before Maurice's time), preparing for entrance to Cambridge, where to his pleasure and relief he made a number of friends, the most important of whom was Charles Blachford Mansfield.

Meanwhile the university life made him certain of one thing, at least: he would never become a clergyman. Although too poor to enter fully in the social life of his fellow students, he saw enough to realize that he had a full capacity for enjoying worldly pleasures and was greatly tempted by the notion of going to America after his degree and seeking his fortune in the West. Every now and then he felt ashamed, reminding himself that a gentleman's son had to assume certain social responsibilities and he did not want to disappoint his mother, 'a second Mrs Fry', as he called her, by turning into a scapegrace son.

One will never know how many, or how few, wild oats he might have sown at university since shyness and poverty prevented this during his first year, and the presence of Fanny Grenfell in his life prevented it thereafter. He met her during the first long vacation, a fateful encounter which he called pedantically 'eye-wedlock', found her to be an understanding companion and listener, and won her heart. They had to battle against her disapproving bourgeois family for several years before they could marry.

Like Ludlow, Kingsley had become first acquainted with Maurice through writing to him, and having come to know him, Kingsley, again like Ludlow, regarded Maurice as an ideal father figure. Ludlow went further than Kingsley, wanting Maurice to be a spiritual and radical leader, whilst Kingsley, less ambitious, was prepared to accept Maurice as a theological teacher and was happy to do what he could to translate Maurice's teaching into popular language which would reach a wide public.

On the evening of 10 April, therefore, the two young men, full of ideas and optimism, confronted Maurice and told him that the time had come to contact the working class. Kingsley spent the night at Maurice's house staying up to write a handbill, or placard, addressed to the 'Workmen of England' and signed 'A Working Parson'. It was a dramatic attempt at communication which did not impress the London workers as much as the friends hoped, but it had a tonic effect upon Kingsley. He could not wait for the next step, but nobody was sure what that should be. They were really trying to break new ground by setting up a dialogue between middle-class Anglicans and working-class atheists. When appealed to, Maurice could only suggest the kind of thing he knew well, which was to write a series of tracts, and it was in fact Julius Hare, who dropped in to visit Maurice that week, who made the obvious suggestion. Start a paper like Cobbett's *Political Register*, he advised, with young Ludlow as editor. Print short, pithy comments on contemporary problems and treat them from a religious angle. He would contribute to it and was sure some of his friends would. Contributions could not be paid for, otherwise the paper could not be financed, and since they would be aiming for a broad appeal they should ask Chartists for contributions and include poetry and Bible interpretation. Their aim was to write about 'Politics for the People', so that should be their title.

The suggestion was taken up at once, with Maurice as eager as Kingsley and Ludlow, and ready to be a co-editor with Ludlow, or rather, an editor-in-chief, with Ludlow doing most of the work. Maurice wrote to Kingsley begging for an article—'Could you not write a working country parson's letter about the right and wrong use of the Bible—I mean, protesting against the notion of turning it into a book for keeping the poor in order . . . ?' Maurice kept Julius to his word about contributing something. 'The working people don't at all cry for easy literature, but scorn it,' he warned his friend. 'I do hope the first number will go forth with God's blessing,' he wrote later to Kingsley.

It was a considerable achievement, by any standards, to get a weekly paper, price one penny, on the market by 6 May, less than four weeks from its conception. The editors were less successful with their readership for the working men did not buy it, being deeply suspicious of its origins and intentions, and the middle class did not buy it as they were scared by its radical political tone. Julius Hare begged Maurice to restrain Ludlow and Kingsley and tone down the editorials, whilst Parker, who was publishing the paper, in respect for Maurice, trembled when he received complaints from his middle-class subscribers to the profitable *Fraser's Magazine*, the backbone of his business.

The contributors to *Politics for the People* were quite distinguished and not frightening, and many of them, along with the contributors to the successor paper, the *Christian Socialist*, became famous in their chosen careers. They included the Rev Richard Whatley, a future Archbishop of Dublin and a pioneer of social science; the Rev R. C. Trench,[1] a colleague of Maurice's at King's College, a stalwart of the Philological Society, and another future Archbishop of Dublin; the Rev A. P. Stanley, biographer of Dr Arnold, and a future Dean of Westminster; Arthur Helps, higher civil servant, and a future Clerk to the Privy Council; James Spedding, another civil servant, who became a well-known

literary editor and critic; William A. Guy, dean of the medical
faculty at King's College; John Conington, a future professor of
Latin at Oxford; Edward Strachey, Maurice's former pupil; and,
of course, the young men who grouped themselves round Ludlow, Kingsley and Maurice. The joint editors of *Politics for the
People* were Maurice and Ludlow, and the editorial meetings,
which were held at Maurice's house, were informal and open to
all the members of the Maurician circle.

In spite of what might be considered as a fairly broad and liberal
policy, the paper alarmed some of Maurice's associates. Such a
one was the Rev S. Clark, who became very nervous when he read
Kingsley's 'Second Letter to the Chartists', expanding Maurice's
original thought that the Bible had been misused so as to keep the
poor in order, as 'an opium dose for keeping beasts of burden
patient while they were being overloaded'. That particular article
aroused great resentment in religious circles without evoking any
corresponding approval in Chartist ones. On the contrary, the
Chartists' papers joined with the religious press in roundly
condemning *Politics*, and all the critics, complained Maurice
plaintively, used arguments which strongly suggested they had
not bothered to read the offending articles.

Shallow criticism of that kind was meat and drink to Ludlow
and Kingsley, who had a tendency to mark their success by the
amount of opposition they provoked, but the publicity harmed
each of them professionally. Bellenden Ker began to have reservations about his clever assistant and Kingsley was quickly and
permanently tarred with the revolutionary brush. Maurice urged
them to be more moderate: Ludlow should learn to temper his
socialism, and Kingsley should learn to forgo those strong
piquant phrases of his, so memorable and so wounding. They
should remember that some rich men, yes, even landlords, did
possess consciences and convictions. And if they both wanted
him to continue as editor, added Maurice, getting warm, they
would have to allow him to exercise some control. Goodness
knows he had enough outside commitments to make him
prepared to relinquish editorship. He sounded like a dedicated
headmaster admonishing his favourite prefects, and the young
men deferred to him, although Ludlow stubbornly insisted that
the group must discuss socialism and its implications because it
represented a reaction against rampant individualism and was

indeed an attempt by good men 'to make society a more thriving and better partnership'.

He could have said a good deal more on this point but was inhibited because he saw that his friends might suffer through 'guilt by association' if he were too outspoken. Kingsley had already suffered, for he had been confidently expecting to be offered a part-time teaching post at King's College when the offer was withdrawn, quite clearly because of the articles in *Politics*. Maurice asked Ludlow to go down to Eversley and explain this to Kingsley, an embarrassing task which Ludlow did not enjoy, and he tried to soften the blow by praising Kingsley's literary gifts. Fortunately for Ludlow, Kingsley was in one of his ebullient, self-dramatizing moods, and took the disappointment in good heart. 'That myth of old Von Trong Hagen, dashing the boat to pieces, by which the Nibelungen crossed the Danube is great and true,' he declaimed. 'Let the unreturning ferry-boat perish. Let us forward. God leads us, though blind . . . Out, out on the wide weltering oceans of thought!' But in spite of his mock heroics, Kingsley had too many responsibilities to venture far on the weltering ocean. His parish duties came first, then some part-time teaching which Maurice had procured for him at Queen's College, and then his writing.

Even Maurice's position at King's College had become insecure as a result of his connection with *Politics*, although for the time being it seemed unthinkable that Maurice would suffer. The last thing Ludlow wanted was to harm his dear 'Master', or his close friend. His relationship with Kingsley was still close although it had to be carried on as much by correspondence as by personal contact, but they were both prolific letter-writers and this literary dialogue led to useful cross-fertilization of ideas. The most striking thing about Kingsley was his immense energy, largely alas undisciplined so that his literary talent was frequently diminished as he attempted every type of writing, and at top speed—poems, stories, sermons, lectures, essays. A discerning critic himself, Ludlow was convinced that Kingsley's gift was for poetry and he implored his friend to abandon the novels and stick to the poems. That did not suit Kingsley, however, for he was full of ideas and opinions which demanded expression and he knew that only through novels and sermons could he reach a wide reading public.

He had to fit that work into his other duties and wrote either late at night, when everyone was in bed, or first thing in the morning, before the household had risen. His wife copied his manuscripts in a legible hand for the printer. She did this for love of her husband, not for belief in the 'glorious work' which he was engaged in, for she had no liking for Chartists and greatly disliked those who habitually called Kingsley by unpleasant names in their newspapers. She was as much a disciple of Maurice as Kingsley was, but she did not care for the rest of the group and was a little afraid of Ludlow, with his stiff manner and uncompromising views. Several of the other friends who arrived unexpectedly from London were definitely eccentric, not quite gentlemen in Fanny Kingsley's opinion.

She was willing to make an exception in the case of Charles Mansfield, who was certainly as uncompromising and eccentric as the rest, perhaps more so, but he had a charm of manner which was irresistible. Cuthbert Ellison, the 'swell' of the group, who shared rooms with Thackeray, said that he had heard the famous author declare that Mansfield must have possessed rudimentary wings hidden beneath his waistcoat, he was such an angel. He was an odd sort of angel, none the less, given to extremes of conscience and with an inquisitive and scientific mind which ranged as extensively as that of his hero, Francis Bacon.

He looked the very pattern of the blond, handsome young Englishman of good family. He was slim and athletic, and an amusing and informative conversationalist, and to outsiders he must have seemed a young man with everything to live for. His friends knew a different Mansfield, a sensitive soul who had barely survived the iron rule of the schoolmasters and the brutal tyranny of the boys at Winchester College, and had been removed from school at sixteen suffering from a nervous breakdown. His father was a wealthy, worldly Hampshire rector who made no allowances for his gifted but unusual son. In 1839 Mansfield had gone to Clare Hall, Cambridge, where he first met Kingsley, both men sharing an interest in science. Mansfield's inventive fancy was as poetic in his world of science as was Kingsley's in the world of language, and like Kingsley, he enjoyed the freedom of the university although he was a martyr to depression and frequently overcome by feelings of guilt.

Not that he gave an impression of perpetual melancholy, for his vivacity and generous nature attracted a circle of admirers, who felt better for being in his company. He was sympathetic towards all living creatures and his years at Winchester left him with a hatred and mistrust of authority and an almost irrational horror of any form of injustice. After leaving Cambridge his first notion was to train as a doctor, but after a short period of walking the wards at St George's Hospital he became revolted by the standards of care and practice. He saw he could never fit in with standard medical orthodoxy and he would have to find other outlets for his idealism and for his interest in science.

Unlike Kingsley and Ludlow he had private means, so to some extent he could please himself what work he took up. He spent lavishly on books and absorbed their contents like a sponge, preferring books on natural history, botany, mesmerism, ornithology, geography and medieval magic. He had one of the best collections in London of books on magic and he practised mesmerism on his friends, Kingsley in particular, who suffered from migraines when he was overworked. During a visit to South America in 1852 he found his knowledge of mesmerism and hypnotism very useful. Mansfield believed that Mesmer's theories about animal magnetism and a magnetic fluid in the body were worth following up, and he thought that hypnotism would be used in surgery (chloroform was not in common use in England until about 1848). He was so successful in this field that it seems most likely that Mansfield was a natural faith healer. Many young men with similar interests to Mansfield and his friends shared the belief that mesmerism would help cure nervous exhaustion, rather as individuals today of roughly comparable type might turn to group therapy or meditation.

Mansfield's important work was in the field of chemistry and he was fortunate in having the time, the money and an encouraging professor so that he could experiment as he pleased. In the mid-1840s Mansfield had enrolled in the chemistry class taken by A. W. Hofmann, the brilliant German scientist who was the first director of the newly opened Royal College of Chemistry. Hofmann had worked in Wiebig under Goeseen in isolating a compound which he called 'aniline' from coal tar. He decided that this must be the basic substance which Otto Unverdorben had discovered in 1826, and he continued this promising line of research in London, where his early experiments revealed the presence of benzene. He directed Mansfield, who was an out-standing pupil, to carry on that research. Mansfield invented and patented a number of processes for the fractional distillation of benzol, isolating benzene and another hydrocarbon called toluene. It became obvious to Mansfield that this work would become vital to the wholesale dye industries and that it was more than probable that one day his patents would make him rich.

Money never played an important part in Mansfield's life and he was ready to put his chemistry experiments to one side when Kingsley drew him into the *Politics for the People* project in 1848. He was not a Christian like the others, being plagued by religious doubts, and as he was on bad terms with his father he rejected the gentrified Anglicanism which his father represented. His scientific studies gave him a vague notion of a 'Divine Idea', some sense that the universe was pervaded by a harmonious order and that human beings were too low in the order of things to be able to comprehend the infinitely wise and good nature of a super-natural intelligence. When his father discovered that Mansfield was writing for *Politics* he promptly stopped his allowance, so the young man was left with a very small sum on which to live. This did not disturb him, for he schooled himself to manage very cheaply on a vegetarian diet and continued to make small donations to *Politics*.

Ludlow first met Mansfield at Eversley Rectory in the spring of 1848 and they were friends at once, Mansfield soon becoming more important to Ludlow than Kingsley. As a friend, Mansfield had a number of advantages over Kingsley, thought Ludlow. For one thing, Kingsley was tied to Eversley whilst Mansfield lived in London; Kingsley had a wife and family but Mansfield was single, and Ludlow did not have to share him. Then Mansfield was more intellectual than Kingsley, free from Kingsley's love of hearty outdoor pursuits like hunting, riding and fishing, and long botanical expeditions. Mansfield was gentler, more refined, less carnal than Kingsley. So he became Ludlow's closest friend, a confidant, and Ludlow reflected with enormous satisfaction that a 'band of brothers' was in the making like Nelson's captains before the battle of Trafalgar.

Politics for the People, although only a penny a copy, did not sell well enough to justify continuation beyond July 1848, which neither surprised nor disappointed Ludlow and Maurice, who looked upon it as a trial balloon to help make contact with working-class readers. In that laudable aim it had apparently failed and a Chartist paper, which was even more short-lived than *Politics*, published an article entitled 'More Friends of the People—Well-fed Democracy in Broadcloth', which was so prejudiced and ill informed about the contributors to *Politics* that Ludlow was actually impelled to make a joke and wrote a reply saying that *Politics* was largely the work of a water-drinking lawyer and not a jolly parson nodding over his bottle of port!

The real achievement of their periodical, as its writers saw it, was to have given the opportunity for a series of discussion meetings held at Maurice's home which continued after the paper was dead. Maurice became the focus and spiritual adviser for the group which attended.[2] Mansfield introduced to the group Dr Charles B. Walsh, who was deeply concerned about lack of sanitation in the slums, and his own cousin, Archibald Mansfield Campbell. The latter, an architect, recruited a professional colleague, Frank Cranmer Penrose, an old Cambridge acquaintance of Kingsley's. Ludlow brought along Bellenden Ker's latest pupil, Frederick James Furnivall, a hyperactive enthusiast who became the most zealous recruiting officer of them all.

They followed a strict drill in vetting possible comrades. Candidates were first taken to have tea with Maurice, then they were taken to hear him preach in Lincoln's Inn Chapel and finally they were invited to one of the weekly meetings, which had become Bible study sessions with emphasis upon contemporary problems.

In this way the band of brothers attained a respectable size, representing different professions and all shades of religious and social beliefs. The common factors were idealism and youth, and the regular Bible meetings kept them united, even the shyest among them being encouraged by Maurice, in his element as a born teacher, to speak his mind. The evenings followed a familiar routine, with Maurice reading some chosen passage from the Bible and then asking for interpretations and for the application of the passage to topical problems. There was only one rule, that a speaker had to address Maurice, a device adopted to prevent any personal argument. If any awkward silence ensued Ludlow would assume the role of devil's advocate and start the ball rolling again. Sometimes the young men appealed to Maurice, who would bury his face in his clasped hands and give an opinion in a quiet but strangely compelling voice. His disciples felt it was a privilege and a life-enhancing experience to share in those evenings.

Not everyone saw Maurice in such a shining light. One day Kingsley sent his new friend, James Anthony Froude, along to Ludlow, in the hope that Froude would be passed on to Maurice in the customary fashion and join the group. Froude was notorious at that time for being the author of a semi-autobiographical novel, *The Nemesis of Faith*, which had attracted hostile reviews and was considered by many to be rather shocking. Kingsley hoped the novel would not turn its readers away from Christianity and he was sorry for Froude, who was to become a life-long friend and a family connection through marrying Fanny Kingsley's sister. Tea with Maurice did not exert the magical power which Kingsley had anticipated and Froude joined other literary and intellectual circles, becoming a close friend of Thomas Carlyle instead. Then there was Arthur Hugh Clough, whose poetry had impressed both Ludlow and Mansfield. They were sure that Clough was really one of them, but he did not take to Maurice and slipped away.

Setbacks of this nature were quite trivial, however, for the young men in the group were sure their work was important and they supported each other in that belief. Mansfield perhaps summed it up for all of them when he blessed his good friends, Kingsley and Ludlow, for showing that there were, after all, honest, decent men with whom he could work. Life had meaning, after all.

Work to be Done

Uprouse ye now, brave brother-band,
With honest heart, and working hand;
We are but few, toil-tried, and true;
Yet hearts beat high to dare and do;
And who would not a champion be
In Labour's lordlier Chivalry?

Gerald Massey

The 'brothers' were too youthful to be satisfied with spiritual uplift alone and longed to get down to practical work, but owing to Maurice's pathological mistrust of formal organizations they were not free to join an existing political, social or philanthropical group, so were forced to create something original. The happiest of them was Ludlow who was quietly confident that his new-found friends would soon join him in Christianizing the workers in the London slums, a form of urban evangelism which was broadly akin to Louis Meyer's activities in Paris. Taking Kingsley's advice to 'do the work that's nearest', Ludlow decided that a start could be made in the squalid quarter called Little Ormond Yard, only minutes from Maurice's house. The vicar alleged that not even a policeman would venture there alone. Obviously something should be done, and as the Mauricians believed implicitly that education was the key to decent behaviour, it seemed to Ludlow and the rest that they should start a night school in Little Ormond Yard.

Furnivall was one of Ludlow's most energetic supporters and he at once wrote to his father for money, which duly arrived but without any parental blessing for the project. 'We can all easily be liberal and generous with other people's money,' wrote Furnivall senior, a successful country surgeon. 'With Ragged Schools, Socialism, or any other ism, you really have no business at all. . . . Don't play at Law and work at School teaching.'

Blithely disregarding the rebuke, Furnivall spent his father's ten pounds on buying desks and furniture and on 21 September 1848 the school was formally opened by Ludlow, Furnivall, Campbell, Penrose, young John Parker and the Rev S. Clark, the parish curate, who read a few verses from Ecclesiastes and repeated a prayer. Pupils were enrolled on the spot and lessons in reading, writing and arithmetic began the same night.

The school succeeded beyond their wildest dreams. Although intended only for men, there was such a local demand for further classes in the daytime for the children that the founders clubbed together to pay the wages of a teacher who would give lessons to boys, and then to girls. Organizing the school had been Ludlow's initiative and that of the men who ran, taught and financed it. It was a surprise to all of them when Maurice introduced a young lawyer who was, the others instinctively felt, too much of a 'hearty' to fit in. Maurice was meek but very firm in his support of the newcomer, and forced the group to accept Thomas Hughes of Lincoln's Inn, destined to become a doughty champion of English working-class causes, although in 1848 nobody could foresee that. As wholesome and country-bred as a Cox's orange pippin, Hughes's chief claim to fame at that date was his reputation as an Oxford cricketer, something which cut no ice with the band of brothers. 'He'll be no good for teaching, a very good fellow for cricket and that sort of thing,' they whispered wisely. However, Maurice thought otherwise, re-calling that the previous year Hughes had written to him, as chaplain of Lincoln's Inn, asking for collections to be taken in the chapel for Irish famine relief, hardly the action of a man whose interests were bounded by the cricket pitch. Subsequently Hughes had inquired about volunteer social work. So Maurice lightly scolded his group, reminding them of his principle that you should trust a man and a volunteer worker unless and until he proved unworthy of that trust; they should give Hughes a job to do and see what he was made of.

Thomas Hughes was a cheerful, well-balanced individual who had been married for about a year and had just been admitted to the Bar. Like Kingsley, he earned about £400 a year, enough to live on very simply. Like Ludlow, he had read Stanley's bio-graphy of Dr Arnold and been enthralled by it, '. . . a most delightful book', he noted in his diary, and of Arnold he wrote,

The young Frederick James Furnivall

'no man I should think ever did more good in his generation'. That comment was made before Hughes met Maurice, for once he was made part of the Maurician circle Hughes felt the unmistakable quickening of the spirit which was Maurice's especial gift to those who worked closely with him, and afterwards Hughes placed Maurice above Arnold. It did not take long for Hughes to find a place in the group and to become one of its spokesmen, bringing a down-to-earth reality to the circle, and he, with Maurice, Kingsley and Ludlow became, to all intents and purposes, the composite public image of their social reforming movement.

Nobody could have come from a more middle class and Tory background than Hughes, or have exhibited fewer of the quirks and crotchets which the other members of the group displayed in such abundance, but his social conscience was explained by his family background. His forebears were English country parsons and he was born at Uffington in the Vale of the White Horse, that animal being an ancient chalk-cut figure and a potent cultural symbol. Hughes was fascinated by it as a boy and as a man. He was one of eight children, the second son, his elder brother George being his idol.

The dominating figure in the family was his grandmother, a formidable and fashionable lady who ruled her husband, a country parson, and her only son, Tom Hughes's father. Young Tom was never afraid of her and he was a favourite and devoted grandson who looked forward to visits to her London house in the shadow of St Paul's Cathedral, where he acquired the social graces by meeting the rich and the famous, the respectable and the raffish. He learned early in life to enjoy dinner parties and other social occasions and nobody ever called Tom Hughes 'shy'. Two heroes encountered at his grandmother's house were Sir Walter Scott and Henry New, the boxer, and they marked the boy for their own. He learned enormous amounts of Scott's poetry by heart and grew up to be an amateur boxer of renown.

His father, John Hughes, was a well-meaning dilettante who dabbled in literature, completely under his mother's control. It was she who chose a wife for him, an admirable choice as it happened, and John Hughes amiably acquiesced. He and his wife were serious people at heart who agreed that they would bring up their children to be industrious, never to take money for granted and to be Christians in the best sense. There is a strongly idealized portrait of John Hughes as Squire Brown in *Tom Brown's Schooldays*. When his father died, he inherited a modest fortune which others might have rejoiced at but which depressed him deeply because he felt that nothing in his pampered and useless existence had led him to deserve good fortune. His children were quite unaware of their father's morbid reaction, for they were simply happy and excited to move into the historic Donnington Priory in the White Horse Vale where life was suddenly more comfortable and where their mother quickly assumed the role of Lady Bountiful in the village.

The Hughes children were friendly with the village children, following the traditional country pattern of Tory semi-democracy in childhood, and knowing that in adult life school and profession would separate the classes. They never questioned their father's teaching that people blessed with money and privilege had a duty to repay it through service to the community. Squire Hughes sent his sons to Rugby School because he approved of Dr Arnold's attempts to Christianize the school. He had known Arnold when they were students together at Oxford, and although Squire Hughes was a Tory and Arnold a Whig, he was prepared to overlook their political difference in view of Arnold's admirable religious attitudes. The school which George and Tom Hughes joined in 1833 was still brutally rough and tumble but it was worlds away from the appalling regime at Winchester which almost crushed Mansfield. Tom's great love was Rugby Football and he was known to say in adult life that one half-hour of good Rugby was worth a year of common life. He studied quite hard at school, maintaining a respectable place in the middle of examination lists, and he very much enjoyed history and poetry. Arnold captured his respect from the very first term, and later on Hughes would insist that Arnold had given education a soul and purpose which it had not possessed since the reign of Elizabeth. There was only one instance when Hughes doubted his headmaster's wisdom and that was when Arnold expelled George Hughes, and it took many years before Tom Hughes could review the incident dispassionately to agree sadly that Arnold had been right.

He found no trouble in accepting the Arnold ethos, and his

naturally democratic outlook was strengthened by the headmaster's lectures and sermons, although those often shocked
him by their criticisms of contemporary society. He had been
blissfully unaware of any glaring inequalities. A decade later,
reading Stanley's biography, Hughes relived his meetings with
Arnold and began to think seriously about the implications of
Arnold's teachings.

After schooldays, Tom Hughes followed his brother George
to Oriel College, Oxford, where John Hughes had gone. The
university had undergone a change since the solemn days of
Keble and Newman, and sport and athletics were the thing when
Hughes arrived. These were greatly to his liking, as they were
to George's, and both young men did well at university sports,
Tom Hughes becoming noted for boxing and cricket, and
George for rowing. Whilst at university Tom Hughes met a
young lady called Frances Ford, fell in love and vowed to lead a
better life so as to be worthy of her. Like Kingsley after meeting
Fanny Grenfell, Hughes considered himself redeemed by the
love of a good woman, a youthful exaggeration, for he was in no
need of redemption. However, his new love had the advantage of
making him work hard as her snobbish relatives did not think
that a younger son with few prospects was a suitable match.

Fanny Ford was a charming girl who had complete faith in her
Tom to make good, but was at the same time obedient in the
Victorian style to her parents. After the routinely long engagement imposed by the parents, the pair were married and Fanny
Hughes proved to be a supportive wife who never complained,
no matter how often her husband was away on his reforming
crusades. He often felt guilty at leaving her while he attended so
many political meetings, but he tried to make it up to her by his
devotion and by sharing with her the busy social life they led in
addition to his social work.

There had been a time when Hughes had secretly considered
becoming a country parson, but he decided he was not a good
enough person and so he went into the legal profession, never
caring much for it, but working hard and conscientiously so that
he became known as a sound equity lawyer.

Like Ludlow before him, he was disturbed by the wretched
living conditions of the shopworkers whose homes he passed
each morning as he walked to his chambers in Lincoln's Inn.

(The area remained largely slum-residential until about the 1870s.) He felt outraged when he watched the urchins playing in the street whilst the gardens of Lincoln's Inn were green and inviting, and one afternoon he used his tenant's key to open the gate and invite the children inside. One afternoon only! He was visited by the beadle of the Inn who threatened, white with fury, to take away his key if he ever repeated the experiment. That incident with the children gave an indication of Hughes's real interests. He was ready to work solidly at the law for a living but his heart lay in his social work.

The Chartist scare of 1848 worried Hughes as it did Maurice and Kingsley, and Hughes enrolled as a special constable, being taken on, although he was not very successful. On 10 April he was assigned to duty in Trafalgar Square where many speeches were being delivered. Like Kingsley, Hughes was more or less in sympathy with the Chartists but he lost his temper as he listened to some of the inflammatory speeches. He protested loudly, a scuffle broke out and the regular police were summoned. The upshot was that Hughes and his friends were arrested for disturbing the peace!

The social unrest of the year preyed upon Hughes's conscience and at last he approached Maurice in person (his earlier contacts with him having been by correspondence), with the result that Maurice at once took him down to the night school in Little Ormond Yard.

In spite of the initial doubts of the group, Hughes quickly fitted in with the band of brothers. Genial, pragmatic, even-tempered, Tom Hughes was an 'endurer', to use his own word, and he had the good coach's knack of being able to make a team out of a bunch of individualistic, eccentric idealists. His contribution was in large measure the assurance and stability which his presence gave to the group. His companionship was comforting to his new friends. Kingsley loved Hughes for his sporting prowess, especially as a fisherman, and Ludlow loved him because he had all the social qualities which Ludlow sadly lacked.

The night school proved by its success that it was filling a need, but Ludlow was still not satisfied and continued his round of parish visiting, usually with John Self. All his instincts told him that society needed radical change, and Self encouraged this idea when he mentioned that he had recommended *Politics for the People* to a number of working men whose early suspicion of the paper had been partly allayed through its closure. One of those working-class friends was a Chartist tailor called Walter Cooper, a Scot whose native Calvinism had not survived a visit to London, where he saw Methodist parsons who reserved a religion of hell-fire and humility for the poor whilst offering a very different kind, full of worldliness and hypocrisy, for the rich.

Cooper joined the newly founded 'League of Social Progress' and had become, early in 1849, a popular working-class speaker, based in London. He was exactly the type of man Ludlow was most eager to meet, and he got Self to introduce him. Cooper agreed to accompany Ludlow to listen to Maurice at Lincoln's Inn, Maurice of course having no idea that a keen-witted Chartist was summing him up. The result was all that Ludlow could have wished, for Cooper said he was impressed by Maurice, and when Maurice was told about this, he was equally pleased and wrote to Georgina Hare, Julius Hare's half-sister, and Maurice's future second wife, on 12 March 1849:

> . . . My dear friend Ludlow has told me a thing just now that I am sure will please you, for it has comforted me. He has got a Chartist acquaintance of his to come and hear me at Lincoln's Inn. He has been for four Sundays, and last Sunday he said that he really began to understand me and like me. He asked why I could not meet the working men and talk to them. (He is a small tailor himself, but a man of really considerable attainments.)

Maurice had immediately taken to Cooper. 'The man is full of honest thought. He has been driven into infidelity from feeling that there were no Christians to meet the wants of his kind. The story is very cheering to me and gives me hopes that I may be some good that way hereafter. Thank God for calling me to it.'

Maurice was in an emotional state because it was Easter, the season which had so often brought death to the Maurice family, and his mind was filled with memories and feelings of mortality. He was also preoccupied with an altercation with Dr Jelf, principal of King's College, who was perturbed to see that Maurice, once in good standing with Church authorities, was being attacked by almost every section of the religious establishment because of his outspoken social views. Jelf had the well being of the College at heart and feared lest Maurice should become a subversive influence at King's, frightening the parents of prospective students. He had prepared a list of complaints against Maurice which the latter answered patiently, although he was hurt to the quick by the utter absurdity of most of the charges.

'I had been accused of not believing in the doctrines of the Prayer Book,' he wrote indignantly to Jelf.

No evidence had been produced for the charge; the writer had been compelled to confess he could produce none. Still he continued to propagate the insinuation and to direct it against me especially as a Professor of Divinity.

Three days later when his irritation had subsided he could see the humorous side, and he told Georgina Hare mischievously that he believed Jelf was suffering more than he was.

He is ill in bed, and I am afraid I have some of his nervous feelings to answer for. One is sorry to be the cause of keeping worthy people in a fever, but that comes of their inviting such dangerous explosive reformers to enter their quiet orthodox schools.

Maurice was honestly amazed that Jelf was raising those points since all Maurice's so-called 'heresies' had been long in print in articles or books, and it was surely inconceivable that Jelf had never glanced at them before Maurice was appointed to the faculty. 'I think on the whole he likes me,' he wrote to his fiancée, 'not perhaps quite as well as you do—but with a fair, reasonable, Anglican mid-way sort of liking; and I have no notion that he will ever throw me off rudely or harshly.' In that last assumption, at least, Maurice lived to be a false prophet.

Meanwhile Maurice promised Cooper to arrange some meetings between working men and the Maurician group, and the naïve ideas of the Mauricians were rather shaken. The 'brothers' could not deny now that thoughtful working-class leaders gave a low priority to religious questions and a high one to social and political questions, a fact which led Maurice and Ludlow to draw different conclusions. Maurice decided that he should be a church reformer and not a political organizer, while Ludlow decided that as a socially committed Christian his duty was to co-operate with the workers in the hope of Christianizing them along the way.

So far the meetings had been social and exploratory with no concrete aim in mind. There was a good deal of interest among the working class in the Robert Owen idea of Home Colonies, and some Chartists asked Maurice to approach government ministers with a view to getting protective legislation which would encourage the formation of such colonies. Maurice was flattered to be asked, but he had no influence in those quarters and had to disappoint his new friends.

The request made the Mauricians look into the whole idea of agricultural Utopias, and Maurice and Ludlow took a day off to visit the eccentric John Minter Morgan at his country home and examine the proposed community village for which he was soliciting funds. Ludlow and Maurice saw nothing in it from their point of view, but Home Colonies of one kind or another continued to be discussed, for they had immense appeal amongst townsmen who had been born in the country. Sometimes Maurice was quite carried away by his enthusiasm, and Ludlow raised his eyebrows when he heard Maurice say in public that it wasn't so much what he should say about Home Colonies, but what he should do about them. Reporting the speech afterwards to Kingsley, Ludlow speculated with a grin whether Maurice were really serious in thus hinting that he was ready to go out and establish one. 'Fancy us all squatting on earth with the Prophet at our head!'

There was no real need to worry. Maurice would never have sanctioned a scheme which involved the abolition of private property, for that would mean putting a secular Communist cart before a Christian horse. Owen's Queenswood community, an agricultural experiment, had failed and his reputation suffered accordingly, but the attraction of Home Colonies in general lingered for many years.

Since it was Maurice who chaired most of the meetings organized between the working men and the Mauricians, there was a tendency for everyone to look to him as a spiritual leader, a position which he tried desperately to avoid, believing most sincerely that leadership inevitably brought corruption. Many of his later twists and turns to leave the group were really inspired by this deep reluctance to take command, but his followers were so devoted to him and so well meaning, that they would not allow him to escape his destiny to be their 'Master' and their 'Prophet'.

Cooper was continually urging Ludlow to arrange entirely public meetings where Chartists could meet the group, and a room was accordingly hired at the Cranbourne Coffee House for 23 April 1849. Maurice agreed to preside, not without inward trepidation, as he was sure he would disappoint the Chartists, but he felt it his responsibility to speak out. He was coming to the conclusion that in some mysterious way God was using him for important work which he had not as yet been able to recognize. His speech was well received and he felt quite ashamed of his fears when he saw the kindness and friendliness of most of the audience. Describing the evening to Kingsley, Maurice mentioned his pleasure at the kindness and good sense of the Chartists whom he met. His tone of surprise was not the product of a patronizing attitude but was a measure of the huge social gap between a middle-class and a working-class man, and indeed Maurice's surprise was matched by similar feelings among the Chartists.

Kingsley had to imagine all these exciting meetings through the details in his friends' letters. Eversley seemed dull in comparison with London, and whenever possible he took a day off to visit the capital. They were not self-indulgent leisure trips but opportunities to talk with tailors about their conditions of labour, material which he was going to use in a new pamphlet, 'Cheap Clothes and Nasty', and in his Chartist novel, *Alton Locke*. Sweated labour was a major theme of that novel, as was sanitary reform which had forced itself upon his notice through his experiences in rural areas, so whilst in London Kingsley also talked with the doctors in the Maurician group.

On one of these London trips Kingsley stayed late in the evening so as to attend one of the Cranbourne meetings, and it was well that he did so, because the meeting began badly and grew worse. The atmosphere was cold and suspicious, and everything seemed on the point of disaster when Kingsley jumped up and stammered loudly that he was a Church of England parson—and a Chartist! His disarming statement took everyone by surprise. It was true, yet it was not true. It was certainly true in the spirit in which Kingsley meant it at that moment: it was not true in the sense that he belonged to a Chartist party. It performed a minor miracle for the Mauricians, the audience giving its attention to Maurice who was free to speak his mind, and win them over. There was agreement that the meetings were productive and should be continued, and Kingsley went to London especially to attend the meeting on 11 July when Maurice rose to new heights as a speaker. The man was inspired, gigantic, declared Kingsley, and even hardened cynics were moved by him.

A few days after that very successful meeting, Maurice had a rare opportunity to contrast his initiatives with the Chartists with the 'what-might-have-been' of worldly fame when he went to Cambridge for a dinner of the Apostles' Club. As usual, he was not particularly at ease among them, but that was no new thing for Maurice, who had never capitalized on his social contacts with fellow Apostles. None the less he was unwilling to break his ties with them, believing that good often came from strange quarters—and who was he to assume it would come from workers' meetings and not from the Apostles' Club?

Although several Chartists were atheists, some of them indeed professional atheists, like George Jacob Holyoake, Maurice was prepared to co-operate with them in special situations. This did not of course prevent him from feeling annoyed when he was attacked in the atheist press, and on one occasion he was so exasperated that he remarked to Kingsley, 'So they mean war', but that was a metaphorical overstatement. Holyoake never intended to declare war on the Christian Socialists in his paper, although it would have been popular, and he had a soft spot for Maurice. A clue to that regard might have been found in an accident to Holyoake's young son, who was run over in the street outside Maurice's home. An unknown clergyman, seeing the commotion, appeared on the scene, rescued the child and carried him, streaming with blood, to the hospital. Holyoake never discovered the identity of that Good Samaritan, who had refused to give his name, but he apparently believed that it was Maurice.

Maurice's charity towards non-believers was not shared by Ludlow who would not accept, far less welcome, avowed atheists. When Furnivall's religious views changed to the point when he could no longer honestly call himself a Christian, Ludlow blamed himself bitterly for having introduced a future atheist into the Maurician circle. Two leading Chartists who attended some of the meetings with Maurice were Bronterre O'Brien and Feargus O'Connor, and Ludlow was cold and unyielding towards them because they were not Christians in spite of the fact that on other issues, democracy and republicanism, for example, he was closer to them than he was to his friends. Most of the Mauricians ranked republicanism with blasphemy, and there was a memorable meeting when the National Anthem was played and some of the Chartists began to hiss. An angry Tom Hughes jumped up on a chair to shout that he would fight the next man who booed the Queen's anthem, and since everyone knew that Hughes boxed very well, the hint was taken, the pianist resumed playing and a loyal chorus took up the strain. Maurice was not present or the incident would never have occurred.

Holyoake was a detached observer of the proceedings and he reflected that it was one thing for Hughes to suggest settling a political point by recourse to fisticuffs, because he was a gentleman, educated at Rugby and Oxford, but suppose the idea had come from a tailor, schooled in Glasgow or London's East End? What then? In general, however, Holyoake was as willing to co-operate on a limited basis with the Christian Socialists as Maurice was with Holyoake's friends. The end was what mattered to both men; they could differ as to the means.

Three Chartists in particular became deeply involved with Maurice. Two were watchcase-joint finishers, Joseph Millbank who worked in silver, and Thomas Shorter who worked in gold. They were intelligent and earnest men who were absorbed easily into the Maurician band. The third man, Lloyd Jones,[1] was a skilled fustian cutter, who could earn enough in two or three days to support his family for a week, so he had the rest of his time free for working-class activity.

Lloyd Jones came from the north of England, where he had become a disciple of Robert Owen. With a few young friends, Lloyd Jones had opened a co-operative store in Salford in 1831, but the shop did not last long and the young men turned their hands to education, opening a night school in Salford which did quite well for six years or so. By the mid-1840s Lloyd Jones had become a typical Owenite missionary, an effective speaker and writer and an experienced organizer. After support for Owen's ideas and experiments dwindled, Lloyd Jones migrated to London, where he resumed his old trade as fustian cutter and turned to Chartism in place of his Owenite work. When the Mauricians met him in 1849, he was a mature, self-educated man, and precisely the type of working man the band of brothers hoped to make contact with. Ludlow and Lloyd Jones hit it off immediately and formed an excellent personal and working relationship. Lloyd Jones was nothing like a Christian in Ludlow's meaning of the term, but he was forgiven because Ludlow liked and admired him.

The summer of 1849 was generally unhealthy, with typhus everywhere and hints of the serious cholera epidemic which was on the way. Kingsley[2] wore himself out nursing the Eversley sick, sitting up nights with patients whose family was too frightened of infection to remain at the bedside. He knew that poverty was as endemic as sickness in his parish, and wished he knew the way to cure them. He agreed with the country parsons in southern and south-west England that emigration was one possible solution for poverty, especially in the case of the girls, and one of Kingsley's duties was to see Eversley emigrants off from Tilbury. Goodbyes over, he would hurry back to London to visit his friends and catch up with all the news. He found London hot, dusty and enervating, not much better than Eversley and was glad to be in the train returning to the country.

The teachers at the night school at Little Ormond Yard decided to arrange a country picnic for the boys who attended the day school, and they begged Maurice to accompany them. He was too shy to accept at first, afraid that he would be a wet blanket and spoil everyone's fun, yet on the other hand if he refused, he would hurt his friends' feelings. He tried to take a more positive stand. The 'smoke-dried boys', at any rate, would benefit from a day in the country, and so, come to think of it, would he. Maurice was in a troubled state of mind again, upset at the news that Carlyle was writing a biography of John

Sterling in response to the respectful and insipid *Life and Letters* written by Julius Hare. Maurice feared that Carlyle would rake over the old ashes of Sterling's atheism. A good deal of Maurice's unhappiness over the Carlyle biography arose from his own memories of being inadequate when Sterling needed him most. It certainly gave Maurice no comfort when in the course of time the Carlyle biography was completed and published and by its brilliant presentation bestowed upon Sterling a literary immortality he had not achieved by his own efforts.

Meanwhile Maurice pulled himself together over the matter of the picnic, accepted the invitation, and once in the country with his friends enjoyed the day tremendously. It was most gratifying to see that his own protégé, Tom Hughes, was the life and soul of the day, inventing game after game and leading the boys in all their sports, with Furnivall not far behind.

There was another personal preoccupation for Maurice, and a much happier one, being his imminent marriage to Georgina Hare. He had every confidence, entirely well founded, that he would be happy with her and that she would be a good step-mother for his boys. It would be a union of adults, quite different from the exuberant youthful marriage of Maurice and Anna Barton, but just as successful in its own quiet way. Furnivall, who was an inveterate sentimentalist, went round the Maurician circle collecting money for a wedding present, and shortly before the wedding left a splendid pile of books at Maurice's home, with the signatures of all the donors. The books included Holinshed, Hall, Fabyan, Hardyng, Rastell, Arnold, Froissart's *Chronicles* in thirteen volumes, Fuller's *Worthies* in two volumes, and Facciolati's *Lexicon* in four volumes.

The Prophet had not expected a wedding gift. Writing to thank Furnivall, he declared that he owed his young friends far more than they owed him, and he was especially grateful for the present because it showed that they were not setting him up on a pedestal as a teacher, but were fond of him as a friend. 'One who marries voluntarily comes down from an oracular tripod and declares that he has nothing to distinguish himself from his fellows,' he said, adding that Georgina would not feel truly married to him if she did not also feel hearty sympathy with the kindest and truest friends a man ever had.

There was, of course, one of those true and kind friends who had profound reservations about Maurice's changed marital status. It was Ludlow, who had often spoken censoriously about second marriages and who did not believe it possible for a member of the well-off Hare family to have sympathy with the working class. Much more likely, he prophesied, darkly pessimistic, that the second Mrs Maurice would entice her husband away from the band of brothers! That was part of Ludlow's misgivings, but a deeper part concerned his own sense of loss and rejection, like a child whose beloved parent has remarried, thus showing in the clearest possible manner that the parent needed more than the child was able to give. Ludlow also felt uncomfortable at the public proof that Maurice was a man, like other men, who wanted a woman's love and a full sexual life. Ludlow wished the Prophet could have lived a celibate life, and said as much in confidence to Kingsley, who also rather disliked second marriages, partly because they would pose problems in a life hereafter which would presumably be monogamous.

Kingsley gave no support to Ludlow over Maurice's second marriage, for he waived all rules in the case of his Master and he felt it was not for him, or even for Ludlow, to criticize Maurice.

So Ludlow had to keep his disappointments bottled up inside himself and Kingsley was soon far away in Devonshire, sent there on doctor's orders to read, fish and sleep. By the time Kingsley was well enough to return to Eversley Maurice was already married and Ludlow had left London for Paris.

The French Connection

France: The economic crisis of 1848 was not solved by the socialist experiments which followed the February revolt, and by May there was a large conservative opposition. In June there was civil war in Paris between extreme socialists and conservatives, put down ruthlessly by the government. In November 1848 a new constitution was adopted, with Louis Napoleon elected president, and conservative ministers in the government. The following year saw a swing away from the socialists towards the conservatives.

England, 1849: Improvements in sanitary reform were seen following the Public Health Act of 1848. Emigration was encouraged by the discovery of gold in California in 1848 and in Australia in 1851. Wordsworth died in 1850 and Alfred Tennyson became Poet Laureate.

It did not take Ludlow long to realize that the Paris he observed in 1849 was very different from the Paris he had seen in 1848, and on the whole he felt pleased by what he found. Of course he regretted the short, sharp bloodiness of the 'June days', and was unhappy that the government put on trial socialists like Louis Blanc, sentencing them to periods of exile, but he had not cared for extremist policies and was reassured that there seemed more moderation now among the revolutionaries of 1848. He was especially interested in the co-operative workshops in Paris, which were protecting the interests of their members but not trying to abolish a competitive society. In 1849 Ludlow was not sure that he supported the workshops, believing that Home Colonies were the best way to socialize society, but he had to admire the co-operatives' spirit of brotherhood and he let himself dream that a moral regeneration would spring from those new collectives. Was he, he wondered, being too optimistic in thinking that the golden age was on its way? The workshops were providing their members with the chance for democratic self-government and fellowship and that, it seemed to Ludlow in 1849, far out-weighed any doctrinaire insistence upon getting rid of the profit motive.

The Utopian appeal of the workshops was strong and persuasive. They were self-governing and independent; each member worked for himself, but each was ready to help another in need; a process of moral as well as material improvement was thereby created. Most of the Paris workshops were on a small scale, an advantage which saved them from the problems inherent in larger enterprises, but which gave a misleading impression that producer co-operatives could succeed in any circumstances. Their social welfare functions were necessary in 1849 when no compre-hensive State welfare system existed.

The workshops which so pleased Ludlow reflected the small size of Paris industry in general, and when he was there they were enjoying a short period of sunny success. No businessman, Ludlow was not aware of the significance of size, and if he wondered about England as a future location for similar work-shops he had only his knowledge of London to guide him, a city which resembled Paris in having small-scale industries. For co-operatives to succeed on a broad basis so that they could make a real contribution to the quality of English working-class life, they would have to succeed in the industrial heartland of the north with its great factories. That was a much more difficult task, as Ludlow would discover.

He returned to London from his Paris holiday quite sure that he had discovered the key to Christian social reform in these co-operatives, and he could not wait to pass on the good news to the band of brothers. At last they could all get down to real hard work, after months of preparation through Bible study and the night school teaching. It never crossed his mind that during his short absence they might have found a new interest. Yet such was the case. He found that they were completely absorbed in a new venture and whenever he tried to talk to them about the producer co-operatives they listened politely, but their attention was else-where. Yes, yes, they said, by all means let Paris have her co-operatives—but what London needed was sanitary reform and they were the group to bring this about.

There was a good deal of sense in what they said, since they could point to 15,000 deaths from cholera that summer. Mansfield, Walsh and Kingsley led the Maurician group in a campaign to teach the general public about the need for clean drinking water and proper sewage disposal. Dr Walsh had just been appointed Superintending Inspector to Southwark and Bermond-sey by the new General Board of Health, and he had been so horrified by the Southwark slums that he took his friends on a conducted tour.[1] Kingsley described it to his wife:

Oh, God! what I saw! people having no water to drink—hundreds of them—but the water of the common sewer . . . At the time the cholera was raging Walsh saw them throwing untold horrors into the ditch, and then dipping out the water and drinking it! . . . And mind, these are not dirty, debauched Irish, but honest, hard working artisans.

He urged Fanny Kingsley to dun their rich neighbours for contributions; twenty pounds would buy a water cart and Walsh would make sure it was properly used. Kingsley went to Oxford to enlist the support of Bishop Wilberforce, a supporter of sanitary reform who impressed Kingsley very favourably. (Ten years later he would change his mind when Wilberforce gained unenviable notoriety in the 'apes and angels' debate with T. H. Huxley over Darwin's theories.)

Walsh had called Jacob's Island, Bermondsey, the 'capital of cholera', and he had his friends publish a twelve-page pamphlet to draw attention to its horrors. Mansfield, who was particularly outraged by what he had seen, said that it was not enough to make the scandal public, they must form a National Health League to force legislative reform. They turned to Ludlow, their expert in drafting, to work out a constitution for such a league, and stifling a sigh for his lost co-operatives, he sat down and got to work. He based his constitution on that of the Anti-Corn Law League, and the Health League was to appeal to all classes and be directed towards the general promotion of public health.

Members would raise money from the public to finance specific sanitary reforms.

Kingsley was sent home with instructions to write his best stinging articles. He took a clutch of government Blue Books with him which he planned to humanize with descriptions of his own experiences in dealing with infectious diseases in rural areas. He felt frustrated, marooned in Eversley, and bombarded Ludlow by every post with ideas for new initiatives, for officials to be lobbied, personalities to be approached, larger print orders for their pamphlet. 'Why are you so confoundedly merciful and tender-hearted?' he complained. 'Do you actually fancy that you can talk these landlords into repentance?' He was impatient to see the League formed and working, seeing it as a useful wedge to push open the door to other reforms not only sanitary ones.

The group had been so absorbed in their new project, clearly an estimable one, that they had quite forgotten to mention it to Maurice and took his approval for granted. They also took it for granted that he would accept the role and title of president of the League, once formed. It was accordingly a considerable and quite incomprehensible shock when he vehemently refused to associate himself with it and by so doing effectively strangled it at birth.

Ludlow could not contain himself. First his friends paid no attention to his workshops, and now the Prophet paid no attention to the Health League. He complained bitterly to Mansfield, who passed his complaint on to Maurice, and the older man realized that in all fairness he must explain himself to Ludlow. It was the result, he said, of his experience years before in the Education League when he was dismayed by the bitter arguments and unpleasant in-fighting. He mistrusted all man-made organizations, and even a league run by his own supporters was bound eventually to show similar tendencies. He begged Ludlow to be content with parish work and apologized for 'pouring tepid water' on the League. But that was his nature, he added. 'I am a cold-blooded animal.'

There was nothing Ludlow could find to say. He had given the League all his time and energy, had indeed been so vehement in his language that Walsh had tactfully toned it down. He never forgot how Maurice squashed the League, and when he wrote about it in 1894, he noted that what Maurice had described as 'pouring tepid water on' seemed to the others as 'relentlessly crushed'. Once again Ludlow was in a situation where he had to bury his frustrations and desires and submit mutely to fate, all the more galling because this time he was sure that the League would have succeeded. His friends had a similar reaction. They were full of suppressed energy like smouldering volcanoes waiting for a signal to erupt. 'I have a wild longing to do *something*,' wrote Kingsley from Eversley.

All through the autumn of 1849 the friends kept hoping that 'something' would appear, and appear it did, in the very unlikely shape of a political refugee from France, Jules St André Le Chevalier, who in England shortened his name to Jules Lechevalier.

He was an interesting and versatile man of Maurice's age, and had been a casual acquaintance of Ludlow's since 1840, when he called at Cadogan Square with a letter of introduction from Charles Liot. Lechevalier was born in Martinique and in 1840 was keenly interested in the abolition of slavery and colonial conditions. Ludlow was courteous to him but the difference in their ages and temperament meant that their relationship remained distant. Lechevalier went to France, where he began to study socialism of various kinds and earned a living as a political journalist. He became attracted to the ideas of Saint-Simon, then moved on to follow Charles Fourier, admiring in particular his schemes for workers' associations. Then his enthusiasm for Fourierism waned and he looked round for something new, a broadly based socialist philosophy which would have a democratic appeal for the working class.

Orthodox French socialists rather mistrusted him, feeling that he was talented but shallow, unreliable, and ready to make compromises in the name of broad appeal. Nor did they believe him when he said he was a lapsed Catholic, for they suspected he was still religious at heart and hostile to the anti-clericalism which was automatic in most French socialist parties. His latest hero was Proudhon, and he had played a minor part in the 1848 revolution, joining the socialists and supporting the working men's associations.

Lechevalier was elected to the National Assembly, co-operating with Proudhon in setting up a People's Bank, but after the 'June days' he had been arrested with other leading socialist personalities and ordered to leave France. England was a natural refuge and as soon as he reached London he called upon Ludlow, to be given a very different welcome from previous occasions. Ludlow was proud to befriend a man who was not only a French socialist but had been sentenced to exile for his beliefs. Not only that, as the two men talked it was clear to Ludlow that Lechevalier shared his dream of wanting religious and moral values to apply to society, and he, too, had some reservations about Louis Blanc's kind of social workshops, fearing they would in the end lead to governmental despotism.

Listening spellbound to Lechevalier, and reliving his own visits to Paris in 1848 and 1849 as he did so, Ludlow felt a resurgence of his former excitement and pride in the French experiment. He told himself that his earlier judgements about the Frenchman had been mistaken. Did it really matter if Lechevalier were inconsistent? He had come round in the end, and would be a splendid addition to the band of brothers, to be borne off in triumph first to Maurice's services at Lincoln's Inn, and then to the famous Bible evenings. The truth was that at this juncture Lechevalier's social and political opinions coincided almost exactly with Ludlow's own, and coming at the moment when Ludlow felt that Maurice had let him down, the Frenchman made an exceedingly strong impression on the young man. Lechevalier's advent was important to Ludlow, and indeed to the whole group.

After the initial introductions had been made, Lechevalier began a careful study of Maurice's theology, his usual custom on meeting new ideas, and almost at once he decided he had at last met a man who combined Christianity and socialism. The Frenchman's intellectual apparatus slightly overawed his new English friends, especially since he also spoke English remarkably well. He was good-looking but rather rotund, and when he grew older became so corpulent that Holyoake described him as 'quite globular, and when he moved he vibrated like a locomotive jelly'. At the time Holyoake wrote that, he had good reason to feel spiteful towards Lechevalier, but in 1849 there was nothing but goodwill towards the exile. When Lechevalier told Maurice that there was a need for 'the Church'—he did not specify which one—to set good social examples in order to win the working class to Christianity, Maurice warmed to him at once.

Then there occurred an event which captured the Mauricians

completely, nothing less than Lechevalier's dramatic conversion to the Church of England. After nearly thirty years of absenting himself from the Roman Catholic Church he felt, it seemed, an urgent impulse to join the Anglican Church as he had learned about it through talking with Maurice. With hindsight, the Mauricians might query the validity of that conversion, seeing that Lechevalier drifted towards the Anglo-Catholics, wondering if his striking conversion might not have been partly dictated by the need to make friends who would help him earn a living to support a wife and children. At the moment of conversion, however, it looked like the finger of God, and indeed it was well within Lechevalier's mercurial nature to have been entirely sincere.

The Mauricians rejoiced over him as if he were the prodigal son and spent hours discussing his suggestions about how to marry socialism with Christianity in the creation of workers' co-operatives in England. Even Maurice was cautiously approving of Lechevalier's ideas, while as for Ludlow, he accepted them wholeheartedly and could not wait to draft outlines of the schemes, and then revise and polish them. In his happy enthusiasm he wrote to Louis Meyer who was, however, unsympathetic, insisting that spiritual rebirth needed evangelical crusades, not workers' co-operatives. Meyer also disliked the name 'Christian Socialism' which the group, under Lechevalier's influence, was about to adopt. To be effective, argued Meyer, a title had to be clearly understood. Everyone knew what socialism stood for; it was workers' associations, people's banks, revolution and so forth. Christianity, or the application of Christianity, had never figured in the aims of socialism.

In short, Meyer was advising Ludlow to continue working in the time-honoured pastoral way, as Maurice had done over the proposed Health League. It was not the first time Meyer had given Ludlow unpalatable advice and it broke the last emotional tie which Ludlow had with France. Thenceforth in all aspects of his life, thoughts and aspirations Ludlow was an Englishman, and Maurice gradually filled, and more than filled, Meyer's place in Ludlow's life. The young man's deepest instincts were gloriously confirmed when shortly afterwards, and quite unexpectedly, Maurice declared that only the name 'Christian Socialist' could truthfully describe the intentions of the group.

The young men were ready to undertake some new enterprise.

They had noticed that the working men who attended the weekly meetings at Maurice's house had taken no interest in parish visiting, or the sanitary reform campaign, or even in emigration. The group tended to split over emigration, with Kingsley and Maurice in favour, following Carlyle's support of it, along with Sidney Herbert in the government. Ludlow and Mansfield agreed with Lord Shaftesbury that it merely exported England's social problems, and Mansfield insisted that the poor had as much right to live in England as the rich. 'God placed them here, not that we should live upon their lives—*eating their blood*—and then should give them as final payment a transportation which costs us as many pounds per head, as we are consuming, many of us, in foreign wine per week.' Not that Mansfield consumed foreign wine, for he, Ludlow and Furnivall were mighty teetotallers.

They begged Maurice to lead them in some well-defined plan, but he characteristically refused, at which they decided they could no longer wait for him to become a leader and it was time to act without him. They arranged to meet at a supper at Ludlow's house when they would attempt to set up some workers' co-operatives. After some hesitation they decided not to invite Maurice in case he doused that scheme, too, with more of his 'tepid water'.

However, the unexpected occurred. Maurice, that gentle, good and guileless man, heard about the supper and without inquiring further assumed that he was invited and went along, not knowing that behind his back Ludlow, Mansfield and Hughes had decided to form a tailors' and shirtmakers' association, and Kingsley was coming from Eversley especially for the occasion. Kingsley's share of the work had to be almost exclusively literary and propagandist, but he was important to the group. *Yeast*, which had made a stir when it was published in instalments, was now being published in book form, and he was half-way through his Chartist book, *Alton Locke*, and had finished his pamphlet 'Cheap Clothes and Nasty'. He was full of praise for an article of Ludlow's in *Fraser's Magazine* and pooh-poohed his own recent pamphlet, which was really a splendid piece of polemical writing. Tom Hughes had noticed before this trait in Kingsley, a paradoxical mixture of diffidence and self-confidence, of aggressive optimism and morbid depression.

The general tenor at this crucial supper meeting was therefore common acceptance of a decision virtually taken. Henry Mayhew's articles in the *Morning Chronicle* had supplied an important emotional stimulus, and now the band of brothers had reached an intellectual conclusion. Those who had missed the Mayhew articles when they first appeared could find the basic facts in Ludlow's article for *Fraser's*, and later in 1850 they were quoted extensively in a sour history of England by Ledru Rollin, another French socialist refugee. Indeed, throughout 1849 and 1850 Mayhew's disclosures were creating a climate of opinion quite favourable to the experiment of working men's associations. Ludlow's supper could fairly be said to have been the inaugural meeting for the Christian Socialists as an identifiable group concerned with setting up associations, and afterwards there was no stopping them and Maurice was swept along on the tide.

Organization was not one of Maurice's talents, nor could he bring himself to elaborate a set of rules, but he did write to Kingsley on 2 January 1850, proclaiming that 'Competition is put forth as the law of the universe. That is a lie. The time has come for us to declare that it is a lie by word and deed. I see no way but associating for work instead of for strikes . . .' He then hedged that categorical statement about with reservations which showed he did not intend to destroy the relationship between employer and employed but wanted to root out deception and immorality in business and industry. As a man with a vocation for teaching, Maurice preferred the literary side of association work and was relieved to allow others to organize co-operatives. He was ready to start a series of tracts, quite distinct from running associations, and asked for them to be discussed at the Monday Bible meetings at his house, which would leave the larger and more general weekly meetings available for discussing details about the associations. He insisted that the tracts should be Christian in character, like *Politics for the People*, and he laid down two conditions: first, there was to be freedom to make it absolutely clear that their work was based on clear religious beliefs, and second, there was to be freedom to invite into the group any sympathizers prepared to work with them, 'viz. all men of honest purpose, whatever their intellectual confusions may be'. Since Maurice's requests were law to his disciples these conditions were accepted, although Ludlow disliked the possibility that he might be called upon to co-operate with someone whose religious views differed from his own.

Within days of the supper at Ludlow's house a working meeting of about twenty supporters took place at Maurice's house, and a tailors' association was set up, with Walter Cooper, an obvious choice, as manager. A committee was elected to raise money for rent, purchase of material and cash in hand for wages, a sum of £350. Operating rules were formulated, a house in Castle Street, just off Oxford Street, was hired, and the association was ready.

The Mauricians were very interested to see from the *Morning Chronicle* that a packed meeting of Journeymen-tailors at Exeter Hall on 17 January had protested against the practices of their trade and voted to petition Parliament to appoint a committee to examine their trade practices. Surely, argued the Mauricians, those were just the men who would jump at the chance of joining producer co-operatives. Unfortunately, when approached, most of these men showed no such interest and merely repeated that they wanted a government committee set up. This was not good enough for Ludlow, who organized a meeting for London tailors with Walter Cooper as the star speaker. He had anticipated that Cooper's famed oratory would win them on the spot, but only a dozen even evinced interest in associations and none signed up.

On 11 February 1850 the Working Tailors' Association formally began operations, and two or three days later Maurice committed himself also by telling Ludlow that the only honest title for the tracts was 'Tracts on Christian Socialism', because it would 'commit us at once to the conflict we must engage in sooner or later with the unsocial Christians and the unchristian Socialists'. Thus the tentative ideas of first Ludlow and then Lechevalier had come to fruition in Maurice.

Meanwhile the Prophet happily canvassed all his friends to gain support for the new tailors' association. He wrote to Daniel Macmillan at his Cambridge bookshop, promising to send a list of tailors' prices as soon as it was compiled, and adding shrewdly, 'Pray make it known in Cambridge, and say how much I feel interested in it to any who may take the least interest in me'. He knew there were many young men who respected him without having a liking for socialism, men like Fenton John Anthony Hort, for instance, student at Trinity College, friend of the

Macmillan brothers and admirer of Maurice.

Like Hughes, Hort had gone to Rugby where he formed the intention, fulfilled in adult life, of becoming a clergyman. He was a studious young man who was destined to be a Cambridge don before he became a parson, and he found that Maurice's books were a helpful guide. A sociable and talkative man, Fenton Hort became a pioneer in the sport of mountaineering, and he enjoyed fossil hunting, botany and photography. He had subscribed to *Politics for the People* and been excited by it although rather nervous about its socialist implications. Since then he had followed through the newspapers, and through conversations with the Macmillans, the activities of Maurice and company, often amused by the press accounts. There had been one in the *English Review* which he enjoyed. It had praised Kingsley as a poet but expressed fears that he might fall into the hands of F. D. Maurice and become spoiled: 'We have heard that Mr Kingsley holds extreme democratical opinions and that he has been even mixed up with the Chartists, but this we cannot possibly believe.'

Daniel Macmillan showed Maurice's letter to Hort the day it arrived, and Hort was impatient to see the new developments and to read the 'Tracts on Christian Socialism'. A self-admitted Tory, he was not sure he approved of Maurice's declaration that the co-operative principle was better than the competitive one, but he trusted Maurice, and was willing to learn, although he promised himself that if they went right over to socialism, he would remain safely on the sidelines.[2]

The first tract, Maurice's own work, was in the form of a dialogue, one of his favourite literary devices, and was based on a favourite theme of his, that brotherhood, fellowship and co-operative work formed the essence of the laws of God and could be achieved without radically changing the existing forms of society. Careful reading of that first tract and careful attention to what Maurice normally said, would have shown that his greatest dread was to find himself, willy-nilly, leader of a Christian Socialist party. As his son put it: 'His great wish was to Christianise Socialism, not to Christian-Socialise the universe'. But his supporters frequently misheard him, for his personality was so magnetic that they desperately wanted him to legitimize their hopes and aims by sharing them, and it was too painful for them to face the reality when he did not share them.

With none of Maurice's dislike of organizations, the young Christian Socialists gloried in their new work. As Tom Hughes said in 1873, reviewing those days: 'I certainly thought, (and for that matter have not altered my opinion to this day) that here we had found the solution to the great labour question: but I was also convinced that we had nothing to do but just announce it and found an association or two, in order to convert all England, and usher in the millennium at once, so plain did the whole thing seem to me. I will not undertake to answer for the rest of the Council, but I doubt whether I was at all more sanguine than the majority.'

It was logical that they should turn to French experience for guidelines, and Lechevalier offered a few hints, but his most practical contribution was to bring Charles Sully into the group, an English bookbinder who had lived in Paris and was now a political exile. He had fought behind the barricades 'till his arms were bloody to the elbows', but he had rejected force in favour of peaceful solutions, a change of heart which annoyed his erstwhile comrades but greatly endeared him to the Christian Socialists.

Sully was a spare, hard-faced man who seldom smiled, which the Englishmen put down to his political background until they discovered it was connected with his private life. He never disguised his want of religion and took no interest in the religious and moral aspects which attracted Maurice and the younger men, but in obedience to Maurice's dictum he was welcomed into the group as a sympathizer and his experience and organizing ability were respected. He was asked to prepare a plan for a Central Board which would run associations and he drew up a scheme founded on sound business principles with no lip service to idealism. Sight of it drove Maurice to despair, and he refused to be associated with Sully's plan.

The situation was delicate and difficult, for the Christian Socialists could not conceive of remaining in any organization which did not ultimately bear their Prophet's seal of approval, yet they had seen that the tailors on their own either could not or would not form a self-governing association. Ludlow stepped into the breach, quietly asking Sully to draft a second constitution, and then himself revising it in such a way that Maurice would approve it, and it would also meet the needs of the associations. The draft was finished by June, and put into print as Tract V, with a caveat that the scheme of organization laid down was not intended to lead anyone into an unthinking worship of social mechanism. Society was not an assemblage of wheels and strings but a partnership of living men, and Christian Socialists were concerned with the spirit which animated society, not just with its form.

The young men, all of them close personal friends as well as committed Christian Socialists, were quite sure that they had found the solution for society's ills, and their constant meetings reinforced those beliefs. They spoke about associations to everyone they met, and believed that all men and women of goodwill were bound to agree with them, once associations had been clearly explained. Yet even among Maurice's admirers there were people who thought that associations were dangerous. Fenton Hort had met the Christian Socialists in May 1850, and was so fascinated by them, and what Alexander Macmillan liked to call the 'Crotchet Club', alluding to the quirks and foibles of the members, that he went to London to see them whenever he could. His first encounter had been at a Monday Bible meeting, where he was especially thrilled to meet Kingsley (who was rushing off to catch a train to Eversley and did not have time to say more than goodbye to him). Hort became very friendly with Ludlow, Hughes and Furnivall, who did everything they could to win him over, but he remained obstinately Tory.

The Christian Socialists had formed 'The Society for Promoting Working Men's Associations' as a step to creating more associations and they unanimously offered the post of secretary to Sully, who was pleased to accept. Unfortunately, his connection with the group had been noticed by the English left wing press, and Julian Harney, the Chartist editor of the *Red Republican*, and a friend of Marx and Engels, sought to blacken the new Society by exposing its secretary as a bigamist. The news astonished the Christian Socialists, as it did most other people, but when they thought it over they realized it explained a good deal of Sully's mysterious manner.

Now that the truth was out, Sully spoke quite frankly about a disastrous first marriage, and of his later bigamous one with another woman. The Christian Socialists were sympathetic and understanding and would have liked to have kept him on as secretary, but it was foolhardy for Sully to remain in London and risk prosecution, so his friends passed the hat round and raised the fare for him and his family to go to the United States.[3] Thomas Shorter took Sully's place as secretary to the Society.

The Association Crusade

Up, up, up and up!
Face your game and play it!
The night is past, behold the sun!
The idols fall, the lie is done!

Alton Locke's song

Setting up working men's associations was a real crusade for the Christian Socialists, who made up in eagerness what they lacked in experience. Ludlow, Hughes and Furnivall, the main London activists, all of them lawyers, looked on associations as instruments of social change: Maurice and Kingsley, educators more than organizers, and both priests, looked on them as instruments of social protest. That was a fundamental difference which passed unobserved in the euphoria of the moment. The associations marked a new stage in the work of the Christian Socialists and was much more than the 'holy water' by which 'the priest consecrated the heartburnings of the aristocrat', to use Marx's contemptuous phrase. Indeed, aristocrats were conspicuous by their absence in the Christian Socialist movement, although two men were shortly to join the group who might come into that category; Edward Vansittart Neale,[1] a wealthy member of the country gentry, and Viscount Goderich, a member of an important Whig family. The Puritan tradition of the seventeenth century was more marked in these two than a nineteenth-century aristocratic one, and any 'holy water' which Maurice might have been trying to sprinkle would have affected the middle-class members more than those two upper-class ones, since neither followed Maurice in his religious ideas. It would be difficult to find two men conforming less to the stereotype of 'aristocrat'. Perhaps in France or Germany a mixture of Christianity and Socialism salved the conscience of the rich, but it was not so in England with Maurice and his followers.

The Working Tailors' Association began operations, and new associations were in the pipe-line. The band of brothers were at last compelled to submit, with some grumbling, to a degree of formality, something they had managed to avoid hitherto. They became Promoters in 'The Society for Promoting Working Men's Associations', with a Council of Promoters, Maurice as president. The Council was made up of twelve ordinary members who did the work, and any number of associated members, these being almost anybody who expressed an interest in associations. Finally there was a Central Board, of managers and representatives from associations, with other delegates, and a paid secretary. The Board's function was to regulate 'all the relations of the Associations with each other, and, with the concurrence of the Council of Promoters, those of the united Associations with the public at large'. It was to encourage the formation of new associations and to organize the exchange and distribution of goods through Labour Bazaars. Ten or so new associations were quickly formed, two more tailors' associations, two builders', three shoemakers', one piano maker's, one printer's and one smith's, all in London, enough to encourage the Christian Socialists, but a pitifully small response from the working class, and they were in London. The message had not spread outwards.

The Council transacted business between the Society of Promoters and the associations; it saw to publicity, collected and distributed money and, in Ludlow's words, diffused 'the principles of Co-operation as the practical application of Christianity to trade and industry'. It met each Friday and its members took turns to attend the office every day. Council and Central Board together, by their relationship and work, in fact implied a policy dedicated to changing the existing economic pattern of society, the very reverse of what Maurice stood for, but he raised no objection, being apparently too busy to perceive the wider implication, and through his position as president of the Council Maurice became in the public mind the chief proponent of co-operative associations, which to many in 1850 were dangerous, not to say revolutionary, bodies.

Maurice anticipated that associations would have a conciliatory, not a revolutionary effect upon industry, arguing that the worst danger came from strikes, because successful ones would give workers a risky and unrealistic sense of their power, whilst unsuccessful ones would frustrate them and drive them to desperate courses. It was surely better to direct them into constructive associations. In any case, his meetings with working-class men had led him to believe that the men were determined to have associations, come what might. Speaking to a responsible middle class, he would say, ''Stop asking: 'How can we prevent associations?' and start asking: 'What can we do to lessen the present evils?' ''

One of Maurice's first positive steps as president of the Council was to introduce a newcomer as Promoter, one Edward Vansittart Neale. It was what he had done with Tom Hughes and the night school. Neale had read of the associations, felt interested in the idea and contacted Maurice, so Maurice had naturally taken him at his word and invited him to join the Council.

The rest of the active Promoters were slightly resentful, Ludlow especially, at having to welcome a stranger into their inner circle. He had not grown up with them, maturing in the charmed weekly meetings at Maurice's house. He was older than they were, contemporary with Maurice, was better read in the works of Continental socialists and was far richer.

To make matters worse, he swiftly attained an important position among the Promoters, working hard and being very generous with money. All the Promoters gave money, that went without saying, but most of them had so little to give! They all went without small pleasures and luxuries so as to have money for the cause. 'Don't fire at me about smoking,' wrote Kingsley once to Ludlow, with a good deal of tartness, 'I do it because it does me good, and I could not (for I have tried again and again) do without it. I smoke the very cheapest tobacco. In the meantime I am keeping no horse—a most real self-sacrifice to me.' Kingsley even economized on his pipes, using clay ones which could be re-baked and used over and over again. As for Mansfield, the golden angel, he lived like an ascetic, virtually starving himself in order to have money for the movement and for his chemistry experiments, these latter being very interesting and making men at the Royal Institution say that he was Michael Faraday's successor.

Amid young men like these, Neale stood out like a sore

thumb, although a closer acquaintance showed that he was not so different after all. Like so many of the Christian Socialists, he had a strong Puritan heritage, prizing his ancestral connection with Oliver Cromwell. He was a nephew of William Wilberforce, the Evangelical and abolitionist. What set Neale apart was the size of his fortune, derived from a much earlier Neale who became rich trading with the colonies. His grandfather in 1780 purchased Bisham Abbey, an historic manor house on the banks of the Thames. Neale's father was an Anglican clergyman with Low Church leanings who had his son educated at home until he was ready for university.

When Neale was sent to Oriel College, Oxford, he was an impatient, lonely and sex-starved young man who kept a detailed diary as a surrogate companion. He tried to join in the social and sporting life of the university, frequenting wine parties and running up large debts which his grumbling father settled for him. But he was too shy to accompany his friends on their sexual adventures and found physical relief in masturbation, although he believed the practice to be wrong and suffered untold guilt over it. His strict Evangelical training made him feel guilty when he visited the London Zoo on a Sunday.

He was at Oriel in the brilliant days of John Henry Newman, who tutored him. He met the talented and enigmatic Hurrell Froude, Newman's great friend, and was briefly tempted by the Tractarians, especially after his cousin, Robert Wilberforce, joined them. He thought their form of religion was warmer and more appealing than the chilly, narrow one of the Evangelicals. He disliked the partisan, and often malicious, atmosphere of many Evangelical meetings which he attended, including ones chaired by his Uncle William. Neale's reaction, indeed, was much the same as Maurice's, at similar meetings. Slowly but surely Neale moved away from the Low Church Whiggery of his family towards the High Church Toryism of Newman, and when Neale left Oxford in 1831 he had learned one thing at least, he was not cut out to be an Anglican clergyman of his father's type—nor an Anglican clergyman at all.

Naturally he went into the legal profession, entering Lincoln's Inn, with no interest in politics beyond a stern disapproval of Parliamentary reform. Young Gladstone, he recalled with pleasure, had made a splendid anti-Reform speech at Oxford.

None the less he was interested, and with his background could hardly fail to be, in social questions, and like Ludlow and Lechevalier, became a man searching for a social cause with a religious flavour. He was as lonely in London as he had been in Oxford, with acquaintances but not friends, and where women were concerned he had strong sexual feelings which his religious scruples told him were wrong. He was always attracted to pretty women, but quickly bored by stupid ones, and it seemed to be his tragedy that the pretty ones he met were stupid as well!

It was in 1836, when he was in his mid-twenties, that Neale received the first emotional shock of his life, no less than the unexpected death of his favourite sister, Caroline. He had been close to her as he had never been close to his parents and he mourned her deeply. He longed for his parents to understand his grief, and comfort him, but was horrified to find that they not only ignored him, they seemed to have no sense of loss themselves, but spent hours bickering over whether the girl had or had not been pious enough to avoid eternal damnation. It was a point of view which led their son to renounce the Evangelical religion for ever. He adopted a new philosophy, that life was lived on earth, and heaven should be sought on earth. If heaven did not yet exist on earth, then man's duty was to create it. Striving to create heaven on earth was to become Neale's mission in life, on which he would spend most of his energies and income.

At the time of his sister's death, however, he had not managed to elaborate a working philosophy for himself, and was reduced to numbness, resolved to shun emotion and to rule his life by reason. As a first step towards this new way of life he would choose a bride, 'a new love, and one which began in reason and judgment much more than imagination, and which offers a fair prospect of marriage in a not very remote distance'. The new love was his cousin, Frances Sarah Farrer, a good match in worldly terms, for the Farrers were well connected in legal circles and could assist Neale's career.

The marriage was a fatal mistake for both of them. The difficulty which many middle-class Victorians had in arriving at a mutually satisfying sex life, lust being incompatible with bourgeois gentility, troubled Neale more than most, and the coldness which quickly arose between him and his wife became glacial after Neale met the Christian Socialists and found in working with them the gratification which happier men would expect to find with their families. Possibly Frances Neale might have tolerated it, had the gratification been merely emotional, but Neale had to place his fortune at the disposal of the movement, and Mrs Neale neither forgot nor forgave.

He had come into contact with Maurice through reading Maurice's book, *The Kingdom of Christ*, which had a liberating effect on him, as it did on so many Evangelicals. He proceeded to study socialism, reading French and German writers, and his English Puritanism slowly crystallized into Utopian socialism. He decided his next step would be to meet working-class people, something utterly removed from his social experience, but he was determined to succeed, hoping in some vague manner that if he could form an idealized relationship with the deprived and under-privileged, this would give him the love which he had craved and which he had not found either as a son or a husband.

All his hopes and frustrations were neatly detailed in his diary which ends, significantly, in 1849, the year he met the Christian Socialists and began his life's work. From that moment until his death, and as Ludlow observed, Neale was a man 'who died young at eighty-two', he was a busy and fulfilled individual.[2]

He had a flair for organization and business and soon noticed that it was the middle-class men in the movement, not the working-class ones, who had the drive and the conviction to promote associations. The working men joined the associations for material, not moral reasons, to Neale's disappointment. The younger Christian Socialists were aware of that situation but not dismayed by it, believing that they must wait for the civilizing effect of association upon men who had been conditioned by injustice, exploitation and lack of educational opportunities. They could point to men who showed the benefits of association, men like Thomas Christmas, of the Tottenham Court Road Shoemakers' Association. When he joined the association he was an illiterate who reserved Saturday nights for heavy drinking, but the Christian Socialists saw he had the makings of a good manager and put him in charge. Their friendliness and trust mellowed him. 'At first rough, suspicious and loudmouthed, the very expression of his face gradually changed till in old age he became kindly and gracious,' recorded Ludlow.

None of these London associations, not even the speed with which they were set up, would have caused any ripple had it not been for the books and articles published by Kingsley and Maurice during that period. From 1850 onwards it seemed as though whatever they wrote was doomed to be criticized not for the actual content but for the reviewers' misinterpretations. Indeed, Parker turned down *Alton Locke*, which was deeply influenced by the Chartist poet Thomas Cooper, author of *The Purgatory of Suicides*, and Kingsley submitted it to John Chapman, who published it on Carlyle's recommendation.

Carlyle had read the novel in the bright September sunshine in Annandale and he enjoyed the portrait of himself, thinly disguised as Sandy Mackaye, but he tut-tutted over other aspects of the book. '. . . I am bound to say, the book is definable as *crude*; by no manner of means the best we expect of you—if you will resolutely temper your fire.' He warned Kingsley, very wisely, to take no notice of reviews, laudatory or otherwise. In general, he praised the book as a new explosion of red-hot shot against the Devil's Dungheap. It was certainly a prime literary example of the Church Didactic, a hotch-potch of ideas, criticism, descriptions, politics, religion and poetry, in a word, Kingsley with all his strength and weakness.

The first hostile review came from the *Record* and was so unpleasant that Professor Nicholay of Queen's College was afraid that the College would suffer if anybody thought that Kingsley was still on its teaching staff. Accordingly he wrote to the paper pointing out that although Kingsley had indeed once taught literature to the girls of Queen's College, he had long since given it up, and so there was now no connection. When Maurice read Nicholay's letter in the *Record* he was so outraged at the man's timidity that he resigned as chairman of the Queen's College management committee. It was the least he could do, he explained, to show solidarity with Kingsley and to prove to the working men whom he was just beginning to know that he was sincere in all he said. Maurice's precipitate action startled the Queen's College administrators, who had not expected Maurice to take such a hard line, and they called in Ludlow, with some others, to draft a new constitution for the

College and to persuade Maurice, when the dust had settled, to rejoin the management committee.

Kingsley could not help being excited by his new status as a controversial author, and was proud that his powerful descriptions of the terrible conditions in the tailoring trade pleased his working-class readers. Not many people thought that the love interest, the characters of the two leading women, or the final religious conversion of Alton Locke were convincing, but those were minor drawbacks judged against the accomplishment of the book as a whole. It was reviewed at length in all the influential journals, and those who did not actually read the book could see what it was about by reading the long quotations. Sweated labour, slum housing, the reasons why men turned Chartist, and associations, were spelled out in plain terms, and if anybody wanted a change from such serious subjects, there were always Kingsley's poems.

Fenton Hort rushed out to buy a copy of *Alton Locke*, read it carefully and sent a copy, with his analysis, to his friend, the Rev John Ellerton, who was sympathetic to the Christian Socialists but lived too far away to be active. He became a corresponding member of the Society of Promoters. Hort could not make his mind up about *Alton Locke*. He had enjoyed *Yeast* very much, but Kingsley's new book, although riveting, also disgusted him, whilst as for its theology—'The book is pure Humanitarianism, with God as the instrument to bring it about,' he complained. He could not agree that Kingsley had popularized Maurice's teaching in that novel, but then, Hort was a Maurician without being a Christian Socialist, and that made all the difference.

The leading article of the January 1851 issue of the *Edinburgh Review* was a long survey called 'English Socialism and Communistic Associations' by William Rathbone Greg, one of the severest opponents of the Christian Socialists. Although hostile, as to be expected, it might have been worse, and it gave useful publicity to associations. So the Christian Socialists were quite pleased, and so was Greg, who later published it in a book. Most of the reviews of *Alton Locke* were sneering, although *Blackwood's* reviewer said that it contained passages of genius, amongst others of preposterous absurdity. In spite of his good intentions to remember Carlyle's advice, Kingsley suffered acutely when he read his reviews and was for ever asking his friends earnestly to give independent advice and criticism of his latest poems and pieces. Ludlow complied, but had to be careful what he said, for he found that Kingsley, like all authors, only wanted to hear his praises sung.

The book had been first published anonymously, but after November 1850 everyone knew that Charles Kingsley was the author. Kingsley wrote to the press defending his opinions and his Christian faith, much to Maurice's distress, for Maurice thought it better that Kingsley kept quiet. The Rector of Eversley also announced his total withdrawal from Queen's College, even in an advisory capacity, and felt pleased with himself for taking the honourable course in making sure that worthy institutions like Queen's College did not suffer from being linked with his name.

All this controversy meant that *Alton Locke* sold, and sold well, so Parker recovered his nerve over Kingsley and published *Yeast* in book form in March 1851. That was more straightforward and appealing than *Alton Locke* and had done well as a serial. Lancelot Smith, who resembled the younger Kingsley and a thousand other young men, was an attractive hero, and indeed the novel was so successful as a book that Maurice remarked, not entirely as a joke, that he was afraid *Yeast* might become *too* popular! It was not the job of Christian Socialists to be popular, he reminded Kingsley.

The Rector was automatically a member of the Council of Promoters through his close friendship with the others, and through his early work on *Politics for the People*, but his Eversley duties prevented him from taking the daily and obsessive interest in associative work that his friends did. To do that, one needed to live in London, for the Promoters took it in turns to meet at six each morning to take routine decisions about the associations before going on to their respective offices. The associations were expected to operate along the lines of Ludlow's constitution, although that constitution could never have been legally enforced, given the current state of the law. It worked well enough, there being a good atmosphere of mutual trust, and most of the Christian Socialists were well pleased with the progress they made in 1850.

Ludlow was the exception. It was not that his convictions

were stronger than those of his friends, but his personal situation was different. As a lonely bachelor living with his mother, he had less to occupy his mind and more leisure than his married friends, and the gospel of associations was psychologically deeply important to him. He was not satisfied and began thinking again about starting a special journal. This time he had an ally in Maurice, who found literary projects more congenial than organizational ones. Ludlow and Maurice together made a formidable team and the proposed journal was soon licked into shape. It was called, boldly, the *Christian Socialist*, with Ludlow as editor, and first appeared at the end of 1850, soon to become, as Ludlow had intended, the mouthpiece of the Christian Socialist movement.[3]

The *Christian Socialist*

Who would sit down and whine for a lost
                                    age of gold,
While the Lord of all ages is here?
True hearts will leap up at the trumpet
                                    of God,
And those who can suffer, can dare.

'Parson Lot'

All the group's shining hopes and excitement, its optimism tempered with sobriety, could be seen in the pages of the *Christian Socialist* which first appeared on 2 November 1850. At last Ludlow was in his element, speaking directly to the working men he longed to serve and make his friends in the pen-name of John Townsend, or 'J.T.'. It was to be a rule of the journal that writers should be anonymous, a common practice of the time, although in the case of the *Christian Socialist* keen readers soon learnt the identity of the contributors. Ludlow's first editorial gave a good indication of his style:

We do not mean to eschew Politics. We shall have Chartists writing with us, and Conservatives, and yet we hope not to quarrel, having this one common ground of Socialism, just as on that ground we hope not to quarrel, though the professing Christian be mixed in our ranks with those who have hitherto passed for Infidels.

The entire spectrum of English life was to be covered; free trade, education, the land question, poor laws, reform of the law, sanitary reform, taxation, finance, and even Church reform.

Chartists who had been suspicious of *Politics for the People* and had not read it for that reason, decided that perhaps they should give this middle-class group a chance, and they began to read the *Christian Socialist*. Many found it to their liking and wrote articles for it. Such a one was Gerald Massey, a genuine people's poet, who had been born in Tring in great poverty, his father being a boatman on the Grand Union Canal, earning ten shillings a week. When the boy was eight, he was sent out to work in some silk mills where, for a thirteen-hour day and a six-day week, he earned one shilling. His mother taught him to read using the Bible and Bunyan's *Pilgrim's Progress* as primers, and for years afterwards Massey believed those were accurate history books.

At fifteen the boy escaped to London, and took any job that came his way so long as it gave him time to browse on the capital's secondhand bookstalls and educate himself. He fell in love with a strange young woman, Rosina Janes Knowles, who was described rather mysteriously as 'the daughter of a professional man in the north', but any family she might have had remained in the north and she was a free soul interested in the occult. Massey discovered that love had made him a poet, and his first slim volume *Poems and Chansons* was published by a Tring bookseller in an edition of two hundred and fifty, price one shilling. The French revolution of 1848 made him a political journalist and since he married Rosina, he needed to work hard. For a while he and a kindred spirit, J. B. Leno, started a republican paper called the *Spirit of Freedom*, but this, like so many similar papers, was short-lived. When the Christian Socialists began their association work Massey was immediately interested and the Christian Socialists, recognizing that he was a man out of the ordinary, snapped him up to serve as secretary to Walter Cooper's tailors' association.

Massey was a handsome young man, with dreamy eyes and flowing hair. Maurice liked him very much, but hoped he would not be taken up by middle-class intellectuals outside the Christian Socialist circle, and spoiled. This fear was not entirely realized, although Massey developed some strange interests, notably in witchcraft and spiritualism, influenced by his wife. He had to work as a hack journalist in addition to his association duties, and it was through his freelance work for John Chapman that George Eliot came in contact with him and was later to use him as a model for her working-class radical, Felix Holt.

Ludlow was eager to have Massey write for his paper but made it very clear, 'bullied' was Ludlow's word, that Massey must stop writing for Julian Harney's *Red Republican*. Massey did not object, for like so many working-class men reared on Nonconformist religious books and ideas, he found the ideas of brotherhood in associations more emotionally satisfying than the cooler and more impersonal socialist dogma. It did not take long for him to succumb to Maurice's charm.

> God bless you, Brave One, in our dearth
> Your life shall leave a trailing glory.

he proclaimed, showing his respect for the Prophet.

Massey was not the only working-class agitator to join the association cause and work for the *Christian Socialist*. There was also James John Bezer, who had been imprisoned for his Chartist activities. When he was released, Harney's *Red Republican* gave him a grand write-up:

> This sterling democrat who suffered nearly two years' incarceration in Newgate, for advocating the principles of the People's Charter, is about to take a tour through the country and proposes to deliver lectures in all the principal towns. The sufferings of himself and fellow-victims in prison,—the principles of democratic and social reform, and the united organisation of democratic and social reformers to obtain the Charter, will form the leading topics of Mr Bezer's lectures. . . . Mr Bezer deserves, and we doubt not will receive, a hearty welcome from the 'Reds' in all parts of England.

Bezer had a successful tour and returned to London in October 1850 to begin business as a newsagent. 'We earnestly solicit our metropolitan friends to give their orders to this persecuted and sterling democrat,' exhorted the *Red Republican*, but not long afterwards Bezer met the Christian Socialists, and with J. B. Leno started a printers' co-operative, the *Christian Socialist* becoming its main customer. Harney was disgusted, seeing this as going over to the enemy, although he was aware that Chartism still appealed to only a small section of the working class and that, broadly speaking, trade unionism and associations were making greater strides than Chartism. Indeed, in August 1850 he had suggested a new Chartist Convention to look into the possibility of broadening the Chartist programme and in December he changed the name of his paper to the *Friend of the People*, judging this new title to be less intimidating than the former one. It is possible that if Maurice had not been so opposed to links with any formal group or party, there might have been some co-operation between him and the Christian Socialists, and he would have found much in common with Ludlow. When Harney convened the Convention it was for 'Chartism and something more', and he had spoken of honest reformers who would join together in a 'band of brotherhood'. That Chartism was losing its hold on the London working class was in great measure owing to the patient work and writings of the Christian Socialists, although outside London their influence was very much weaker.

Even Charles Kingsley felt woefully out of touch in Eversley, in spite of letters and occasional visits to London. He rather envied his friends, supervising associations and running their periodical, but on the other hand he was beginning to have second thoughts about the cause. He maintained a 'gallant front' before his Christian Socialist friends, whose integrity and energy he deeply admired, but lamented his own shortcomings. He was ashamed of his laziness, his longing to forget social problems and chase butterflies or catch trout, to play games with his children, enjoy his wife's company and, not least, to be well regarded for a change by his respectable country neighbours. He would try to shake off these unworthy emotions and write to Maurice, imploring him to write or visit and make the Rector a better man. He wrote for the paper and, as 'Parson Lot', was a great draw, but he was not involved with organizational work in the way that Ludlow, Hughes and Furnivall were.

The new paper had a dual purpose. It was to be a vehicle of Christian Socialist propaganda on the one hand and a 'Journal of Association', giving news of current associations and instructions on how to form new ones, on the other. Millbank and Shorter, now joint secretaries of the Society of Promoters, wrote in the paper. Their first article hinted at reasons for poverty in England, and suggested that the workers were partly to blame: 'We have become rivals where we ought to have become brethren, and have competed with each other when we ought to have co-

operated;—rivals, with more or less of hate, and hosts of
expedients to disguise its hideousness and make it respectable.'
Christian Socialists lectured up and down the country on associations, Cooper, Massey and Lechevalier being in great demand.
Requests for legal advice came to the paper, like one from the
Bury General Labour Redemption Society, a very vigorous
organization, which wanted to start a Working Men's Bank to
finance its General Store. Bury was a lively centre for association,
and the Bury Society promised to circulate the *Christian Socialist*
in the district. Ludlow printed news about co-operatives in
Edinburgh, and there was a letter from Charles Sully in New
York stating that there was 'more idolatrous worship of
Mammon, in this country, than in Europe'. Co-operatives were
doing quite well in the States, he said, but they were stores, not
producer co-operatives, and there was nothing morally uplifting
about consumer stores. Ludlow wrote a brief history of the Arm-
chair Makers' Association of Paris, to show his readers that they
were not alone: working men in foreign countries were also forming associations.

There was a certain amount of light relief, not very much, in
the way of fiction, sketches and poetry, for education in its broad
sense was always an important aim of the Christian Socialists.
Some of the poetry was from living poets, Tennyson, who was an
admirer of Maurice; Kingsley and Massey, of course; but the dead
classics were not neglected.

Lloyd Jones was appointed as manager of a new London Co-
operative Store which was soon to open at 76 Charlotte Street,
and he advertised it in the pages of the paper, asking associations
to send orders. The address must have struck a chord in Owenite
hearts, for it had been in Charlotte Street that Robert Owen had
opened his Equitable Labour Bazaar in 1832.

The paper was remarkable value at a penny a copy, for it was
about 16,000 words of closely packed material with no paid
advertising. It sold around 1,500 copies a week, in spite of its
difficulties in finding any distributors to handle it. Anyone who
bought the first copy, and continued to buy it each week would
find he had embarked upon an adult education course of a highly
specialized nature. The second issue displayed the dual nature of
the Christian Socialist group, a religious side represented by
Kingsley with a series called 'Bible Politics, or God Justified to

the People' wherein he sought to explain the aggressiveness of the Israelites in the Old Testament, and a practical side represented by Ludlow in his report, the first of many, about the activities of a government committee, headed by R. A. Slaney, M.P., inquiring into the savings of the middle and working classes.

'My friends,' wrote Ludlow, amazingly free of inhibitions, 'we are yet but at the very outset of a long and stormy voyage, wherein you and I and many whom we know not yet, may be wrecked, before the new world of association be reached.' He mentioned the problems which the associations had run into—'straitness of resources, a few pressing debts, an occasional act of dishonesty, a few internal squabbles, such have been our worst evils. What are these to the giant struggles which our Parisian brethren have had from the first to carry on?'

English co-operatives were hampered by legal restrictions, and to protect association funds the Christian Socialists arranged that any property owned by or loans granted to the associations should be held by Trustees, men like Hughes and Neale. The Promoters considered registering the associations either as joint stock companies or as friendly societies, but rejected both ideas because nobody had enough money to form joint stock companies and because friendly societies were forbidden to trade with the general public. When Hughes heard by chance about Slaney's committee, he saw that the scope of that body could be enlarged to survey the whole field of companies and partnerships and the need for new laws. Ludlow agreed that the committee could be made use of, and he instructed readers of the *Christian Socialist* to present evidence. Slaney knew nothing of co-operators, had no connection whatsoever with the Christian Socialists and was astonished to find that suddenly his committee was overwhelmed by working men, queueing up to give evidence about their savings. Indeed, Slaney's work was virtually master-minded by Ludlow and Hughes from behind the scenes, and as it was carefully reported in the *Christian Socialist* and intensely interesting to co-operators throughout the country, the progress reports on the committee gave the *Christian Socialist* great status and popularity within the co-operative movement.[1]

The legal expertise of Hughes, Ludlow and Neale was useful in other ways, for the managers, picked more for availability and willingness than for ability, or even reliability, were in constant difficulties and it fell to the lawyers, 'none of whom was over-burdened with regular practice', as Hughes put it, to solve the problems. Many respectable solicitors who called at Hughes's chambers at 7 Old Square, Lincoln's Inn, were put out when told to wait while Hughes gave free legal advice to his Chartist friends and co-operators. Not that Hughes cared.

'We were young, saucy, and so thoroughly convinced we were right, that we cared, shall I say, not a damn.' In any case, he did not do too badly at the law, being exceptionally punctual and hard working, and gaining the reputation of being a sound equity lawyer. One of his friends, W. E. Forster, who married Dr Arnold's daughter, Jane, thus becoming brother-in-law to Hughes's friend and swimming companion, Matthew Arnold, was amused by the Christian Socialists. 'Well, for a set of revolutionists, I must say you are the pleasantest ones I know,' he commented, and even John Stuart Mill had kind words for them, and gave evidence in their favour to Slaney's committee. As for an earnest German student[2] who was in England to study social questions and co-operatives, he fell in love with them as a collective and wrote an ecstatic description of a cricket match between a Christian Socialist eleven and a team from Price's factory at Belmont.

Ludlow had learned in Bellenden Ker's chambers how legisla-tion could be used or amended to bring about social reforms and he wanted to have the existing Friendly Societies' Act amended so as to include producer associations. Indeed he had drafted a possible amendment and in June 1850 had sent it to Lord Ashley (the future Earl of Shaftesbury) hoping that he would introduce it in the House. Nothing came of that venture, to the disappoint-ment of the Christian Socialists, who concluded that the noble lord was happy to promote factory acts but disliked associations because he thought them nothing less than socialism.

In the autumn of 1950 Neale had gone to Paris, on behalf of the Christian Socialists, to look at the association picture there, and returned deeply impressed with profit-sharing partnerships. He wrote a long article about it for the paper, proving Ludlow's point that the Christian Socialists did not fear to discuss different ideas. Nor did they fear to print criticism. A correspondent wrote asking why, since Christian Socialism was only Christianity carried into real life, did they add that other word 'rendered horrid in men's ears, and stinking in their nostrils, because indissolubly associated with those French vagabonds who include Sobrier and ravens like him'. To which Ludlow replied: 'We are not deterred from calling ourselves Christians because Henry VIII or Alva bore that name.'

A basic difference of opinion began to emerge between Ludlow and Neale over the respective merits of producer and consumer co-operatives, Neale having a strong business streak which predisposed him to favour co-operatives which were successful, which meant the stores co-operatives, not the producer associations. They had been especially successful in the north of England, where the Rochdale Equitable Pioneers had opened their store in Toad Lane as early as 1844. Stores, argued Neale, would heal the conflict of interests between buyer and seller; a network of stores could be brought under the umbrella of a central agency, a Co-operative League of Commonwealth, including the producer co-operatives as well. This would attract secular co-operatives in addition to the Christian Socialist ones, and bring Chartists, atheists and trade union members into the movement. Lloyd Jones supported Neale in this idea, and it was noticeable that both these men paid little attention to the Christianizing aspect of co-operatives, which Ludlow felt was paramount. Hughes felt there was a good deal in what Neale said, although he did not want to make any break with Ludlow, and Lechevalier was also in support of Neale, who proposed to go ahead with a London store, and found a grocer and co-operator, Joseph Woodin, who would be their buyer.

Neale and Ludlow shared chambers, so Ludlow knew all about the progress of Neale's plan. Nothing changed his point of view, There was no morality in stores, he maintained; a successful consumer co-operative would attract middle-class people who knew a bargain when they saw it, but it would do nothing to help the working class. Maurice agreed with Ludlow. None the less Neale continued, and there was a public meeting on 5 November 1850 to interest people in the store. Henry Mayhew was the star speaker, and said that although he was neither a Chartist, a Socialist, a Protectionist or a Free Trader, he was ready to tell the truth, that the only hope for the country was combination amongst the working classes. To approving calls of 'Hear, hear', he moved a resolution supporting 'co-operation amongst the people', and Lloyd Jones moved a resolution that the producer associations should support the new store.

Ludlow tried to put the annoying matter out of his mind and concentrated upon his self-imposed task of educating the masses. His most serious reflections were contained in his 'Letters to the Working Men's Associations of London', printed in the paper. Discipline, he said, must be founded upon mutual trust, and whatever might work in the competitive world, in associations only trust would work. As for a manager, 'his whole authority is a moral one; he cannot rule by force, still less by fraud. It is far better to trust him, unworthy, than to distrust him, if there is the least chance of his not deserving your distrust.' It was Maurice speaking with the tongue of Ludlow. However, Ludlow did warn against giving trust too readily, and advised caution.

Interest in co-operatives was spreading and a Norwich clergyman wrote to the *Christian Socialist* asking how a group of Norwich weavers could start a co-operative. Their chief problem was lack of money. The Promoters replied that they had no cash to spare but would forward money received at the paper, and wished the weavers well. The Norwich Weavers' Co-operative was finally formed, but was not very long-lived.

International items were always popular and readers learned that the Paris Piano Makers' Association was sending a piano to the Hyde Park Exhibition opening the next year, and more seriously, readers were alerted to the new political trials being held in Paris and reported with considerable emotion by Ludlow. 'That hell-hound, the Public Prosecutor, is striving every nerve to pin his victim to the ground; no calumny is too gross, no invention too cruel for his purpose.' The accused appeared to have been guilty of holding the sort of meetings which the Promoters held routinely twice a week. No wonder Christian Socialist blood was up and that for evermore Napoleon III was damned as a hypocritical tyrant!

It was relatively easy to form co-operatives but a very different matter to keep them going. A correspondent wrote, 'I have seen one club of co-operatives broken up, and have just heard of a secretary of another cheating his friends, and at last becoming insane under the reproaches he met,' and this was not uncommon. The monthly meetings of Promoters and Associates were reported in full in the hope that it might be helpful to other associations. The change of emphasis which took place four years later on the part of the band of brothers from associative to educational work, becomes very understandable in view of the constant setbacks in the co-operatives. The Central Board was finally compelled, reluctantly, to agree that nobody should be appointed manager of an association unless he could read, write and do simple sums. Mere willingness could no longer serve. One manager, a Mr Howson, begged to be allowed to be an ordinary workman again, and spoke pathetically of 'the misrepresentation to which all his acts were constantly liable, and the little sacrifices of personal feelings which he was daily called upon to make'.

Christian Socialist speakers were in great demand, especially Walter Cooper and Lloyd Jones. The latter had an odd experience in Ashton in December 1850, when, having an hour or two free, he dropped into a Protestant meeting being held to protest against Pius IX and the so-called 'Papal Aggression'. During the discussion which followed the speeches, Lloyd Jones rose to make the commonplace Christian Socialist point that Roman Catholicism had increased in England because so few Anglican ministers cared about the needs and wishes of the English people. If Anglican clergymen, by supporting co-operation, showed a true desire to help the working class, that would be the best possible defence to foreign encroachment. His argument was considered in Ashton to be so provocative that he was, in his own words, 'attacked by clergymen and gentlemen, and all sorts of men: I was collared, and cuffed, and shouted at . . .', and he only escaped in one piece because a stranger helped him. Religious prejudice and conflicts were not confined to the north of England. Ludlow had been inside the church of St Barnabas during one of the Protestant riots against the church's High Church rituals and, like Lloyd Jones, he was startled by the passions shown by 'gentlemen-ruffians'.

The trouble about Walter Cooper's popularity as a national speaker was that he could not be away on tours and look after his tailors' association at the same time, and the Promoters were appalled to receive a deputation from that association with complaints that there were sixty false items in the accounts. An immediate examination of the books showed that only four items could be said to be wrong, and those seemed to be the result of inexperience and sloppiness, so that any insinuations of fraud were baseless. The association crumbled, nevertheless, owing to 'those internal causes which no success can prevent, which no improved legislation can put right', but the tailors were sturdy at heart and they reformed their co-operative. The Promoters called a special conference to discuss the general matter of managers, associates and their various duties, but so few members attended the meeting that the Promoters had to agree, regretfully, that on the whole working men did not want to be managers.

Difficulties of that nature gave Neale further ammunition for his argument that there was a real need for his consumer store in London and Ludlow, whilst still passionately disagreeing, was fair-minded enough to let Neale have space in the *Christian Socialist*. The paper was well known in the co-operative movement, if nowhere else. One could learn from it how to start an Association Bank (forerunner of the C.W.S. Bank), read about Walter Cooper's latest lecture tour, or Maurice's views on education. Fenton Hort thought that Maurice's articles were the best thing in the paper. There were sections about the successes of foreign consumer co-operatives, particularly in the United States, an account of one in Belgium called *La Solidarité*, and a history of the noted cheese associations of the Jura mountains, the *fruitières*, already famous through Fourier's writings. Frank Penrose wrote about architecture, taking the Ruskinian view that there was an indissoluble link between morality and art so that bad morals produced bad art. Short quotations from Ruskin often appeared as fillers, although Ruskin was never a Christian Socialist in the Maurician sense, nor indeed involved with the association work. His connection with the group would come later, through his personal friendship with Furnivall.

Ludlow persevered with his lecture course to the readers, telling them that associates had to do two things; first, find the man best fitted to be manager, and second, work under him in a disciplined manner. It was almost as if the manager could have dictatorial powers, and indeed Ludlow was prepared to accept that, believing that associations would effect such a profound moral improvement in men's characters that they would have nothing to fear from dictatorship. It was an example of Ludlow being ahead of his time, although a generation or so later there would be a number of English Socialists ready to agree with him.

It was a tribute to the integrity and determination of the
Promoters, all middle-class professional men, that they had been
able to transcend class barriers through their association movement, which in the mid-nineteenth century was quite an exceptional accomplishment. Working-class atheists resented the small
but increasing success of the Christian Socialists and Holyoake
complained in his paper, the *Reasoner*, of the dual aspect of the
Christian Socialist. 'This periodical abounds in proselytising
articles, in very bad taste. . . . To mix up Christianity with
Socialism is to shelter its errors from legitimate attack, and to
take an unfair advantage of us,' he wrote, to which Ludlow
replied through the pages of his paper that nobody expected the
Christian Socialist to be satisfactory to the *Reasoner*. He rejected
Holyoake's idea that their Christianity should be limited to the
'Tracts', insisting that any Christianity worth its salt was a
'bread and butter question', and he was supported by Shorter,
who wrote that the 'Great Want of the Age' was a moral one, the
want of 'a spirit that shall quicken the dead bones, a living
soul—an active and enlightened conscience, a deep, abiding, ever-
present sense of the dignity and worth of human nature, of
our duties and responsibilities in relation to it;. . .' Ludlow
and Shorter sounded the Puritan revivalist note so characteristic
of the band of brothers, and it found a response in the northern
working classes whose religious influences tended to be Nonconformist rather than Anglican. Years later it would be
strongly echoed in the Independent Labour Party.

On the practical side, Ludlow reminded his readers that the
work of Slaney's committee was almost finished and a bill to
legalize industrial associations was ready to be introduced into the
Commons. He urged his readers to besiege their M.P.s with
letters, deputations and petitions and to 'create that pressure of
public opinion which alone is generally capable of stirring Whig
ministers to action.' A model petition was printed for readers to
use.

The liberal-minded Promoters wished to help all working men,
co-operators or no. Take, for instance, Mr Weston and his model
railway engine, the Novamotive, and the trouble he had getting a
patent for it. Mansfield wrote a series of articles about patents,
with which he was personally familiar, and discoursed lengthily
on the philosophical or other right of an inventor to own his

patent. Patents were a form of property, said Mansfield; could one morally justify ownership? Ludlow even found space for mention of James Pierrepoint Greaves, founder of a singular group of English mystics who called themselves Sacred Socialists.

In March 1851 the Working Tailors' Association celebrated its anniversary, the first of the associations to do so, with a festive gathering. Maurice presided genially behind the ubiquitous tea urn and made an appropriate speech about the duty of Promoters and Associates to proclaim the right principles and to teach men how to fight against the wrong ones. Everybody had the chance to make a speech and the gathering closed with community singing of liberation songs. It was all simple stuff, with little of theory and nothing of sophistication, but it warmed the hearts of the associates, rewarding them for past work and encouraging them for the year to come and it set the pattern for other associations when their own anniversaries arrived.

When things became too pleasant or too successful Ludlow could be relied upon to sound the solemn call for self-sacrifice. In one of his serious articles in the paper (these could be distinguished by the heading, 'My Friends') he said:

> And I believe . . . that the associative spirit has always shown itself and always will show itself in exactly two opposite tendencies; on the one hand, a determination to spread association far and wide. and whilst spreading it, to unite the various associated bodies more and more closely. For self in everything is the great divider and weakener; self-sacrifice, the strengthener, the binder together of all things. I accuse no one: I only warn: I warn myself as well as others.

Self-sacrifice was not meant to spell misery, and jokes and community singing were part of the social side of the group and their friends, They were proud that John Hullah, whose popular music systems educated the nation's singing teachers, was a Christian Socialist who organized singing classes for them.

> Surely the young men of our metropolis and other large towns would be much better employed in Hullah's part singing than in midnight polking with courtesans in casinos. . . . Every musician should become a Socialist, and, let us add, every Socialist, as far as possible, a musician.

Hullah was not their only musician. There was also Alfred Nicholson, a professional oboe player, full of horrendous stories of exploitation in orchestral circles. Previously the band of brothers had assumed that sweated labour was confined to trades like tailoring and they were startled to find it could apply to musicians, indeed to clerks as well. Mayhew had listed clerks among the London poor and one such poor clerk wrote to the *Christian Socialist*: 'They are paid in the barren coin of *position*, when they want *money* to purchase necessaries,' he wrote of his fellows.

The 26 April 1851 issue of the paper had an article from Charles Sully in New York, where at the request of the Promoters, he had compiled a shilling pamphlet which set out the rules, regulations and constitutions of many American associations and trade unions. The Christian Socialists were happy to put on record their affection for 'an old friend and fellow-worker still in the cause of association', and they did all they could to welcome articles from working men. Richard Isham, of the Printers' Association, took over from Ludlow the 'Letters to Working Men', addressing his readers not as 'My Friends' but as 'Fellow Workmen'. Gerald Massey, always to be counted on for purple effusions, wrote an article called 'The Brotherhood of Labour' which was sprinkled with sentences like 'For thee the stars—vestal daughters of the night—God's thoughts written on the leaves of the blue heaven—preach through the eternal centuries their religion of silent work-worship.' Parson Lot's articles always generated a good deal of steam, and the Rector could also be trusted to answer correspondents in the paper in fine thundering style.

When they reviewed the apparently insoluble problems of small associations, the Promoters could not help wondering whether it would be better to amalgamate them into one large General Industrial Society, but a change of that magnitude would amount to a change of principle, so the idea was referred to Maurice, who promptly referred it to the Central Board, where it was tabled for future discussion. Where fundamental changes were concerned, Maurice always preferred to make haste slowly.

The Christian Socialists believed in healthy bodies as well as healthy minds and souls, and they disapproved of heavy eating and drinking. Some of them were rabid teetotallers. Mansfield cited the Bible in support of abstinence: 'There is nothing in the Bible recommending beer,' he would say, and warned that he would fight to the death any attempt to set up a co-operative beer-shop. When Charles Sully, working with an American friend called Joseph Stansbury, sent some samples of Indian corn flour, with a booklet of recipes, Neale had his wife cook it for the Neale family first, and then offered it for sale in the co-operative store. He begged Christian Socialist readers not to be prejudiced against the new flour, but to try it out, as he had done. His words went unheeded, another example of the Christian Socialists being ahead of their time!

The Promoters continued to organize public meetings on a variety of subjects, but experience soon taught them they could only get a good attendance when they had a well-known speaker and a practical subject. Kingsley gave a closely reasoned two-hour talk on how to organize agricultural co-operatives, and the Concert Rooms in Mortimer Street were jam-packed. His talk was published in the paper, and reprinted as a pamphlet, which sold very well. It was a popular subject, for interest in agricultural co-operatives, evocative of the Owenite 'Home Colonies', or the 'lost communities', in Holyoake's nostalgic phrase, was perennial. By contrast, when Walsh gave a lecture on sanitary reforms and epidemics there was such a poor attendance that the organizers had to apologise to him. Ludlow was not prepared to let things stand there, and he printed Walsh's lecture in full in the next edition of the paper. The workers were certainly going to be educated if Ludlow had anything to do with it!

The associative cause and the editorship of the *Christian Socialist* had become the most important part of Ludlow's life, but it was a different matter when it came to Maurice. He was deeply concerned in the cause, and approved it strongly, but he had other duties, and he had family interests and responsibilities, so he did not write for the paper unless he felt compelled to take a public stand. This was the case in June 1851 when Kingsley, with ill-judged impulsiveness, had entered into public correspondence with the *Guardian*, a paper of the High Church party. It had criticized Christian Socialism and Kingsley hurried to defend the cause. Maurice intervened, partly to save Kingsley from going too far, and partly to be seen to take a public stand with his fellow Christian Socialist. Writing in the *Christian Socialist*, he gave short shrift to the *Guardian*.

> A religious newspaper is bound by its office and calling to prove that all the evils of the Church and of the nation, proceed not from the party who reads it but from some other. It lives, therefore for the promotion of self-deception and flattery: . . .

That marked both Maurice and Kingsley as men to be closely watched in establishment quarters.

By this time the Ludlow/Neale dispute over producer associations versus stores was coming into the open in the *Christian Socialist*. Neale wrote a long article in praise of his London store, which had not flourished as he had hoped, mainly owing to poor publicity, and Neale hinted that the *Christian Socialist* could have done more to publicise the store. He planned to turn it into a Central Agency supplying branch stores with goods at wholesale prices, with Woodin as chief buyer and Lechevalier as manager. Hoping to forestall Ludlow's criticisms, Neale stressed that his Agency was not an attack on associations: 'I wish only to put in a claim for the other, to be regarded *equally* with the sister institution as a true product of co-operative feeling.' Ludlow made out his case in the next issue, expressing his fear that, because a consumer store dealt only with distribution, it could not avoid an anti-social bias unless its central management could instil a spirit of brotherly love in the enterprise. In this ideological struggle were the seeds of future disunity in the group, which both protagonists hoped to avoid, neither having any ambition to become a leader, and it was understood that so far as possible they would carry on their argument in a low key behind the scenes.

Meanwhile the Great Exhibition opened in Hyde Park, attracting throngs of visitors to London, many of them working-class families taking advantage of the cheap railway fares. Mansfield was very cynical about it. 'I saw there all the riches of the world, all with names of the owners, blazoned forth in letters of gold, but almost nowhere the names of them that had wrought the gold, the precious wood, and the silk,' and he spoke of it scornfully as 'the Hyde Park slop-built tabernacle'. Kingsley, on the other hand, was so moved by the splendour of the Exhibition that his eyes brimmed with tears when he entered the glittering hall. The Exhibition lent a general air of festivity to the London summer and the Promoters held a Whitsuntide party for almost three hundred Promoters, co-operators and their families in St Martin's Hall. They tried to keep speeches to a minimum but could not prevent Walford, one of the associates, from riding his favourite hobby-horse, that drink was destroying brotherhood and that temperance would do more than anything else to restore it. He was quickly hushed in favour of community singing, and everyone went home at nine o'clock in a jolly mood of self-congratulation.

The Christian Socialists believed in sharing their enjoyment, and families were welcomed at the socials. Nobody doubted the sanctity of marriage or the pleasures of home and children and even Ludlow got married in the end, and counted his wedding day as the happiest of his life. When Mansfield had a nervous breakdown because his emotional life was in a shambles, Ludlow confided to Kingsley that all would be well if only they could find some nice girl who would fall in love with their friend! Frequently, however, Ludlow sounded too austere and authoritarian for his English friends, although he had enough romance in him to be attracted by exotic experiments like the Icarian community in Illinois, founded by Étienne Cabet, a picturesque French socialist who took the fancy of all the Christian Socialists.

Cabet was the son of a cooper who was determined that his boy should have a good education. The young man studied law and went into legal journalism and then politics, taking part in the 1830 revolution and being appointed procurator-general of Corsica. Unfortunately he had an acid tongue which made him so many enemies that he was dismissed his post, but he was elected to the Chamber of Deputies, and he began to edit a left-wing paper, *Le Populaire*. His political articles earned him a sentence of exile, so he came to England, studied the ideas of Robert Owen and became inspired by a dead visionary, Sir Thomas More, whose *Utopia* led Cabet to write a similar book called *Voyage en Icarie*. In it he discussed progressive taxation, obligation to work, old-age pensions and sharing goods and commodities, and the book enjoyed a vogue in France. When

Cabet returned home following a political amnesty in 1839 he found he was famous. A group formed itself, ready to live by the ideas in his book, so he began to raise money to purchase land in the United States. In March 1848 he led a band of sixty-nine prospective settlers on the first stage of their journey, but as soon as they reached New Orleans they discovered that Cabet had been swindled, for the Texan land he had purchased, unseen, was worthless. Some of his supporters turned against him, and a cry arose for him to be arrested for fraud.

Quite unperturbed, Cabet negotiated to buy land at Nauvoo, Illinois, which had been settled by the Mormons until neighbourly disapproval forced them to trek westwards to Utah, and Cabet left the remnants of his troop there whilst he prepared to return to France to stand trial. On his way home he stopped briefly in London, and called in to see his old friend, Lechevalier, at whose office he met several of the Christian Socialists. Tom Hughes felt considerable admiration for the colourful Frenchman, and when Hughes promoted his own agricultural Utopia in the States, the township of Rugby, Tennessee, many years later, he was influenced at least in part by his encounter with Cabet.

The Frenchman crossed to France, stood trial and was acquitted. When news reached the settlers in Nauvoo they celebrated with 'the greatest pleasure party we had taken since the departure of Citizen Cabet'. To the Christian Socialists, reading the accounts in their paper, the Icarian settlement sounded like Arcadia, but it was subject to the same strains and dissensions as the London associations and was held together only by Cabet's forceful personality. When he died in 1856 the settlement collapsed and its members became absorbed into ordinary American life, until today the only traces of their vision are a few buildings in the Nauvoo State Park and some references in books and articles.

In July 1851 the Castle Street tailors held their summer 'bean feast', taking a party up the Regent's Canal from Paddington to the country village of Alperton. One of the tailors quipped that London would be a very agreeable place if it were only situated in the country! A large marquee was erected for a dinner of ham and beef and there was great laughter when an uninvited pig strolled into the tent. Later there was singing and dancing to a harp and violin.

The presence of so many working men and their wives in London for the Exhibition gave the Rev G. S. Drew, Vicar of St John's, Charlotte Street, in the heart of Association-land, the notion of organizing six sermons to be of especial interest to a working-class congregation. He would give one, and Maurice would give two. The other three were to be divided among Kingsley, the Rev Septimus C. H. Hansard, a Marylebone curate and friend of Hughes and the others, and the Rev F. W. Robertson, all of them being well-known Christian Socialists.

Kingsley took great pains with his sermon, entitled 'The Message of the Church to Labouring Men' and based upon a text from St Luke which described the practice instituted by Moses among the Jews of releasing debtors and bond-servants at given periods, and of returning land to its original owners. He used the text to prove that any system of government which favoured the permanent accumulation of capital in a few hands must be contrary to the Kingdom of God as indicated by Jesus.

His audience listened with approval, for Kingsley was preaching to the converted and his hearers knew what to expect from their 'Parson Lot'. Drew, however, was horrified. He had never heard Kingsley in full spate or noticed the mesmeric effect he had on listeners, and he suddenly realized why Kingsley was considered a dangerous influence. Anxious not to be taken as a Kingsley man himself, Drew stood up at the end of the sermon and admonished his guest preacher. Kingsley was too stunned to protest, the congregation was wisely silent although highly indignant on his behalf, and the Christian Socialists hurriedly whisked Kingsley away for a soothing cup of tea at Maurice's house. By late evening the Rector was sufficiently calm to take the train to Eversley, but far too agitated to go to bed, and he spent the night pacing the Rectory lawn and composing a poem destined to become rightly famous, 'Three Fishers', a sublimation of his tensions.

The other sermons went off without incident, but then the other preachers were not Kingsley. Hansard was typical of the younger Christian Socialists, something of a character even then, and developing into a special mould later on. A friend of Tom Hughes's sister, Jeannie, met Hansard in 1862 and described him candidly:

. . . a toad in beard and spectacles and he is so frightfully vain
and conceited and boastful it is quite absurd. But behind all his
snarls and growls and snappishness and *rudeness* even, he does
work like a dray horse, and never fails one.—He will give up
every engagement to come and help, and the navvies literally
worship him—(beard and all)—He is a real treasure—a
sincerely good, useful, sensible, excellent worthy creature, and
such a socialist!

The description could have been applied to many of the Christian
Socialists.

An interesting new writer for the *Christian Socialist* was A. H.
Louis,[3] one of Ludlow's discoveries, a Jewish convert to
Christianity. He seemed a romantic character, was certainly very
able, and he showed an interest in Christian Socialism and the
association cause, so Ludlow introduced Louis to Maurice. He
was the last in the trio of men brought by Ludlow into the Maurician group who rendered important service to the cause for a time
but who all, for various reasons, drifted away from Maurice, and
it was one of Ludlow's lasting regrets that he was the one to have
introduced all three. The other two were Furnivall and
Lechevalier.

In September 1851 Ludlow and Hughes went on a lecturing
and investigative tour of Lancashire leaving Furnivall to edit the
paper. Ludlow's descriptions of the tour were forceful and enter-
taining and like the Webbs, with whom, religion apart, he would
have found much in common, he deeply appreciated the value of
solid facts and surveys. Some of his comments were to be used
years later in a history of the working class by G. D. H. Cole, a
member of the younger set of Fabians who succeeded the Webb
generation. More socially conscious in 1851 than when he had
accompanied his mother on an earlier trip, Ludlow now believed
that the standard of living in Lancashire had declined. He wrote:
'Cities like Manchester, I say it deliberately, are a national
crime; human beings are not to be condemned to breathe
smoke and poison for their life-long, that cotton-stuff may be
cheap.'

Furnivall so enjoyed Ludlow's articles, which for once were
relaxed and often amusing, that he printed Ludlow's name as
author, which produced a starchy rebuke by return of post that

such a practice might lead to 'offensive egotism' and if Furnivall persisted he, Ludlow, would be compelled to return to his usual dry style. Poor Ludlow! His conscience was so tender that he had to embrace austerity at every turn. Furnivall tried to curb his own exuberance and began printing a series of extracts from Dr King's *Co-operator*, a journal printed in Brighton some twenty years earlier. Dr King's pioneer experiments in co-operation had marked the beginning of the English movement, and although there were failures, the reasons for their failure were of immense interest to co-operators in the 1850s.

Indeed, national interest in co-operatives was growing to such an extent that Ernest Jones attacked them in his paper, *Notes to the People*. Jones was a Chartist who had been sentenced to two years' imprisonment after the 1848 disorders, a sentence so manifestly unfair that it had been debated in the House of Commons, which agreed the trial had been unjust. None the less Jones had to serve his sentence, and when he came out of prison he was surprised and irritated to find that the Christian Socialists were gaining support and their paper was successful, except in the financial sense. It was a year old and £300 in debt, but the Promoters were confident that appeals and a Fighting Fund could deal with the debt.

The main thing was that associations were increasing in number and everyone connected with the *Christian Socialist* took it as axiomatic that if only they were better known, they would increase in size and importance. After all, Bishop Wilberforce had invited Walter Cooper to Cuddesdon Palace and given him orders for the Tailors' Association. It was true that the bishop was related to Neale, but he was not the only prelate to order goods from co-operatives. It was becoming quite the fashion even if, as the joke went, you could always tell a sympathizer by the cut of his co-operative trousers.

The clash between the Christian Socialists and Ernest Jones came to a head over a meeting in Bradford where Jones, as a member of the Chartist executive, attacked the co-operative and Christian Socialist movements in general and Bradford co-operators in particular. This aroused loud protests, but the rowdy nature of the meeting was not recorded in *Notes to the People*, so a Bradford joiner called Robert Ryder redressed the balance with a blistering account sent to the *Christian Socialist*. Ludlow was delighted to receive it but judged it editorially judicious to tone down the language somewhat. Ryder wrote:

> The thinkers among the working class are heartily tired of the hackneyed representation of their grievances, to which they have been so often and so abundantly treated by declamatory orators. Such conduct is calculated to make us think that Mr Jones has objections to our working out our own salvation lest 'Othello's occupation should be gone'.

It was a shrewd blow which did not make Jones any better disposed towards co-operators and Christian Socialists.

Ludlow replied to Jones through the paper:

> I have to charge Mr Ernest Jones with a thorough misconception of the character of the present co-operative movement considered as a whole: with an apparently complete ignorance of the distinction that exists between its two currents, that of consumption, and that of production, and, as a natural consequence, with a total inability to perceive either how these two currents may be made either to harmonise together, or what evils now result when they clash.

By the end of 1851 the continuing debate between Ludlow, purist of the association cause, and Neale, pragmatist of the stores cause, was coming to a head but the Christian Socialists were great ones for 'washing their dirty linen at home', as Ludlow put it, and in the pages of the *Christian Socialist* which staggered on until the close of the year, there was little hint of the fight behind the scenes. The 8 November 1851 issue carried a leading article by Hughes summing up two years of abortive work to help the ballast-heavers of the Thames, men whose conditions had first been highlighted by Mayhew. Hughes singled out for praise Thomas Flynn, a ballast-heaver who had worked many years for the betterment of his fellow workers, giving up two or three days' work a week in order to do that, although he had no other income but his trade. The Whig government, dominated by Free Traders, argued that to give job security to the ballast-heavers would be a restriction on trade, and a Bill which would have helped the men was accordingly thrown out. Disillusioned,

Flynn, in company with many of his mates, left their jobs and took other employment. The result was that the employers and middlemen were free to take their pick of the unskilled unemployed and the conditions of work for these men remained disgraceful.

Hughes and Furnivall had worked with Flynn over the two years, and the failure disheartened them. Politics and Parliament were a dirty business altogether, Hughes declared, and unwilling to shelter any longer behind initials or pseudonyms, he proudly signed his article in full. 'I think it high time that we should all begin to do so, whenever we write,' he explained. Why should the press attack only Maurice and Kingsley, he asked; the rest of them demanded their right to be attacked for what they believed in.

As a circulation booster, issue No. 56 of the paper gave away a lithographic portrait of Kingsley, autographed. The edition sold out and 'Parson Lot' was framed and hung proudly in many working-class homes. In the main, however, circulation remained a problem. A friend from Uttoxeter wrote to tell the Promoters that he had offered to present the *Christian Socialist* to the Uttoxeter Literary Institution, free of charge, but his offer was refused because the paper was likely to cause 'undesirable disputes and discussions'. The Weybridge Mechanics' Institute excluded it because it was 'political', although the Institute took *The Times*. Kingsley sniffed at that item of information, recalling that more than one Mechanics' Institute had refused to buy his *Alton Locke* because it was 'political'. Gerald Massey proposed the draconian solution that all association managers should impose a levy of one penny a week upon members and give them a free copy of the paper, which made Ludlow smile but drew from him the comment that support not given voluntarily was worthless.

It was quite infuriating for the Christian Socialists to skim through the autumn issues, knowing that the interesting ideas, letters, articles, reports and literary pieces were not reaching their intended readership, especially when to the world at large they seemed to be doing so well. Mrs Southwood Hill, an admirer of Maurice, like her clever little daughter, Octavia, wrote to the paper pleading for the formation of a Society of Ladies Promoters. Charitably inclined middle-class ladies began visiting London's

East End not so much 'slumming' as investigating the possibility of setting up women's associations there. A royal accolade was bestowed upon associations when Prince Albert visited the Dean Mills' Co-operative Stores near Bolton, and one of a different colour was bestowed when French authorities banned the *Christian Socialist*. 'It is an honour to receive persecution at such hands,' wrote the paper's Paris correspondent, but the Promoters worried about the fate of the French associations under the Emperor's new régime. At least the age of words has gone, trumpeted Ludlow bravely, but those were empty words, and when the *Daily News* of 4 December, from Paris, reported that all the *Associations Fraternelles* in the working-class areas had been shut down, Ludlow wrote more sombrely: 'No more ominous tidings could have been received. The flower of the working classes are thus turned adrift, no doubt in order that they may be mown down at one blow.'

In the 20 December 1851 issue Ludlow was delighted to give pride of place to a report from the *Preston Guardian* of a coruscating display of debating skill by Ernest Jones and Lloyd Jones. Prefacing the extract, Ludlow wrote:

> After long reluctance to ascribe unworthy motives to an opponent, I am bound to warn Mr Ernest Jones that the virulence of his attack on the profits of the co-operative bodies looks far too much like the anger of a mere demagogue, whose interest it is to keep the working-classes poor, in order that they may remain his slaves.

It was Ludlow's last rocket. The quarrel between him and Neale was so bitter that Ludlow felt he must resign, and resign from the Society of Promoters, and in the interests of unity Maurice stepped in to end the paper as Ludlow had shaped it and allow it to continue merely in a truncated form as a bald 'Journal of Association'. The last issue under Ludlow's editorship gave the numbers and types of co-operatives in operation in Britain at that date: 35 working men's producer associations and 14 flour mill societies; but there were 145 towns and villages which reported one or more co-operative stores. In spite of all Ludlow's missionary endeavours, the working classes, especially in Scotland and the north of England, were giving their loyalty and their pennies to the consumer co-operatives, just as Neale had predicted.

The decision to close the *Christian Socialist* was more important than it seemed at the time because to the public at large the paper *was* the movement, and when it ceased, and Ludlow had no platform from which to continue his dialogue with his readers, it was assumed mistakenly that the Christian Socialists had gone out of business.

The Price of Success

So die, thou child of stormy dawn,
Thou winter flower, forlorn of nurse;
Chilled early by the bigot's curse,
The pedant's frown, the worldling's yawn.

'Parson Lot'

Slaney's Bill, largely drafted by Ludlow, became law in June 1852 as the Provident Society Act, passed by the Tories who were in power briefly as a result of Palmerston's 'tit for tat with Johnny Russell'. The Christian Socialists were not disconcerted by having the Conservatives as allies, since they had a poor opinion of Whig administrations and their one 'swell', Cuthbert Ellison, was a Disraeli 'Young Englander' as well as a Christian Socialist. Ludlow was not sure yet about Disraeli whom he called 'a great Jew revolutionist in a Tory wig'. Passage of the Act cleared the path for future protective legislation for co-operatives, associations and unions, and the Christian Socialist lawyers drew up a set of model rules for submission to John Tidd Pratt, the Registrar of Friendly Societies.

Paradoxically, this success of the group made much of their work redundant, for in the future any persons wishing to form an association had only to write to the Registrar for the printed rules under which they could operate legally, and there was no longer any need to write to the Promoters for help. At the time, however, the Promoters did not realize this because two other issues engaged their attention, the great engineers' strike of 1852 and the Ludlow/Neale clash which came into the open that year.

The Promoters had been friendly with some of the leaders of the Amalgamated Society of Engineers, formed in 1850, and were hopeful that at least two of them, William Newton and William Allan, would put society funds into backing engineers' co-operatives. In the summer of 1851 they heard that the bankrupt Windsor Ironworks in Liverpool was for sale, and although the Christian Socialists, even with Neale's wealth, could not afford to buy it, they hoped the engineers would do so. Allan went so far as to start raising money, and named six trustees, three of whom were Hughes, Ludlow and Neale. The link between Neale and the engineers was fairly strong, and he was committed to working with the trade societies, forerunners of the trade unions, believing that they would support his Central Co-operative Agency. Indeed, Newton and Allan, along with Alexander Fleming of the National Association of United Trades, sat with co-operators on Neale's Agency committee.

Such evidence that the Agency and the irreligious Neale were forging ahead was anathema to Ludlow, who determined to have a showdown with Neale at the Promoters' Council meeting of 6 November 1851. For some reason he was unable to fight his battle there in person, but he prepared his case in a strong letter which he sent to Maurice with the request that Maurice would present it to Council. The letter demanded the expulsion from the Society of Promoters of Hughes, Neale, Lloyd Jones and Lechevalier, the four mainstays of the Agency: either they went, or Ludlow went. If Council backed the Agency men, Ludlow would also resign his editorship of the *Christian Socialist.*

He felt no hesitation or self-doubt and was convinced that he disliked the Agency only because its prospectus did not mention the word 'Christianity' and because he could not see any moral benefit deriving from its work. Such was Ludlow's reputation for total honesty that nobody in the Society would question his motives. One cannot, of course, help wondering how far his stiff-necked attitude was dictated by natural disappointment that his articles and lectures, his years of self-denial, seemed to count for so little. Along had come Neale, with money, energy and enthusiasm, and—one should be fair—dedication and learning, and the associates were off and away, cheering Mr Neale and forgetting Mr Ludlow.

In leaving the potentially explosive letter in Maurice's hands Ludlow was subconsciously avoiding a real split in the group, for Maurice's instinct was to compromise in the name of unity. He read Ludlow's letter and destroyed it before going to the Council meeting where he persuaded the Promoters to agree that the

Agency should operate, but as a separate entity from the Society. He had to persuade Furnivall of the correctness of that course, because Furnivall wanted the Promoters to support the Agency. Then Maurice wrote to Ludlow about what he had done. 'This is accomplished without a schism, Neale and Hughes perfectly concurring in it.'

Having brought the Promoters round to his way of thinking, Maurice applied himself to the more difficult task of making Ludlow agree. He begged him to subdue the divisive tendencies in his heart and suggested he was risking the whole principle of association and brotherhood for the sake of his notion how to carry out that principle, and outsiders might even think he was moved by jealousy, not principle. Finally, Maurice assured Ludlow that he sympathized with him over the Agency, and would certainly not let it swallow up the Society of Promoters. In other words, he was saying, 'Trust me', and Ludlow readily acquiesced.

The fracas among the Promoters could hardly have come at a worse time for Maurice, who was having his own battles with Dr Jelf. The press attacks upon Maurice and Kingsley and the Christian Socialists in general made Jelf afraid that King's College would suffer through guilt by association. Maurice must either disavow Kingsley, or make Kingsley disavow Maurice, Jelf demanded:

> otherwise it may be said justly, 'Mr Maurice is identified with Mr Kingsley, and Mr Kingsley is identified with Mr Holyoake, and Mr Holyoake is identified with Tom Paine . . . There are only three links between King's College and the author of the *Rights of Man*'.

Maurice replied calmly but at length, challenging the council of King's College to dismiss him. He refused to give up his connection with the Christian Socialists whose great aim, he explained, had been to take the Bible as simple truth and to try to prove to working people that the Bible could be a better practical guide to everyday living than the advice of political demagogues as ignorant as themselves. The College shrank from acting publicly against Maurice but hinted strongly he should be more cautious in his friends and in his writings, an unsatisfactory outcome from Maurice's point of view, for he had no intention of deserting his friends, particularly now that the engineers' strike had begun, followed by the employers' lockout.

The strike had been inevitable since the end of 1851, when the leaders of the A.S.E. gave formal notice to the employers that its members would not do piece-work, and overtime would be worked only if machines broke down, and then at double pay. The employers replied that this was an interference in business, and formed a Central Association of Employers of Operative Engineers, preparing to enforce a lock-out. By 10 January, 1852 most of the country's iron works lay idle.

The establishment press, led by *The Times*, took the employers' side, accusing the engineers of being Chartists in disguise. No popular paper had a good word for the men, so the Christian Socialists sprang to their defence through meetings, lectures and the *Journal of Association* which, under Hughes's editorship, was strongly partisan. They put the case for the engineers and pressed for arbitration, and the younger men thoroughly enjoyed making strong speeches, to the dismay of Maurice, who scolded Furnivall and Louis for being so outspoken. One reason why the Christian Socialists put so much vigour into their support of the engineers was that at last it looked as if the A.S.E. was turning to producer co-operatives, which in view of the intransigence of the employers began to seem extremely attractive as a means of improving working conditions. The Executive asked its members to allow £10,000 of society funds to be set aside for funding co-operatives. The Christian Socialists regarded that as a welcome turning away from early materialist demands. The engineers were getting ready to build the temple of Brotherhood on the foundations of Righteousness, said Ludlow, without the hint of a smile.

Behind the scenes he was still nagging at Maurice for having reneged on the original intention of Christianizing socialism while Maurice continued to turn the other cheek. Incapable of being a leader himself, Ludlow desperately tried to make Maurice assume that role, even though it would have made Maurice what he most feared to become. When the Prophet spoke with authority, it was not to lead men forward but to hold them back. Ludlow could not bear this for he, like the other younger Christian Socialists, was seized with a kind of fervour, convinced that they were all personally involved in a crucial phase of working-class history. Neale and his rich cousin, Augustus Vansittart, showed what they were made of by working closely with the A.S.E. leadership and financing a foundry in Cambridge Road, Mile End and the Atlas Works in Southwark. They were quite sure that when the engineers, the cream of the working class, formed producer associations, their inevitable success would make the association cause irresistible.

The Promoters at last had their own conference hall and offices, designed by Frank Penrose as a conversion of space of a floor at the Castle Street Tailors' Association. The work, at a cost of £230, was carried out by the North London Builders' Association, a splendid team of punctual, hardworking men, and the hall became an invaluable meeting-place for the group and its friends. On the surface, things were still going well, but the group felt uneasy as the bitter doctrinal dispute between Ludlow and Maurice spread to the rest of them. Maurice insisted that human relations had to improve before industrial relations could be any better; Ludlow considered it was more a question of property relations.

Even less publicized than the ideological debates were the personal problems of some of the members. That lovable genius, Charles Mansfield,[1] seemed to live on the edge of emotional chaos. His work with the associations and his chemistry research, including a book on the theory of salts, were impressive but his private life was a momentous failure. He had made an impulsive early marriage which soon failed and his wife left him. He met another attractive girl but she spurned him because he was a married man. Almost suicidal, he decided to desert his own class, and to Ludlow's stern disapproval he took a young working girl for his mistress. That was like a rich man claiming his *droit de seigneur*, declared Ludlow, a barbed shaft at Mansfield's wealthy family. The two friends had their first quarrel, for Mansfield thought his motives were being questioned and unknown to Ludlow, he intended to marry the girl when his divorce came through, and educate her in the meantime. As for Ludlow, he had a sense of loss as well as moral disapproval, and he was led to say far more than was wise. Mansfield should cut the girl out of his life at once, he declared; how could he have taken advantage of an underprivileged creature?

Mansfield's altercation with Ludlow, his religious doubts and the uncertainties of his relationship with the girl were driving him to a nervous breakdown, and his friends persuaded him to go away. He had recently read a book about Paraguay,[2] then a little-known country which sounded like a corner of Paradise, so he arranged to go there, visiting Brazil on the way. He planned to take copious notes and photographs and write a book on his return. Maurice was surprised to hear that Mansfield was actually leaving England.

> Ludlow said something to me about it, but I understood from him that you had abandoned it . . . I shall miss you very much; more than you would easily believe, seeing I had done so little to help you, and to show that I had some interest in your troubles and in your work,

he wrote just before Mansfield left. The change did Mansfield a world of good and his heart lightened with every mile away from England. Ludlow, however, missed him more than he could admit on the personal level and also as a stout ally in the continuing feud with the Agency men, especially with Lechevalier, who was emerging in a rather unexpected manner.

He had proved a surpassingly incompetent manager of the Agency, hardly surprising in view of his background, but the Christian Socialists were in no mood to make allowances. They were shocked to learn he had borrowed £600 from Neale, and disapproved of his habit of airing his grievances in public and touting for custom among the trade societies. It did not seem quite gentlemanly. With mounting distaste they watched his progress towards the Tractarians, which began when in June 1852 he published a pamphlet, *To the Clergy and the Laity*, in which he praised the Tractarians so highly that one of the best known of them, the Rev Charles Marriott of Oriel College, sent him a donation. He left Neale's Agency and scraped together sufficient money to set up in competition with a store called the 'Universal Supply and Demand Establishment', explaining that he had to earn a living to feed his family, but the Christian Socialists neither sympathized nor forgave. Did he *have* to compete with Neale? they asked.

Lechevalier could not leave matters where they were, and tried to vindicate himself with a pamphlet entitled *Five Years in the*

Land of Refuge. Even its dedication page seemed provocative to the sensitive Christian Socialists, being addressed first to 'Maurice, Kingsley, Ludlow, Hughes and Neale, Collectively' and then to Charles Marriott!—and when the author wrote: 'This my best manner of testifying what I really am, Their most sincere and faithful friend', the Christian Socialists were deeply sceptical. He complained that the group had discriminated against him because he was a foreigner, had called him ungrateful and a 'man of unsociable and despotic temper'. He told them that the producer co-operatives had failed because the middle-class Christian Socialists had done all the work and handed the men the benefits of association on a platter. The group was deluding itself, he declared, 'with a communistic and pantheistic fallacy' in believing that a conciliation between conflicting interests could be achieved by spontaneous mutual understanding, and it was simply not true that any relaxation of that belief would produce moral corruption.

At that last remark Ludlow joined in, telling Lechevalier that he was ready to gamble a great spiritual movement on the workings of a piece of intellectual machinery. Once Maurice had said something of the kind to Ludlow: now Ludlow was speaking with the tongue of Maurice to Lechevalier.

The altercation dragged on, and Lechevalier became more petulant month by month. 'You have got rid of the ungrateful friend, of the troublesome and scolding companion,' he said bitterly, 'You are now all Anglo-Saxon gentlemen together!' The Anglo-Saxon gentlemen bit back their hasty replies, and when Lechevalier indeed joined the Tractarians they said they had expected that all along. So much for his religious conversion to the Anglicans!

A sad result of this quarrel was that the Christian Socialists, when reviewing the movement, consistently underestimated Lechevalier's contribution. Maurice summed up their conclusions when he wrote in 1866 that participation in the commercial side of business would have weakened any moral influence the Christian Socialists might have had on the working class—the danger was that they might have 'become the victims of clever sharpers like Lechevalier, and should bring disgrace upon a principle which we felt to be sound'. Holyoake went further than Maurice and called Lechevalier a 'buonaparte spy'.

As a professional dissident and atheist Holyoake knew all about being under police surveillance, was aware of the activities of police informers and had never liked Lechevalier. His accusation was not backed up by evidence, and Holyoake frequently used some licence in his reporting. Hughes once remarked to Ludlow that if Holyoake wrote there had been mutton for supper, he, Hughes, would take it for granted there had been pork on the table.

The Christian Socialists felt that the loss of Lechevalier to their group was more than offset by the gain of Lord Goderich, who had been aware of Christian Socialism for some time but had not had the opportunity to take part hitherto. He was a young aristocrat of impeccably Puritan credentials, being directly descended from Oliver Cromwell on his father's side, and from other Puritans on his mother's. His birthplace was No. 10 Downing Street, no less, owing to the accident of his father becoming a brief caretaker Prime Minister upon the sudden death of George Canning.

Lady Goderich was a pious lady with Low Church leanings who supervised her son's education in a very strong-minded way. The boy developed entrenched habits of solitary reading and decision-making, but fortunately he grew up in the country, living close to boisterous cousins, and learned also to enjoy outdoor sports. He became a fisherman equal to Kingsley and Hughes, and a renowned beetle-hunter. When Baron Bunsen, the Anglophile Prussian ambassador, and an admirer of F. D. Maurice, met Goderich in 1850 he described him as 'a young man of German cultivation, eager for improvement'.

The process of improvement really started in 1848 when Goderich, just twenty-one, accompanied his cousin, Robert Ellis, on a tour of Italy, Switzerland and France. It was an exciting year to be abroad and when he was in Paris Goderich made it his business to visit the workers' co-operatives, which impressed him deeply. He was well to the left of his family's Whiggishness, but was a 'loner' by temperament and not attracted by any political party. He chanced upon *Politics for the People*, took out a subscription and even thought of writing an article for it, but never completed it. Mayhew's articles in the *Morning Chronicle* made him realize that he ought to join a group which would take some positive action to remedy society's ills, but his problem was finding such a group. Although tending towards Free Trade theories, Goderich did not think that *laissez-faire* policies were likely to help the sweated workers, and he did not think that Disraeli's 'Young England' group of the 'Manchester School' would take any positive action. He flinched from the atheism of the Chartists and Socialists and felt he could not join them. He nearly met the Christian Socialists in 1850 when Hughes sent him an invitation to one of their public lectures, but as he was unable to attend, he sent them two shillings instead, with a note to say that if the group was really hard up, he would send a further five pounds. That was quite a sizeable sum for Goderich in those days, but he was ready to send it if required, and he looked forward to becoming friendly with them all, including Kingsley, whose *Alton Locke* he was just reading: '. . . many parts of it have delighted me more than anything I have read for a long time, and it has greatly increased my desire to know Mr Kingsley.'

The trouble was that Goderich lived in the country, and in addition at that time he was busy courting his charming cousin, Henrietta Vyner, whom he married in April 1851. She came from the politically powerful de Grey side of the family, and Goderich's Whig relatives, who disliked his Radicalism, hoped he would forget his politics once he was married. Instead, the reverse happened. Lady Goderich did not complain of his new Christian Socialist friends, accommodating herself gracefully to their crotchets. She was the most captivating of all the Christian Socialist wives and she enchanted the bachelors in the group, especially Furnivall, whose admiration for her was so unbounded that Goderich and Hughes enjoyed a long-running joke at Furnivall's expense.

The engineers' strike and subsequent lock-out triggered Goderich into action. He wrote articles on their behalf, organized meetings and donated five hundred pounds to the strike fund when it needed cash very badly. That was about as much as one private individual could do, but it occurred to him that as an M.P. he would have a captive audience in the House of Commons and could speak to influential men about the engineers and Christian Socialist causes. Accordingly he resolved to stand at the next election and in preparation, and to clear his thoughts, he drafted a long article which set out his political views and submitted it to Hughes, as a possible Christian Socialist publication.

Hughes, who had a rather proprietary air over Goderich

because he was Hughes's recruit, read the manuscript with pleasure and approval. Goderich wrote that he despised a Britain
divided into Disraeli's 'two nations' where the rich minority
governed the poor majority, and equally he mistrusted an 'aristocracy of talent' where clever men lorded it over duller ones. Each
man, he declared, had the right to share in the government of his
country, but each man should understand that self-sacrifice was
the noblest principle of politics and also the safest foundation for
the State. He concluded with a peroration worthy of his Cromwellian ancestry (he named his eldest son Oliver):

> But let us beware lest any folly or any sin of ours retard that
> triumph, and let us remember that the old Puritan spirit is the
> only one in which we can hope to conquer; that spirit which
> told our ancestors that they *must* fail if they should ever sepa-
> rate 'God and the cause'.

Goderich sent another copy to Kingsley, asking for general
criticism and advice on the title. The Rector, who dearly loved a
lord, was thrilled to have a genuine aristocrat in the group, and he
replied, truthfully, that in his opinion the article was ideal for a
Christian Socialist Tract, and that 'The Duty of the Age' was the
right title. He hoped that Goderich would put his name to it. The
manuscript went to Ludlow, who approved it generally and made
a few minor amendments, and then it was sent to Maurice for
what Hughes expected to be a pro forma approval.

To the surprise of Hughes and Goderich, Maurice raised some
pedantic points, such as Goderich's use of the word 'self-government'. Did it mean government over self, or government by self,
or both, or neither? This was the first time that Goderich had
been exposed to the Prophet's style of argument and he was
completely baffled, but he buckled to, rewrote some sentences in
the hope he was doing what Maurice requested, and sent the new
version to Hughes. By that time Maurice had gone on holiday
abroad so he could not be consulted, and without a second's
thought Hughes sent the article to the printer as a new Tract.

The Tracts, indeed, were taking on a new importance because
it was obvious that very soon they would be the only Christian
Socialist publications left, for the *Journal of Association* was cost-
ing the Promoters so much that Hughes and Maurice decided to

close it in April 1852, and continued with it only after Ludlow objected on the grounds that some subscribers had paid for it until June. Ludlow personally raised enough money to carry the journal until that month and resumed editorship, bringing a temporary revival of the old Ludlow fire to the paper. It was proof that Ludlow was ready to work for the movement although, in spite of Maurice, he had resigned from the Council. Kingsley sent a farewell poem for the last issue, with a personal note to Ludlow to cheer him up.

All the Christian Socialists, except perhaps Maurice, felt a pang when their paper ended. The Prophet was a Christian Socialist but not exclusively so, and he was secretly a trifle relieved that the group's public propaganda was ending. If it had become too successful he might have found himself in a real political party, a Christian Socialist Party, something which he dreaded. Perhaps now, too, his disciples would give up trying to drag him into the forefront of their latest Christian Socialist endeavours. He never quite understood that, because he commanded such respect, his admirers longed to have his approbation and participation.

He had a similar effect on many of the younger generation, people like Octavia Hill, a socially committed teenager who was manager of a semi-co-operative, financed by Neale, for women who made a modest income by toy-making and glass-painting. She had an almost gushing admiration for Neale, Hughes, Furnivall and Ludlow but her attitude towards Maurice was one of matchless reverence:

> . . . as to Mr Ludlow, certainly there is not (excepting Mr Furnivall) such a person in the whole world. He has the largest, clearest, best-balanced mind joined to the truest, most earnest wish to help the working classes I ever met with (of course excepting Mr Furnivall's).

In the case of Maurice she suspended all intellectual judgement, and although she frequently failed to follow him when he was elaborating some subtle argument, his voice and his expression had a profound emotional effect upon her, so that in the end all she had to do was to believe him when he said that something was right or was wrong. It was not only adolescents who reacted in that way, most of his admirers did the same thing, assured that

Maurice was such a good man that he must know better than
they did.

By contrast there was also a number of eminently sensible
persons on whom the fabled Maurice charisma had no effect, like
Sir Mountstuart E. Grant Duff, who frequently heard Maurice
preach at Lincoln's Inn and never fathomed what he was saying,
nor even felt that Maurice knew what he was saying. Grant Duff
agreed with Aubrey de Vere who said that listening to Maurice
was like eating pea-soup with a fork.

But there was no mistake about Maurice's meaning when he
returned to England to find that 'The Duty of the Age' was
printed as a Christian Socialist Tract and about to be loosed upon
the world. He ordered the edition to be forthwith suppressed,
gave Hughes 'a precious wigging' and Goderich a stiff reproof.
Goderich replied that he had acted in good faith, assuming that
Ludlow had passed the amended manuscript, whereupon Maurice
turned upon Ludlow and reopened their ideological debate.
Hughes ruefully parcelled up the Tracts with string and brown
paper and left them in a corner of his office, letting the two intellectuals of the circle hammer out their differences.

Maurice kept repeating that his Bible study had convinced him
that an earthly society ought to have a hierarchical structure: 'I
must have Monarchy, Aristocracy and Socialism, or rather
Humanity, recognised as necessary elements and conditions of an
organic Christian society.' In reply, Ludlow begged Maurice to
use his great talents to build, to construct, to which Maurice
replied firmly, 'I am only a digger'. His destiny was to lay solid
foundations for men's thoughts and future actions.

Few people outside the circle were aware of this continuing
argument and, ironically, the man whom the public thought was
the chief Christian Socialist leader, Charles Kingsley, was the one
least involved because of his residence in Hampshire. In any case,
if Maurice were involved in any controversy it was Kingsley's
habit to support the Prophet without more ado. His national
reputation was based on his books; he had finished an historical
novel, *Hypatia*; he was in the middle of a dialogue called
'Phaeton: or Loose Thoughts for Loose Thinkers'; he was
immersed in poetry; and he was for ever firing off squibs to the
papers in defence of Maurice.

What the incident of 'The Duty of the Age' showed was the

virtual impossibility of the individual Christian Socialists agreeing together on a definition of democracy or socialism, let alone being unanimous on the desirability or otherwise of either of those states. Socialism for Maurice was 'the acknowledgement of brotherhood in heart and fellowship of work', not any kind of economic system, from which his 'systemphobia' would send him recoiling in horror. Ludlow, of course, had no such qualms about systems and authority but needed Maurice to approve them, and the couple exchanged long, emotional letters which gave no concessions to the other's point of view and caused pain to the recipient, to the distress of the sender. It was a relief for Maurice to open a letter from Tennyson and see he was being asked to stand godfather to the latest Tennyson baby.

It was even a relief to talk to George Grove about Sunday concerts at the Crystal Palace. Grove was part of what might be called the fringes of the Christian Socialist circle, having been recruited first by Hansard and then by Ludlow. An engineer by training, Grove had been appointed secretary to the Society of Arts and now, in 1852, was secretary of the Crystal Palace, moved from the Hyde Park Exhibition out to Sydenham in south London. Grove had discovered that Sunday was the only day the working man had free and he wished to run regular Sunday concerts at the Crystal Palace. What did Maurice think? Could Sunday be used for such a purpose? Groves was sure that Kingsley would support him, for in *Politics for the People* 'Parson Lot' had argued that galleries and museums should be open to the public on Sundays, but when approached Kingsley said that his gut reaction was to say 'yes' but he would not commit himself publicly unless Maurice did so. Maurice was typically ambivalent, not wishing to support any activity which might diminish Sunday churchgoing, or even the possibility of Sunday church attendance, but on the other hand not wishing to deprive the workers of recreation. Why not have the concerts at times which would allow the audiences to go to Church at other times of the day?

An attitude like that merely meant that both supporters and opponents of Sunday openings attacked Maurice, and when strangers wrote to him on the topic, his search for an absolute answer made his answers so confusing that his correspondents were left no better off. As for Grove he began his concerts and indeed forsook engineering for music, to which he devoted the rest of his life, and is now remembered as the first director of the Royal College of Music and the editor from 1878 to 1889 of the *Dictionary of Music and Musicians*.

One positive step which the Promoters had to take was to amend the aims and rules of their Society in light of the new legal situation following Slaney's Act, and naturally the group turned to Ludlow to draft the new constitution. He accepted the task with enthusiasm, hoping to use it to strengthen the Christian element in the movement, for he saw that future co-operatives might be formed which were entirely secular, and indeed Neale was already working happily with Holyoake and Thornton Hunt in the co-operative movement. The two last-named were as devoted to the co-operative cause as Neale was, but they were in Ludlow's view beyond redemption because of their anti-clericalism. It was bad enough, he felt, that the Positivist ideas of Auguste Comte were filtering through to England, a form of Christianity without God, but at least that was marginally better than atheism. Ludlow knew he was a voice crying in the wilderness but that did not stop him. Mansfield would have backed him up, but he was still in Paraguay. Maurice understood his feelings but did not encourage them. Lloyd Jones agreed that Neale's Agency had no moral force, but he continued working for it all the same. Kingsley made vague sympathetic murmurs but was engrossed in his own activities. Hughes and Hansard agreed that the Society of Promoters was in a muddle, frequently unable to muster a quorum at Council meetings, but they offered no solution. Well-meaning individuals drifted into the Christian Socialist orbit, worked with them for a while and then drifted out, not disillusioned but just unable to give the degree of commitment that Ludlow and the others did.

It was all highly unsatisfactory, complained Ludlow, warning his friends against the 'Mammon-spirit' and 'the devil's opposition', lurid terms which he chose to describe the Co-operative Conference which Neale was organizing. The Promoters had 'begun to build, without being able to finish', commented Ludlow and he decided it was his responsibility to regenerate the Society as a brotherhood of fellow-workers with its priest-king—Maurice, of course—and a religious test required.

So Ludlow put his 'Thoughts' for a constitution on paper and sent them first to Maurice, the normal procedure in cases needing serious consideration. Maurice read them through and asked Ludlow if he might hold on to them for a while, explaining that if he showed them to the Promoters at once it could easily lead to more confusion and dissension. Ludlow was agreeable, expecting that Maurice was intending to bring the Promoters round to Ludlow's point of view in his own time and in his own way, and did not appreciate that what Maurice was really doing was imposing a cooling-off period so that tension could be lowered. The collective soul-searching which Ludlow had been fondly anticipating never materialized, nor did the other Promoters understand his feelings. Neale thought that Ludlow would be appeased because Lechevalier was out of the group, all the Promoters joined him in wanting Ludlow back on the Council and on the Central Board, and Maurice added his magisterial weight to that plea.

It was never possible for Ludlow to hold out against Maurice so he returned to the fold, an action which aroused the Promoters to endless hours of discussion as to the kind of constitution they really wanted. In the end they asked Maurice to draft one, using Ludlow's 'Thoughts' as a basis. Ludlow made no objection, confident that Maurice would preserve his ideas.

Nothing, however, was further from reality. Maurice was a man of true originality and absolute integrity, always striving to act in the very best way. His deepest desire was for unity, including unity with all social classes, and he believed that the Christian element in the Christian Socialist group should be sufficiently elastic to include everyone, Christian or not, willing to fight the destructive forces in society. The Christian Socialists should not concentrate solely upon helping the working classes because society itself was not composed entirely of the working class. Therefore the group must be inclusive and not exclusive, and although its work had a moral base, no religious test should be demanded of its members and associates.

Maurice's thesis suited Neale perfectly but left Ludlow lonely, frustrated and bitterly disappointed. Nobody sympathized with him. Kingsley was shocked that anyone should be so unkind or so intellectually arrogant as to question Maurice's moral judgement and authority and told Ludlow he would rather cut off his right arm than write the kind of letters Ludlow had been sending to Maurice. Hughes tried to patch things up.

For the life of me I can't understand you and I don't suppose I ever shall. I wished thoroughly to put myself, you and all of us under the Prophet; well, he evidently will take the rule tho' not exactly in your way and I am infinitely convinced that he knows best—I wish you would unfold,

he wrote.

Maurice went to great pains to make his position clear to Ludlow. 'I know I have said hard words to you which have given you pain. It gives me very great pain to recollect them, and to think that I have in any way alienated you.' He worked on the draft constitution until he hit upon a formula which even Ludlow could accept. The other Promoters never knew how close Ludlow came to resigning for the second time, and in March 1853 the amended constitution was accepted.

Turning-Point

1852, Louis Napoleon became Emperor
Napoleon III; Palmerston dismissed for
having congratulated the Emperor; gold
rush in Australia; talks with Boers in S.
Africa; Death of the Duke of Wellington;
Gladstone's first budget, 1853.

They changed the name of the Society to The Association for
Promoting Industrial and Provident Societies, stating in the pre-
amble that the Promoters had united to apply Christian principles
to trade and industry. According to Huber, the Promoters active
or corresponding numbered about seventy, including nine clergymen, nine lawyers, two M.P.s, two peers and ten or more
members of the upper middle class. Men like Walter Cooper,
Gerald Massey and James Bezer, Christian Socialists by reason of
their activities, were associates not Promoters, and the addition of
their number made the group much larger.

They could not afford to finance as many projects as they would
have liked and Neale, whose generosity was legendary, had to
endure chilly disapproval at home and everlasting complaints
from his wife that his money should be reserved for the family.
The sad fact was that producer associations lost money. The
Atlas Works and the Mile End Works which were to have proved
conclusively that skilled workers could make a success of co-
operatives had shown themselves in the end to be no different
from associations of unskilled workers, and the A.S.E. executive
reconsidered their bold decision to back producer co-operatives
financially as well as morally. Neale and his cousin had been persuaded to underwrite these two factories to the extent they did
mainly because of the A.S.E.'s policy decision and it was up-
setting to learn that the A.S.E. was pulling out on the advice of its
president, Joseph Musto, who had an intimate view of the Mile

End ironworks through his brother, John Musto, who was manager. Joseph Musto rightly concluded that the problems of the Mile End Works were duplicated at the Atlas Works.

John Musto had noticed early on that self-government in the co-operative was leading to inefficiency, and he had himself appointed manager, tightened up discipline, brought in two of his brothers to help on the managerial side and licked the works into shape. Thereafter it prospered, but it was not a Christian Socialist model of a co-operative, and in light of the stories told by his brother, Joseph Musto changed his mind about risking union funds in co-operatives. In 1853 the works submitted an absurdly low bid for a large contract, winning the order, but it meant that they completed the work at a substantial loss. Augustus Vansittart, who had been drawn into co-operatives by his cousin's persuasion, not by any personal conviction, said that enough was enough, he would not put any more Vansittart money into co-operatives. Without his continuing support the Mile End Works soon closed. Vansittart withdrew to Cambridge, stoical over his losses, to spend the rest of his life as a worthy but rather dull don.

To the immense disappointment of the Christian Socialists, the Atlas Works followed a similar pattern. Money on an unprecedented scale had been poured into these two co-operatives in the expectation that failure was unthinkable. In Hughes's words:

> We had thought now, when the pick of the artisans of England had come into association, we should have great examples to hold up to our tailors and cobblers, who never seemed able to get through a month without a crisis. We found the engineers at least as jealous of each other, as difficult to manage, as ready to shirk work, as their humbler brethren in comparatively unskilled trades.

Showing what Hughes called 'a patience verging upon obstinacy', Neale continued to finance the Atlas Works. Anything less would have been a public admission that his painfully acquired political ideals, now the basis of his life, were Utopian visions impossible of fulfilment.

The smaller associations were usually in some kind of a mess. The Amalgamated Shoemakers' Association was typical, always in difficulties but struggling gamely on, so that the Christian

Socialists continually found a little money and a lot of time to keep them going. It was no more viable than the Mile End works, and finally their manager, Thomas Christmas, took it over as a private enterprise, employing the same men.

The Printers' Association also faced problems, particularly when the Christian Socialist publications ended, for those had been its main customers, and in August 1852 the manager, Richard Isham, took the business over and ran it as a private concern. He even refused to produce accounts or distribute profits, to the intense disapproval of the Promoters.

In the days of the *Christian Socialist*, and the meetings between Promoters and associates, Isham would have been asked to justify his autocratic conduct. In the last resort there would have been an appeal to Maurice to act as peacemaker, but Maurice, like Musto, was now disenchanted with co-operatives. He agreed with Kingsley that education was the key to a better life for working people. Kingsley had emphasized it in his first handbills, that the working class needed education so that they would be fit to be free.

The swing away from work with associations, thus dictated by events, gave each of the Christian Socialists the opportunity to follow individual paths in working towards their broad common goal, and the path or paths differed according to the character of the person involved.

In the case of Goderich it consisted in standing for Parliament. He had no intention of moderating his political opinions and still viewed the world through democratic spectacles. At the Royal Academy he admired Millais' *Huguenot* and *Ophelia* for the 'true democratic painting' which he detected in the delineation of flowers and brickwork. In the depths of Nottingham forests he met a beetle-hunting shoemaker, a kindred spirit, 'most pleasing to my democratic soul'.

Since his worldly relatives, to his disappointment, refused to find him a safe seat, Goderich had to go ahead on his own, and he stood for Hull in the election of 1852 in tandem with the sitting Whig member, James Clay, whose insipid liberalism filled Goderich with contempt. They made an ill-assorted pair, Clay fighting a routine campaign as befitted a seasoned politician, and young Goderich making every mistake of the novice. Shrill-voiced, painfully earnest, under average height, he faced his hecklers bravely, but fell into all the traps set by his wily Tory opponents.

The attractive figure of young Lady Goderich, loyal and devoted, was a decided advantage but it was somewhat outweighed by the unnerving presence of 'Citizen Bezer' from the Printers' Co-operative, acting as Goderich's agent and organizer. He had undertaken to win the support of the labour strongholds in the port and he had impressive contacts with the working class and the radical press. Goderich had every confidence in him, although some instinct for self-preservation prompted him to warn Bezer against infringing the laws on bribery and corruption. That done, he dismissed the possibility from his mind and passed over the modest sums requested by Bezer without question. Clay and Goderich were duly elected, and Goderich wrote exultantly to Hughes—'We did win a good fight, I take it, the chief praise whereof is due to Burgess and Bezer. I earnestly hope I may be able to do some good in this Parliament.'

A fond hope.

At the very instant when Goderich was glorying in his self-styled description as a working-class Member with his Radical and Christian Socialist principles still intact, he received a nasty inquiry from Julian Harney as to Bezer's whereabouts. Harney's republican paper *Star of Freedom* had strongly backed Goderich's campaign and Bezer had asked Goderich for a donation to send to that paper. Goderich gave the money and forgot the incident. It now transpired that Harney had never received the expected sum and was highly suspicious. Where was the money, and more to the point, where was Bezer, or Monops, as the classically-educated Christian Socialists had blithely dubbed their one-eyed printer?

Goderich sought out Mrs Bezer and was alarmed to be met by a tearful and imploring wife who begged his help. Bezer had bolted! Would Lord Goderich assist a loyal and deserted spouse in tracing an errant husband? The young M.P. was exceedingly uncomfortable, such a situation being completely outside his experience. He promised to do what he could and left, and when he told his friends about Bezer he found that although they shared his dismay, they were case-hardened to stories of delinquency.

It was bad enough to think about Bezer and Mrs Bezer, but what about his seat in the House if the scandal became public, he wondered. Would some Tory unearth it and query the entire election? That was exactly what happened and Goderich and Clay were unseated.

Extensive inquiries as to where Bezer had gone eventually brought the answer that he had emigrated to Australia.

Some months later another seat fell vacant and Goderich again offered himself as a candidate. Blooded in political warfare he fought hard, but there was no joy in it this time. In spite of Tory jeers that he was a communist, a socialist, a Chartist, a cosmopolitan, and an associate of foreign revolutionaries like Kossuth, Mazzini, Louis Blanc and Ledru Rollin, he won the election, but his satisfaction was not quite enough to counter the shock he had received over Bezer. His faith as a Christian Socialist was badly shaken.

'It seems to me', he wrote to Hughes—for writing and talking to Hughes not only cleared his mind but helped to strengthen his faith:

> that if the working men only care for co-operation when they are in distress, they don't much, in truth, care about it at all, with here and there exceptions of course. Our Utopias will need to be built on foundations which can only be laid deep in men's hearts.

He clung to his dreams, however. The magnificent ruins of Fountains Abbey were part of his Yorkshire estate and once he remarked wistfully that it would be fine to transform the Abbey into a working-men's university. At that time he could not afford it: much later, when he could, the impulse was gone.

So Goderich's path now lay in the Commons and he hoped to spread the Christian Socialist vision from that centre. He was a conscientious M.P., in spite of complaints to Hughes about the 'perpetual jaw', and he headed a minuscule anti-Whig, pro-Christian Socialist group which included two M.P.s, A. H. Layard and Henry Bruce, and two men later to become M.P.s, W. E. Forster and Tom Hughes. He disliked Palmerston, saying he was the most unprincipled man in the Commons next to Disraeli, and was saddened that Kingsley, whose books he greatly admired, had anything good to say about the Whig leader. Goderich did not share Kingsley's passion for sanitary reform and his antipathy towards Palmerston was not lessened by being told that

Palmerston was faintly sympathetic to sanitary reform. Set Gladstone alongside Palmerston, retorted Goderich, and could there be any doubt which man to choose?

Another strike and lock-out, in Lancashire this time, depressed him profoundly. 'How deep and wide is the separation between the two classes, how terrible their alienation.' The masters needed education so that they could behave fairly towards their workers, he asserted. He still felt that associations were desirable, but for the moment it was perhaps more practical to work for an extension of the franchise. The hard world of politics was taking the young lord some distance from 'The Duty of the Age' and pure Cromwellian ideals.

Indeed the Christian Socialist dream was ceasing to be a strong, unified vision. The disappointments which were apparently inseparable from the associations, the need to make a living, the claims of family—those were the main factors forcing members of the group to re-assess their services to society.

Neale, for instance, concentrated on establishing a national co-operative league which would include stores and producer co-operatives, and he was sure that Slaney's Act could be employed to unify the two types of associations. The London-based Christian Socialists had to accept that co-operatives, especially the stores, had prospered more in the north than in the south and that they owed more to Robert Owen's socialism than to Christian Socialist morality. Northern associations had often started on a shoestring, with money they raised themselves, and were strong because the members were friends and fellow-workers who had known each other since childhood. They were located in small, closely-knit communities where their activities were in full view of family and friends, and failure would be shameful.

Things were rather different in the sprawling anonymity of London. The Christian Socialist associations were made up of men picked at random for their willingness to try an experiment. They had no history of shared companionship in good times and bad, no enduring friendships to see them through difficulties. Furthermore, the middle-class Christian Socialists were always there to bail them out or to resolve problems.

Such were the reflections in Neale's mind as he sat at his desk, organizing his conference and dreaming of a noble vision of society. He had concentrated upon consumer stores in London because they appeared to be practical, but he looked ahead to a time when a combination of such stores would create a stable market for the goods from producer co-operatives. He hoped that his co-operative conference, held in the Promoters' Hall of Association at 34 Castle Street on 26 and 27 July 1852, would lead to great things. The main item on the agenda was to consider how best Slaney's Act could be used to further the co-operative movement and Ludlow approvingly described the conference as 'the first Session of a real Labour-Parliament'.

Attendance was very disappointing, the London associations being strongly represented but not the northern ones. Some of those societies were reluctant to be seen working with the Christian Socialists and others could not afford to send delegates. Nevertheless something was achieved. The conference agreed that co-operative bodies should enrol according to the provisions of Slaney's Act, that a set of model rules for co-operative societies should be drawn up by the Promoters and that a Co-operative Friendly Union should be formed. Lloyd Jones proposed that an executive committee be formed to prepare for a conference next year in Manchester, and also be empowered to take any action it considered in the best interests of the co-operative movement generally.

Ludlow looked at all the empty seats and protested that the conference was 'too thin to represent the movement at large', so he would support the first part of Lloyd Jones's resolution, but not the second part. The only action such a committee could take, he added, was 'the purely moral and voluntary one of the Promoters'. Correct though Ludlow's stand was, it proved too honest and uncompromising for the conference, which passed both sections of Lloyd Jones's resolution. A committee was accordingly formed, made up of Promoters, members of Neale's Agency and five members from provincial co-operative societies as corresponding members.

This first co-operative conference was important enough to bring Kingsley up from the country. He enjoyed entering the hall to the cheers of delegates and listened intently to the proceedings. One thorny problem concerned the moral obligation upon associations to give a truthful description of goods for sale. Most traders seemed to have no scruples on that score, but co-operators had higher standards. The pages of the *Christian Socialist* had

Charles Kingsley

been full of complaints about shops selling fraudulent or adulterated goods. Amid all the debate Kingsley sat quietly scribbling and he rose to read a resolution which was adopted:

> That this Conference entreats all co-operative establishments, for the sake of the general good, to sell all articles exactly for what they know them to be, and to abstain, as much as possible, from the sale of all articles publicly known to be adulterated, even if demanded by their customers.

In later discussions on more general topics, Kingsley urged the societies to undertake welfare activities as well as production or distribution, declaring that 'mutual help was not adjunct to co-operation, but lay at the very root of it'.

Attendance apart, the conference was judged a success, at least by the audience and organizers, and it closed in Christian Socialist manner with a party open to delegates and guests. Maurice had not attended the conference but he made a point of going to the party, which was the most ambitious social event yet held in the new Hall, and many guests arrived as much to see the Hall and gape at famous faces as to congratulate the delegates. Octavia Hill, with her sister, Miranda; her mother; Emma Cons, her friend and helper; and two others, made up a party. They knew many of the Promoters and associates but it was a thrill to be introduced to Kingsley, and Miranda wrote to her friend, Joanna Graham:

> I think I never saw such a face as Mr Kingsley's. That face was the chief pleasure of all, though there was a most splendid collection of people there . . . I think Mr Kingsley's face extremely suffering, and full of the deepest feelings. But there is such a sublime spirituality; he looks so far above this earth, as if he were wrapt in grand reveries; one feels such *intense* humility and awe of him. I hardly dared to look at him . . .

Maurice was called upon to make a speech and Miranda Hill tried to follow his train of thought but failed. 'He seemed as if he felt a great deal more than he could express, and therefore left feelings rather than ideas in one's mind,' she remarked, thereby speaking for more people than she knew. Before Maurice could step down there was a little ceremony, one which he had not expected. The associations had clubbed together to buy him a silver inkstand and a gold pen case, a token of regard which touched him deeply and helped banish some of the self-doubts he had felt during the long arguments with Ludlow.

Association and its educational influence was bound to progress at a snail's pace, as the Christian Socialists had found out, and one of the problems with Lechevalier was that he was too impatient to understand that fact. Most of the quarrels in which he was involved concerned methods and timing, not aims of the group. As Furnivall said, the nature of association demanded a 'long course of practical forethought and self-denials, in order to accumulate capital, learn business habits etc. on the part of working-men'. It was far easier for professional middle-class men to discipline themselves than for deprived working-class men to do so, and when the Christian Socialists formed later associations they tried to be more discriminating in picking the associates.

Several of the Promoters noticed Maurice's apparent loss of interest in association work, but did not know that the reason was his preoccupation with an important collection of essays ready for publication. These had originated in letters to a Unitarian who had asked him for advice on religious topics, and as Maurice expanded his ideas the letters became essays. They were in fact the product of years of correspondence and discussions with many other people as well, and Maurice was fairly certain that when the 'Essays' were in print they would provoke the fiercest criticism yet and give Jelf the weapon he needed to rid King's College of its notorious professor. 'I knew when I wrote the sentences about eternal death,[1] that I was writing my sentence at King's College,' he told Kingsley, to which the loyal Rector responded:

Well, dearest master, I shall not condole with you. You are above that; . . . You know what I feel for you. But your cause is mine. We swim in the same boat, and stand or fall henceforth together. I am the mouse helping the lion—with this difference, that the mouse was *out*-side the net when she gnawed it, while I *am inside*. For if you are condemned for these 'opinions', I shall and must *therefore* avow them . . .

Foreseeing a good deal of unpleasant publicity once the new book was reviewed, Maurice considered it might be to the advantage of the Christian Socialist movement if he discreetly withdrew, but as he gave no hint of his reasons when he embarked upon what Hughes called 'a cholera of resignations', he merely left his friends hurt and puzzled.

His first attempt at resigning was a dismal failure. He announced that he was appointing two assessors to serve in his place as president of the Promoters during his frequent absences from London, and with characteristic insistence upon unity he named Neale and Ludlow to serve jointly. This was a commendable idea on the face of it, each man being a leading theoretician and activist, and together they represented the two separate wings of the movement. Maurice intended that this shared responsibility would bring Neale and Ludlow closer together, a gentle Maurician hope strengthened by an equally Maurician determination to have his own way.

Ludlow started to protest, at which Maurice snapped that if Ludlow wished him, Maurice, to remain president, then Ludlow must obey Maurice's presidential decrees. When Ludlow meekly suggested that Hughes and Walter Cooper be chosen as joint assessors, Maurice replied that Ludlow must co-operate with Neale. After digesting the Prophet's moral rebuke, Ludlow hastened to assure him that he and Neale were now on perfectly good personal terms and did not need any yoke to improve them. If Maurice resigned, just when the Society had adopted a new constitution, it might harm the Society severely. Maurice took the point, named Hughes and Cooper, and with a secret sigh, continued as president for a little longer.

Punishments and Rewards

1853, Britain and France declared war
on Russia; 1854, start of Crimean
campaign.

Maurice presided at the co-operative conference held in
Manchester in August 1853 and was impressed by Neale's
speech and by the adroit way he handled questioners. Co-operation, declared Neale, aimed at constructing a society ruled by
fellowship and mutual trust where man could develop his
physical and spiritual powers to the full. He was talking about a
possible Co-operative Commonwealth, his dearest dream, and it
was a theme to which he would return repeatedly throughout
his life.

Thomas Shorter presented a low-key executive committee
report, low-key because there was very little to report, one
reason being that its committee members were fully engaged in
earning a living elsewhere. The Manchester delegates were
urged to join the Promoters in the Industrial and Provident
Societies' Union, and in their turn they requested a co-operative
journal. Leeds was picked as the venue for the next conference,
Lloyd Jones was elected to the executive committee, and the
business closed with the traditional Festival, Maurice taking the
place of Goderich[1] there.

To any outsider the Manchester conference would appear
proof positive of the successful work and growing influence of
the Christian Socialists, but with hindsight it must be seen as
symbolic more than actual. In reality the group was on the point
of dissolution and even if everything had been running
smoothly, there would have been the need to pause for breath.
When time, money and energy runs low in a movement, and its
leaders agree only on the vaguest and broadest of aims, some
slackening of momentum can be predicted.

Such was the gloomy background against which the short but intense drama of Maurice's dismissal from King's College was about to be enacted. The controversy between Jelf and Maurice centred on the latter's interpretation, especially in his recently published *Theological Essays*, of the phrase 'eternal life'. Maurice said it meant being in communion with God and Jelf said it meant everlasting life in a hereafter. A corollary of the Jelf view, and the one which many people accepted, was that individuals needed to behave themselves in this world to gain 'eternal life' in the next, a system in fact of rewards and punishments. This was the view which had led Maurice and Kingsley to declare that the Bible had been misused as a constable's handbook to keep the poor in order. If Maurice's liberating doctrine were established, Anglican ministers would lose one of their established holds on their congregations.

Jelf had to keep in mind the effect of Maurice and his unorthodox opinions upon the parents who sent their sons to King's, particularly to the divinity department, where the boys were supposed to be taught orthodox theology so that they equipped themselves to become orthodox Anglican ministers. It would be much more convenient if Maurice would quietly resign, and enough letters passed between him and Maurice that summer to fill a book, as Maurice told Hare, trying to make a joke of it, but without much success. He definitely refused to resign, and told Jelf that he had worked at the College for thirteen years and had the right to be investigated by the Council and declared honest or a scoundrel. In the latter case the College risked rather unpleasant publicity, but that was not Maurice's concern. A footman dismissed by his master for drunkenness and pilfering had that right, and Maurice claimed it too.

His impending doom preyed upon his mind all summer and his letters to family and friends were full of the affair. Congratulating his parents on their fifty-ninth wedding anniversary he was philosophical, if not jaunty:

I cannot tell you, my dearest mother, how much your good and brave words about King's College have cheered me. I am quite certain that I shall be dismissed from it, and I do not wish to remain in it, because I believe my giving up will do more to promote the principles I have maintained than my stay in it could do. Therefore I shall go, when the time comes, with hearty good will and, I hope, in charity towards all men.

Ludlow, Kingsley and the rest, and Fenton Hort in Cambridge, rallied support for Maurice. Ludlow was eager to show that, in spite of the social and political differences between him and Maurice, on the personal level they were still close, and he published a pamphlet which gave the facts of the dispute, and planned two more to follow, but Maurice stopped him, saying it was a form of self-advertisement which he loathed. Highly coloured inklings of the trouble came to the associates and when Walter Cooper spoke about it to young Octavia Hill she gained the impression that Maurice's book contained heresy and he was likely to be expelled from the Church. 'What all this betokens, I cannot guess; but I fear something sad,' she wrote. Meanwhile she cheered herself by reading Kingsley's famous sermon, 'The Message of the Church to the Labouring Men' and then read 'The Duty of the Age', which somebody had lent her from Hughes's famous pile of censored Tracts. She enjoyed it, to her surprise. 'I did not think Lord Goderich was so nice,' she confessed to her sisters.

The Christian Socialists, individually and collectively, were her respected mentors, but her secret love and inspiration was John Ruskin, hovering on the fringes of the group through his friendship with Furnivall.[2] 'About Ruskin, it matters very little to me what *The Times* or anything else, says of him. I see much, very, very much, to admire in him, and several things which I could wish different,' she declared on the eve of Ruskin's first visit to the Ladies' Guild, and after that longed-for event had taken place, she was even more vehement.

If it be prejudice to love right and beauty, if it be conceited to declare that God had revealed them to you, to endeavour to make your voice heard in their defence, if it be mad to believe in their triumph, and that we must work to make them triumph, then he is all four, and may God make us all so!

she wrote to her sister Gertrude, with all the fierceness of an emotional fifteen-year-old. It was the start of a relationship with Ruskin which became very important to her, personally and professionally.

As if Maurice did not have enough worries at this time he was approached by Captain Sterling with the request that he should become official guardian of John Sterling's orphaned daughters. Naturally he agreed, although it meant additional dependants at a time when his income was likely to drop, and the Sterling girls grew up as part of the Maurice family. They joined in the later work of the Christian Socialists and became much valued helpers to Octavia Hill when she embarked upon her slum housing schemes.

Meanwhile the Council of King's College was not unanimous about Maurice, and Gladstone led the pro-Maurice faction. He tried in vain to get an adjournment of the case, hoping to have time to enlist the support of the Bishop of Lichfield and Dean Milman of St Paul's, but the anti-Maurice group rushed its proposals through in the hope of avoiding any further adverse publicity. Everyone who knew or had heard of Maurice followed the duel with keen interest and the Maurice/Jelf correspondence was printed in pamphlet form and sold in bookshops.

Maurice was formally dismissed on the issue involving everlasting punishment, with the result that many people who would not normally have taken any notice of the matter, now spoke out for Maurice. The *Spectator*, the *Daily News* and the *Globe*, which had once vilified Maurice as the leader of Christian Socialism hailed him as a martyr for free speech, whilst Holyoake's atheist paper, the *Reasoner* and the anti-Anglican paper of the Unitarians, the *Inquirer*, supported King's College. Maurice received many letters of support, including one from his pupils at King's, and was characteristically surprised by the tokens of sympathy. A sentence of dismissal he had anticipated, but evidence of high regard from strangers was unexpected.

He hoped to remain as professor at Queen's College but made it clear that support for him had to be unanimous, and when he heard that one or two members of the College committee were doubtful about him he resigned instantly, severing a happy working connection of almost six years. He donated to the school his share of the fund raised to pay for its new charter, for which his friend, the Rev R. C. Trench, chairman of the school committee, thanked him, and his Queen's College students gave him a silver inkstand. Again the Prophet was modestly taken by surprise, and told his 'dear friends' that he only hoped he had taught them as much, or half as much, as they had taught him. That good teaching was a double process wherein the teachers learned from the students as well as vice versa was a fundamental belief of Maurice in his role as educator.

The King's College expulsion actually freed Maurice from all restraints. It barred him from preferment in the Church of England but he counted that a blessing in disguise, and now he need not worry about any adverse effect words of his on other subjects might have on King's or Queen's College. He suffered financially, of course, but he had always looked on money as the very least of his considerations.

However, the outcome was much less fortunate for Jelf who, except where Maurice was concerned, was a kind and patient man. He gained the reputation of being a rigid persecutor out of touch with modern ideas, and nobody thought of offering him any promotion. Able though he was, the Maurice controversy blighted his career. King's College, as an institution, also passed under a cloud and, when Jelf finally retired, his successor, by a neat piece of irony, was the Rev Alfred Barry, a disciple of Maurice, who ushered in a breezy new liberal epoch for the College.

Maurice had apparently come through unscathed, but beneath a calm exterior he was on fire to prove to the world the correctness of his religious views, and he discussed with Kingsley and with Daniel Macmillan the possibility of writing new pamphlets which he thought of calling 'Cambridge Tracts'. It was interesting that he turned to Kingsley, the priest, and not to Ludlow, the barrister, but in the end the idea was dropped. Nevertheless it showed that Maurice was groping towards some as yet undisclosed sphere of usefulness which would be educational in a broad sense. The new venture was to be a Working Men's College.

Such an institution was not original. Mechanics' Institutes, catering for working men, had operated for many years but mainly taught vocational skills, and were managed by middle-class committees as suspicious as Jelf of Christian Socialist aspirations. There had been some more interesting experiments in adult education, such as the 'People's College' in Sheffield, which

Lloyd Jones had come across. A Working Men's College on Maurician lines would be a natural development from the night classes in Little Ormond Yard and from lectures and classes in the Hall of Association. Indeed Charles Mansfield had tried to win support for such an idea in 1852 but, typically, had not pursued it. He was a mine of inventive suggestions but, except in chemistry research, never had the time to carry them out.

It was really owing to Mansfield's insistence that the Christian Socialists had arranged their first series of lectures in the winter of 1852. Maurice lectured on the historical plays of Shakespeare; Walter Cooper on the life and genius of Burns; John Hullah on how to start a singing class; R. C. Trench on Proverbs; William Johnson, a teacher at Eton College, on rivers and geography; Penrose on architecture and its influence on the working class; Nevil S. Maskelyne on photography; Goderich on entomology, and Hansard on popular astronomy for children. Seats were bookable at 6*d*. or unreserved at 2*d*. and the lectures were printed afterwards in the *Christian Socialist*. The series proved so popular with the associates and their friends that the group started regular weekly evening classes, at which Hughes and Augustus Vansittart taught English grammar; Maurice, Neale, Louis and others taught English history; Newling taught book-keeping, Ludlow French, and Hullah singing. The moment they could find suitable teachers, the Christian Socialists intended to offer drawing classes and classes in political economy. The classes were restricted to men, at a charge of 2*s*. 6*d*. per quarter, with the exception of the singing class, to which women were admitted. Both men and women were welcome at the lectures.

The success of that series, and the availability of the new Hall of Association encouraged the group to hold a second series in 1853. Maurice's Sunday Bible evenings were transferred to the Hall of Association, where they had a bigger audience than in his home, and he enjoyed conducting his unique brand of lecture-cum-seminar. As Ludlow put it: 'These lectures and classes were the germ of the Working Men's College'.

Among the 1853 lecturers were George Grove, E. Mountstuart Grant Duff, H. J. S. Smith, Charles Pearson, J. Llewelyn Davis, Charles Buxton and Lloyd Jones, and two trump cards, Charles Kingsley and the Rev F. McDougall, calculated to draw capacity audiences.

McDougall was a medical missionary from Borneo, the area which became a household word in Britain in 1849 when James Brooke and some units of the British Navy led a bloodthirsty punitive expedition against Malay pirates and their Dyak crews. The Sultan of Borneo showed his pleasure at Brooke's exploits by making him Rajah of Sarawak, but in Britain there was considerable indignation over the degree of slaughter that had been involved. Kingsley and Ludlow took opposite sides over Brooke, the country parson supporting the Navy and the new Rajah, whilst Ludlow, always sympathetic to native peoples, supported the Dyaks. When Kingsley reminded Ludlow that Cromwell, for example, had not hesitated to slay the Irish, Ludlow drew on his strongest vocabulary to condemn the harshness of powerful rulers: 'whether their name is Charlemagne or Cromwell, Dominic or Calvin . . . no lapse of ages will ever wash from Cromwell's name the blood of the Wexford massacres,' he replied, a judgement which cut deep because his own ancestor, Colonel Ludlow, had been assigned with Ireton to carry out the final massacres in Ireland when Cromwell left that country to deal with the Scots.

In 1851 in the House of Commons Joseph Hume and Richard Cobden charged Brooke with having used undue severity but the 'white Rajah' defended himself successfully, and when later on the British Government purchased the island of Labuan from the Sultan of Borneo it appointed Brooke as governor of the island. McDougall was a great admirer of Brooke and in line to become the first Bishop of Labuan when the Church of England should designate that island as a colonial bishopric.

All that was recalled in 1853 when McDougall was billed as a visiting lecturer and his name attracted a crowd, so that even Ludlow was glad to have him on the Christian Socialist roster. As for Kingsley, he listened like an eager schoolboy to McDougall's stirring tales from the outposts of empire, and could not stifle a pang or two of envy. Parish work was so often just a dull grind among the 'Hampshire clods'. In Eversley a spectacular achievement was getting a National School started, rather different from risking your life among Dyak head-hunters!

Education then, had always been a distinct if minor side of the Promoters' activities and the associates fully appreciated the importance of education in their own lives. They organized an address to Maurice, signed by over a thousand of the working men, representing about a hundred occupations. It was ceremoniously presented to him at a meeting in the Hall of Association on 27 December 1853, and ended:

> That you may long continue to pursue your useful and honourable career: that the eminent services you have confessedly rendered to the Church and to the cause of education, may meet with a more generous and grateful appreciation; that those who at present misunderstand and misrepresent you may learn by your example and that they may at least emulate you in the wisdom and zeal with which you had advocated the cause of the working-man, is the sincere and earnest desire of those whose names are hereunto appended.

Maurice was visibly moved, for his constant anxiety was that he never managed to do as much as he wished for the working class, and the address could not have given him greater pleasure.

Then somebody remarked casually that he hoped that Maurice 'might not find it a fall to cease to be a Professor at King's College and to become the Principal of a Working Men's College'. In the charged emotional atmosphere of the hall that suggestion came like a call from God, and in a spiritual sense Maurice's college was founded there and then.

From that instant on Maurice began to clarify his ideas for the College, a therapeutic activity which allowed him to consider he was already involved in a new enterprise when he received a letter from the Honourable Society of Lincoln's Inn in which the members hoped his present troubles would be 'but a passing cloud in your useful and honoured life'. On 10 January 1854 he wrote to Kingsley that he hoped 'my college' would soon be established, and the next day the Promoters gathered at Maurice's house to hear Neale read a letter from Mr Wilson, Secretary of the People's College in Sheffield, describing the origins of the College and its progress. At once Hughes proposed, with Lloyd Jones seconding, that the Promoters' Committee of Teaching and Publication be empowered to frame, and if possible carry out, a plan to set up a People's College in connection with the London Associations.

The resolution was adopted unanimously, the committee got to work and Maurice was asked to draft a constitution which he gladly completed in record time. Just as the Christian Socialists believed that the operations of trade and industry should be subject to a moral law, so they believed that 'human studies' rather than vocational skills should be the primary part of the education offered by the proposed College. Maurice went even further and would have liked all the teachers to agree that theology should be the true basis of human studies. A College founded by the Christian Socialists which omitted theology would seem like fraud, he pointed out, but although he hoped that the teachers would share his view, no similar obligation was placed upon the students because they, unlike the Christian Socialists, were not pledged to proclaim God as the ground of society and of all human life.

It went without saying that the College would be independent and that the teachers would be unpaid volunteers. Maurice reminded his teachers that teaching adults was quite different from teaching clever boys, for even the most ignorant and humble adult had an experience of life unattainable by a schoolboy. An ideal education should produce a framework of freedom and order which would make working people feel that they belonged to a harmonious society, therefore the new institution must be a real College, not simply a night school, and it should provide fellowship, association and unity.

In June and July that year Maurice gave lectures on education at Willis's Rooms to awaken interest in his College and to appeal for funds. The collection amounted to £87 and his lectures were later printed in a book called *On Learning and Working*. By October most of the teaching staff had been selected, a syllabus of lectures and a prospectus had been drawn up, and Maurice was named as Principal. He gave an inaugural address to a packed audience in St Martin's Hall. The circular which advertised the College made an especial point that it was being opened 'especially for Manual Workers', an indirect reference to the Mechanics' Institutes which had also been set up originally for manual workers, but which in many cases had ended by attracting the clerical class.

Maurice's College was to cater as far as possible for the needs of the poorest and most deprived, though its function was not limited to teaching the elementary skills of reading, writing and simple arithmetic, but was to stretch the mind and provide opportunities for discussion and friendship with the teachers as well as with fellow students. Uninhibited talk over tea or coffee in the commonroom after or before classes was to be an integral part of College education.

As the audience filed in to listen to Maurice Furnivall busied himself, in his capacity as usher, distributing reprints of Chapter VI of Ruskin's *Stones of Venice*, for the graduate of Oxford was Furnivall's recruit to the new College. Furnivall's endless stories about conditions and campaigns in the Christian Socialist movement had awakened Ruskin's interest in working-class deprivation. He heard how Furnivall had worked with Hughes to try to help the ballast-heavers of the Thames; of the time when Furnivall sold his books to raise £100 for the woodcutters' strike in 1851; and of the deep moral significance of co-operatives.

Chapter VI was 'On the Nature of Gothic', a piece destined to exert great influence upon the way people looked at public buildings, especially churches. Art, declared Ruskin, could not be produced except by artists, and architecture also must be designed by artists, and executed by artists. When an age succeeded in producing workmen who were artists, and artists who were workmen, the golden reign of art would commence. It was a manifesto which was entirely in keeping with the spirit of the Christian Socialists.

When puzzled visitors asked Furnivall why he was giving out Ruskin's pamphlet at Maurice's meeting Furnivall answered bluffly so that they could see for themselves 'what sort of a fellow one of our Teachers was', an artless reply, characteristic of Furnivall. He was never a solemn do-gooder, but a cheerful, gregarious and energetic man, loving company and gossip, a demon for strenuous exercise and a keen music lover. He had been an admirer of Jenny Lind, whom he once met, and had listened to Chopin, lost in admiration. The pianist was, declared young Furnivall dramatically, 'consumed with the fire within'. He was bored with the conveyancing work which was his livelihood, but could not afford to give it up until 1873, and his real life was lived in the hours he gave to the associations, to the co-operative movement, to the new Working Men's College, and to the learned literary societies which he would form in years to come.

Perhaps Furnivall was successful in drawing Ruskin into the Maurician orbit because Effie Ruskin had just lately left her husband, preparatory to the nullity suit and her subsequent marriage, after a decent interval, to the handsome young painter, John Millais. The experience of meeting working men face to face, and teaching them, led Ruskin into a new field, that of social criticism, and it helped him assert an intellectual independence in the face of his father's bitter hostility to the change in his son's interests. Ruskin, warned his father, would be flayed alive if he mixed in Radical politics.

The first home of the Working Men's College was fixed at 31 Red Lion Square, home of an association which had failed, and Maurice had assumed responsibility for the rent, so it was available for the College. The Promoters could not help noticing that Maurice spent more and more time fussing over details concerned with the College and less and less time at the executive meetings of the Promoters. Nobody was really surprised and certainly nobody dared complain. Maurice must have his reasons, they said, and that was good enough for them. Ludlow was unhappy about it, but kept silent.

For if 1853 had been a spectacularly critical one for Maurice, it had proved equally so for Ludlow, but in a quiet and private manner. It had started well when his brother-in-law repaid the loan made him in Martinique, which made Ludlow feel sufficiently secure financially to tell his cousin that he loved her and to beg her to marry him. He had remained silent about his love until then and it did not occur to him that he would be refused. Yet she not only refused him but most emphatically forbade him ever to speak about it again. He was stunned by her implacable refusal. Was it that she did not love him, or that she disapproved of Christian Socialism, or that she would not leave her ageing father, or that she felt her duty was to continue to provide a home for numerous nieces and nephews whose parents were in India?

It was not in Ludlow's nature which, though disciplined, was fiery and stubborn, to take 'no' for an answer, and his first impulse was to go to her again and compel assent. Fortunately Charles Mansfield had returned from Paraguay and he convinced Ludlow that dictatorial tactics would not succeed with Maria Forbes. Let things be, urged Mansfield, and sooner or later she would recognize Ludlow's true worth and grow to love him. Some of the best and sweetest women he had ever met, said Mansfield, thinking especially of Fanny Kingsley, completely misunderstood Ludlow because of his stern manner which frightened them. Perhaps Maria Forbes had made a similar mistake. Ludlow must be patient and try to let Maria see his sunnier side. Well-meant advice, although Ludlow was too depressed to have any sunnier side to show, but he gritted his teeth and promised to face the future with grim determination.

It did not seem fair to burden Maurice with his personal disappointments, for 1853 had been one of family sadness for Maurice, apart from the King's College problems. His sister Priscilla died, his dearly loved mother was dying, and his wife, Georgina, was in poor health. How could Ludlow intrude? Besides, he was still rather cool, being disappointed that Maurice was apparently deserting the true cause, associations, for the new one of education.

That was not to imply that Ludlow had no friends. On the contrary, he was close to his Christian Socialist friends and had many good acquaintances in legal and journalistic circles. His interests extended to literature and to the arts, and he wrote on those subjects, as well as on Christian Socialist ones. Mansfield was still his most intimate friend, but Ludlow got on splendidly with Tom Hughes, so well indeed that the two men agreed to share a house. It happened that at the moment when the doctor was telling Ludlow's mother that for health reasons she should leave London and its polluted air to live in the country, Fanny Hughes was telling her husband that the family had outgrown the Marylebone house and they should look for something bigger. The notion of joining forces, of trying a 'Communistic experiment', as Ludlow joked, liking the idea, was most appealing and Frank Penrose was ready to design the house which the builders' co-operative would erect.

They chose Wimbledon, a countrified area in those days, and land was purchased from Lord Cottonham at Copse Hill. By the spring of 1854 the house was finished, two separate homes linked by a fine common library which did double duty as a joint family meeting-place, and on Sundays it became a family chapel where Ludlow and Hughes took it in turn to read prayers. Those were their 'Conventicles', they said, using the Puritan name, and they held them because neither Hughes nor Ludlow approved of the type of services held in neighbouring churches. There was a huge garden which the Hughes children quickly took over for family games and for the Hughes family pets. Ludlow became a surrogate uncle enjoying the pleasures of children's company without the responsibility. When the Working Men's College was open and thriving, the garden at 'The Firs' became a favourite spot for week-end College lectures, teas and socials, and visiting lions would descend to give talks. Kingsley lectured on botany, Goderich on beetles, bringing part of his famous collection with him.

The great success of the new College was the Art Department, presided over by Ruskin, who recruited Dante Gabriel Rossetti, and his other assistant was C. Lowes Dickinson, recruited by Mansfield. Lowes Dickinson was a young artist who had worked in Italy since 1850, enjoying the artistic and Bohemian life until the day he met Archie Campbell, who was also living in Italy. Campbell, who was Charles Mansfield's cousin and a Christian Socialist, persuaded Dickinson that the pursuit of art and happiness alone was an ignoble aim, and he should make his life more positive. When in England, Lowes Dickinson formed the habit of visiting the Campbell family home in Weybridge, where at some time or other he met most of the London Christian Socialists with the notable exception of Maurice.

During the summer of 1854 he happened to be in London and one day he was peacefully strolling towards Russell Square, musing on the contrast between the sharp shadows cast by an Italian sun and the blurred impressions left by an English one, when his arm was suddenly but gently taken by Charles Mansfield, and he was borne off, vainly protesting, to Maurice's house a few yards away. 'We are meeting to discuss his proposal to found a Working Men's College, and you must come to help us, and give what you know to fellow-men who want to know and who haven't had your opportunities,' explained Mansfield. It was quite enough to make a shy young man turn tail and flee but Mansfield was firm and before he knew it, Lowes Dickinson was meeting the famous Maurice. The older man's warmth and charm melted his fears and Lowes Dickinson became part of the band. He was very impressed by the calibre of the men eager to work for the proposed college. 'There was something dramatic about it; it recalls King Harry and his captains on the dawn of Agincourt. Only the object of our fight was a better one than the King's,' wrote Lowes Dickinson fifty years later.

The Founders of the College became defined as men who attended the meetings before its opening and who also taught regularly in its first year. By that definition Lowes Dickinson was a Founder; Ruskin, who taught but had not attended the early meetings, and Kingsley, who had attended the early meetings but did not teach, were not.

Kingsley approved the idea of the College and popularized it wherever he could, but during the crucial years of 1853 and 1854 he was mainly in Devonshire, whither he had taken his ailing wife. The Kingsley family settled in Torquay, where Kingsley intended to write articles and where he certainly hoped to preach a sermon or two in Torquay's fashionable pulpits. It was a hope left unfulfilled for, as his wife said: 'the attacks of the religious press, perhaps happily for him, had so alarmed the clergy of Torquay, High Church and Evangelical, that all pulpit doors were closed against the author of *Alton Locke*, *Yeast* and *Hypatia*.' Making the best of a bad job, Kingsley occupied himself with his children on the beach collecting shells, animals and plants, for classification afterwards. These formed the material for a long article in the *North British Review*, and became a book under the title *Glaucus*. Marine natural history was very popular and many people bought *Glaucus* who would never have purchased the Rector's Christian Socialist works.

His crusading instincts were not as sharp as in the heady days of 1848 and 1849 and he set his sights considerably lower, concentrating upon sanitary reform and education. A variety of factors not all within his control had led to thorough scepticism over producer associations, and when he observed his prime example, Maurice, turning to other things, Kingsley felt justified in behaving in a similar way. He importuned Lord Palmerston about new laws to combat future cholera epidemics (cholera in 1854 was especially severe) and he accepted an invitation to lecture at the prestigious Philosophical Institute in Edinburgh.

He worked himself up into a cold sweat before he was due to walk on to the platform, but everything went well and he wrote

proudly to his wife: 'I have been heaped with kindness. I have
got my say said without giving offence, and made friendships
which I hope will last for life.' He enjoyed being fêted by
Edinburgh's titled intelligentsia and his lectures were collected
and later published.

Associations, colleges and sanitary reform were perennial
causes for the Christian Socialists but in 1854 there was really
only one burning national topic, and that was the Crimean War
over the quarrel between France and Russia about the Christian
shrines in the Holy Land. England was gripped by a nationalistic
fever and Kingsley was not immune. Again writing to his wife,
he said: 'The Guards march to-morrow. How it makes one's
blood boil! We send 10,000 picked men to Malta, *en route* for
Constantinople, and the French 60,000.' He returned to
Eversley from Edinburgh excited and frustrated by the war
news, wished he could go to the Crimea, and in his spare
moments he took pot shots at the rabbits pretending they were
Russian soldiers.

He engaged a curate for the summer and rejoined his family
in Devonshire, renting a house in Bideford for a year, a comfortable, rambling place with a room overlooking the quay, ideal for
writing and dreaming. Every stone in that historic North Devon
town spoke to him of Elizabethan sea-dogs, the kind he was
reading about in a new edition of Hakluyt's *Voyages*, lent him
by Froude, who had the book for review. Whenever the war
news sounded depressing Kingsley lost himself in the sixteenth
century when English seamen were trouncing the Spaniards,
and if that mental stimulant failed him, he opened his heart to
Maurice in long, questioning letters.

The Prophet approved of the Crimean War. Tennyson had
pointed out the moral in *Maud* that hard action was necessary to
awaken England from her materialistic sloth. Tom Hughes was
full of patriotic pride, like a schoolboy cheering on his team.
Even Ludlow, a pacifist at heart, favoured the war because, like
all the Christian Socialists, he was greatly opposed to the Tsar,
not having forgotten Russia's reactionary policies in 1849.
Although not entirely happy that the war entailed two Christian
countries allied with a Muslim one in a war against a third
Christian country, Ludlow was thrilled by the charge of the
Light Brigade. Like Tennyson, Ludlow wrote a poem in com-

memoration: Tennyson's poem lived, Ludlow's was soon forgotten.

Maurice wrote to Kingsley:

> I do hope something from the war in spite of all the feebleness with which it is prosecuted and with which we feel about it; but chiefly as a sign of what God is doing. It is more like the commencement of a battle between God in His absoluteness and the Czar in his than 1848 was, though that might take a more agreeable and popular form.

He added that he was glad that Kingsley was writing an Elizabethan novel (*Westward Ho!*), but Kingsley must never forget that what he was called upon by God to do above all was to preach and to write sermons.

Kingsley was accustomed to Maurice warning him that his true mission was to be a popular preacher fighting for a just society according to God's plan, and he did not quarrel with it, but did not mention it when he replied:

> We think of nothing but the War. . . . The novel is more than half done, and a most ruthless bloodthirsty book it is (just what the times want, I think.) I am afraid I have a little of the wolf-vein in me, in spite of fifteen centuries of civilisation; and so, I sometimes suspect, have you, and if you had not you would not be as tender and loving as you are.

Hughes wrote to beg Kingsley for a poem which would inspire the soldiers at the front, soldiers whom Hughes compared to Cromwell's Ironsides, which Kingsley considered some exaggeration. He was too emotionally unsettled to write poetry, he told Hughes, but he could manage prose and wrote a tract, *Brave Words to Brave Soldiers and Sailors*, which was published anonymously and distributed in the Crimea. It owed more than a little to a striking sermon by Maurice, a fact which Fenton Hort noticed at once, and when it became known that Kingsley was the author it increased his standing among a completely new group—the military, rather to his pride.

Although the Christian Socialists seemed to make the new

College the focus of their attention in 1854 they did not abandon their work for the co-operative movement, and Neale was certainly more interested in co-operatives than in the College. He chaired the Co-operative Conference held in Leeds that year, a conference which had been widely publicized in the new monthly *Co-operative Commercial Circular*, started in reply to the resolution of the 1853 conference. Neale had drafted a plan for his Co-operative Industrial and Commercial Union, one of his cherished ideals, and was determined to have the conference debate the Union.

About twenty-five delegates attended the Leeds Conference, with another twenty-five or so as guests. Maurice sat quietly as an observer. Under Neale's strong chairmanship, the conference debated his new Union, with its strong moral basis, and, as he had hoped, resolved to support it. Christian Socialist delegates were in the majority at this conference, as they had been at the previous ones, although more non-Christian Socialists than before had sent representatives, and further societies had sent letters of support or of information. The Equitable Pioneers in Rochdale sent two delegates, and so did the Leeds Redemption Society. Of the twenty-three co-operative bodies represented, nine were producer associations, and the rest were consumer stores. The Leeds Conference gave a fairly accurate picture of the co-operative position, that there were more co-operatives in the north of England than elsewhere (eight represented societies were based in London), and that most of the northern co-operatives were stores. Producer associations, strengthened by the idealism and money of the Christian Socialists, were strongest in London.

Neale won the day at the conference, on paper at least, for the delegates voted to support his Union, also to hold the next annual conference in Rochdale and to make the existing executive committee, the executive committee of the proposed Union working from London.

Maurice had deliberately taken no part in the conference, but whilst in Leeds he gave a public speech in the Stock Exchange Hall about co-operation generally as applied to industry and education, and spoke about the soon-to-be-formed Working Men's College, stressing that this would be separate from the co-operative movement and from the producer associations. The reason for this, said Maurice, was to avoid turning willing helpers away from the College if they did not want also to assist with association work. The lecture was a clear indication that Maurice was moving away from association work in favour of education, but his Christian Socialist disciples did not understand it at that moment.

Reviewing the Leeds Conference, indeed, the other Christian Socialists were still calmly optimistic. There were ten active associations in London, an interest in producer associations was spreading outside the capital, there were new producer associations in the provinces, and even several abroad. They did not imagine that the new college could be detrimental to the association cause, had not read between the lines of Maurice's talk in Leeds, and were therefore surprised and upset when Maurice, in his report to the Promoters in November 1854, said that they should allow the association work to continue by its own efforts and to turn their energies into establishing the College on a firm basis.

Neale immediately made a counter-proposal, that the Promoters, instead of disbanding, should spend more time developing the social and educational side of association work. He reflected quite accurately the feelings of the active Promoters and a committee was quickly set up to draft a plan along those lines for submission to a special meeting of the Association of Promoters fixed provisionally for 1 February 1855. Indeed, the pro-Neale Promoters actually met a week before that date to debate the plan, and they agreed to start a series of monthly social meetings which would include talks and discussions of an educational nature to be held at the Central Co-operative Agency (Neale's Agency), beginning in March 1855. In the event, however, the unexpected success of the College pre-empted Neale's proposal, and the Christian Socialists, who were less dedicated than Neale and Ludlow to the co-operatives, decided that Maurice's policy was the right one. They were as ready to follow the Prophet into education in 1854 as they had been to follow him in everything else, and to many of them it was something of a relief to be free to work in a social or educational field as individuals, instead of working collectively as a group.

A few continued to do both. Hughes did not drop his work in the co-operative movement or trade unionism just because he followed Maurice enthusiastically into the Working Men's

College, and he continued to insist until his death thirty years or so later that the College on one side and the co-operative movement on the other represented twin threads in a pattern of social development which was helping to make England a better place to live in. Even Neale was ready to work in the College as well as in his beloved co-operatives, but his trouble was that he could only teach political economy and not enough students signed on to make his course worth running. He returned quickly, if not thankfully, to co-operative work where he laboured steadfastly until his death in 1892.

Things were entirely different when it came to Ludlow. He also offered himself for work with the College although almost heart-broken by Maurice's unmistakable move away from associative work, for Ludlow agreed totally with Neale that the College ought to have been a natural development of the educational side of the associations, and remained part of them.

Ludlow asked himself why Maurice was going out of his way to make the College separate, and why he was ostentatiously invit-ing men to work with the College who might have no liking for Christian Socialism or for the cause of associations. Could it be that in truth Maurice was not dedicated to the task of Christian Socializing the country, as Ludlow was?

For the first time, Ludlow examined the words and deeds of Maurice dispassionately and at last admitted to himself that, although Maurice was still as true and honest and unselfish as ever, he had never, except in Ludlow's eyes, worn the trappings of a leader of a social party. For six years Ludlow had been delud-ing himself, hearing and seeing in Maurice what *he* wanted to hear and see, not what was actually said and done.

It was a shattering revelation, made harder because Ludlow kept it to himself and Maurice never suspected he had dealt a crushing blow to his loyal lieutenant. In those bleak days Ludlow felt that every worldly sacrifice he had made for the cause had been for nothing. He had lost the favour of Bellenden Ker, he had failed to win his bride, he had given up a hundred little pleasures, and it was not as if anyone, Maurice for instance, had ever demanded those sacrifices. Ludlow had chosen to make them and felt fulfilled by doing so. Nor had Maurice ever remotely claimed to be the man and leader whom Ludlow longed for; indeed, at every tiff and turn Maurice had said he was emphatically *not* such a man. If blame there was, it had to be placed squarely on Ludlow's shoulders.

In that sad moment Ludlow conformed to his old pattern, allowing his infinite capacity for self-sacrifice, for shrinking into the shadows and into second place, to take possession of him. If he could have at that instance broken the familiar mould, Ludlow might have donned the mantle of the leader of the Christian Socialists, but he could no more do it than he had been able to assert himself independently against Neale and the Central Agency. It was another spiritual crisis which drove Ludlow silently back into his shell in meek acceptance of Maurice's wishes, and when one or two of the Christian Socialists came to him, offering the crown, he refused gently, saying that as Maurice was wiser and greater than all of them put together, they had better follow him as they had done before.

The association side of the work of the Christian Socialists gradually faded away and when associates joined the College, they enrolled as private students, not members of an association. No proselytizing for the associative cause was carried out inside the College, although some years later Hughes and Ludlow formed a new association, the 'London Guilders Association' from College members.

The passage of years gradually tempered Ludlow's original antagonism towards the Central Co-operative Board, and few people then even remembered the Association for Promoting Industrial and Provident Societies, so Ludlow rejoined the Board and joined Hughes and Neale to make a trio of battle-seasoned and hard-working idealists in whom, happily, the flames of idealism still burned bravely.

That was still far in the future, and in 1854 the picture was that the Working Men's College, after only a few weeks of operation, showed every promise of being a pleasant change from the squabbles and disappointments of forming associations, so much work for so little lasting result. The College Founders had decided that the new venture would be a success if thirty students enrolled in the beginning. They also agreed to insist upon a basic standard of reading, writing and arithmetic before admitting men to the regular classes which followed a systematic course. Six evenings were devoted to matriculation testing, and students below that standard were directed to preparatory classes. Indeed an 'Adult

School' was opened soon afterwards to bring applicants up to the required standards.

When the College opened its doors in November 1854 in Red Lion Square, 120 students at once enrolled and more kept coming. By the end of the first term there were 145 and by the end of the last term there were 174. Little wonder that Maurice took those figures as evidence that his College was answering a need, and little wonder, too, that he considered the College more successful, and certainly more congenial, than setting up and thereafter propping up, producer co-operatives.

New Directions

1856, Peace made in Crimean War;
1857, Palmerston's policy against China
in 'Arrow' war; 1857–8, Indian Mutiny;
1858, Government of India Act.

1855 opened sadly for Maurice with the death after months of pain of Julius Hare. 'My whole life for the last eighteen years had been closely bound up with him, and nearly every joy or sorrow I have had has been connected with his home and with him,' wrote Maurice to Daniel Macmillan. The Archdeacon had many friends in Cambridge, including men like Fenton Hort[1] who were too young to have been his students but admired his scholarship, and Hare's magnificent library of German books was bequeathed to the university.

Hardly had his death faded into the background when another, much more dramatic, took its place, one which affected Maurice less than it affected the younger members of the Christian Socialist group, but was a shocking and tragic loss to them all—Mansfield's death in a scientific accident.

One reason why he had taken a relatively small part in the College although the original impulse for its very being had come from him, was that he was occupied in preparing samples of benzol for the forthcoming Paris Exhibition in response to a request from the exhibition organizers. Unworldly in many other ways, Mansfield was fully aware that his process would arouse great interest in Paris and that fortune as well as fame was probably awaiting him. Early in 1855 he hired rooms in St John's Wood, London, engaged an assistant and began the laborious process of preparing his samples. The pair worked long hours during a cold, snowy February, watching over the hot, fume-laden apparatus, often exhausted but buoyed up by anticipation of success at the Exhibition.

Then the unthinkable happened. The naphtha boiled over and caught light with the risk of an explosion at any moment. Mansfield seized the burning still in his arms, intending to carry it into the street, but the door jammed, imprisoning him in the room. Clasping the burning still, he staggered across the room to the window, meaning to throw it out, but the sill was high and the window stiff, and with his hands and arms flayed with liquid fire he lacked the strength to open the window wide enough to throw the still clear. By the time he managed to push it out both he and his assistant were badly burned. They scrambled out of the window and dropped to the snow-covered pavement. Mansfield's clothes were smouldering, his head badly bruised and he rolled in the snow to smother the flames. His assistant was not much better off.

They looked for a cab but none passed them, and they walked and stumbled to the Middlesex Hospital, where the doctors could not do much for them as their burns were so severe. Mansfield lingered for nine agonizing days, his friends taking it in turns to sit by his bedside. The assistant died also.

It was a terrible experience for Ludlow to watch his friend suffer. Only a year or two before, he had been threatening suicide and Mansfield had talked him out of it. Now Mansfield lay dying and Ludlow was still alive, and in the years ahead would have to soldier on without his closest friend. Their relationship was intimate and complex. As Ludlow told Kingsley, the only other person who could come even close to suspecting the depth of Ludlow's grief:

> He came to me at a time when I never expected to have another intimate friend, and surpassed all conceivableness of intimacy. He was to me almost what a wife should be, a better and more delicate conscience . . .

In an emotional and private poem he described Mansfield as 'woman-man', subtle and simple at the same time, 'manly soft' and 'tender strong'—

> The riddle of his life was all at once
> Wise madness, joyous anguish, holy sin.

The shock of Mansfield's passing assembled the group at his funeral and then at a memorial sermon preached by Maurice on 25 March. The scientist became for the younger Christian Socialists what John Sterling had been for Maurice's generation. For several years they gathered together on the anniversary of Mansfield's death to renew memories and fellowship.

In 1856 they collected the letters he had posted from Brazil and Paraguay and published them, with a prefatory memoir by Kingsley, whose affection for Mansfield almost matched Ludlow's, except that as Kingsley had a wife and children to answer his emotional needs, his emotion was not as intense as Ludlow's. Kingsley had some odd stories to illustrate Mansfield's unusual personality, like the one about the seal which he had shot on holiday in Cornwall when a boy. It was Mansfield's albatross. Kingsley wrote:

> That thing haunted him in later life. He deplored it as all but a sin; after he had adopted the notion that it was wrong to take away animal life; and he used to scold me in his sweet, charitable way, for my fishing and entomologizing. He has often told me that the ghost of the seal appeared to him in his dreams, and stood by his bed, bleeding, and making him wretched.

Mansfield kept the seal skin as a perpetual reminder of his thoughtless cruelty.

That was his sombre side, but most people only knew the happy face he showed to the world. Kingsley went on:

> It was wonderful, utterly wonderful to me in after life, knowing all that lay on his heart, to see the way he *flashed* down over the glebe at Eversley, with his knapsack at his back, like a shining star appearing with peace on earth and goodwill to men.

The book on Paraguay made a certain impact and the section about Brazil was translated into Portuguese, the translator declaring that Mansfield was 'a great soul stirred by mighty conceptions and the love of mankind'.

In the winter of 1855 Kingsley's *Westward Ho!* was published,² an event which heralded his inevitable progress into respectability, a progress to which Mansfield's death contributed not a little. He had been Kingsley's best friend and certainly Fanny Kingsley's favourite among the Christian Socialists. Both Kingsleys were fond of Tom Hughes—as who wasn't?—but he was too busy to visit Eversley often, and Furnivall had never been a close friend, whilst Ludlow, though still a good friend, sometimes disagreed with Kingsley on social and political issues. Maurice was not a contemporary and friend in that particular way, being several notches above ordinary mortals, and he had other interests besides Christian Socialism. Fanny Kingsley saw a chance to edge her husband into fields of social endeavour which were still worthy and Christian, meriting Maurice's approval, but would not be categorized by that hateful word 'Socialist' and might take her sensitive husband out of the firing line at last.

The critical and popular success of *Westward Ho!* rather disturbed Maurice, who mistrusted worldly acclaim and preferred to live in the odour of disapproval. Ludlow was even more perturbed but for a different reason. He disliked Kingsley's exuberant and bloodthirsty scenes and was not pacified when he heard that Kingsley was mischievously insisting that he had inserted those scenes especially to shock Ludlow. Kingsley often sent Ludlow drafts of his poems, for Ludlow's able criticism and advice, and Ludlow would reciprocate. Ludlow's poetry did not have the soaring quality of Kingsley's, and the Rector was tactful when he returned his friend's verses, approving the sentiments but not always willing to give high marks for the poesy. 'Beautiful,' he wrote in the margin of one poem, and against 'Death, Rest, Labour' he pencilled—'Most noble, dear old man,' and rightly so, for beneath Ludlow's censorious and prim façade there was unselfishness, intelligence and real nobility of heart.

Those attributes kept him loyally at Maurice's side after the producer co-operative work ended to become the self-effacing organizing secretary whose administrative ability kept the Working Men's College afloat. He hinted that the College teachers should submit to a religious test, harking back to his old dream of a religious brotherhood, but Maurice quickly vetoed the suggestion, nobody except Ludlow wanted it, and the upshot was that, as the years went by, the College teachers showed a wide variation in social and religious opinions.

The first success of the College, to everyone's surprise, was not Maurice but Ruskin, whose art department flourished. He had his own ideas about teaching which did not always coincide with his students' preconceived notions. Take the wheelwright who asked if Ruskin would teach him to draw a cart wheel. 'I don't teach anything special or technical,' answered Ruskin patiently. 'I teach drawing in general', and he explained that after mastering general drawing a student would be able to draw some particular object, like a cart wheel. The man remained unmoved. 'It would help me in my trade to learn how to draw a wheel,' he persisted. 'If that's what you need, you should go to the government School of Design,' advised Ruskin and the man, with only one idea in his mind, left the classroom and the College.

Such incidents were exceptional. Ruskin was a popular teacher, partly because he taught very thoroughly and partly because of his friendly, interesting conversation. Frequently shy with members of his own class and much given to underestimating his social graces—how he envied Tom Hughes's ease of manner, he once confessed—Ruskin was entirely at ease with his art students and won their respect and gratitude. If a student had any skill at all, Ruskin recognized and developed it.

The art rooms at Red Lion Square, as at Great Ormond Street, the College's second address, were gas-lit, which made them uncomfortably hot and dry. Ruskin liked to make himself heard, and when he praised a student he practically bellowed. He would set his students to work drawing a sphere in pencil, using shading, and he explained that he chose a sphere because it was so regular that even an untrained eye could see any mistakes in the drawing. After that, they were given plaster casts of leaves to draw, and finally actual leaves, pebbles and other life objects which Ruskin brought from his personal collection.

As interesting to the students as the sketching was the broad art education they received from the class discussions. One evening a student remarked that he knew a shop near Leicester Square which was selling Dürer engravings for eighteenpence each. 'Then now's the time to lay out your money,' observed Ruskin genially. The student was doubtful. Were the engravings

John Ruskin

genuine, he asked, at which Ruskin cooled. 'You should never buy a work of art merely because it has some great man's name attached to it,' he said sternly. 'If you acquire it, it ought to be either because it's true to nature or is otherwise beautiful in itself, or has some quality in it which gives you genuine pleasure.'

His classes were limited to drawing in black and white, but not so the classes of Dante Gabriel Rossetti, whose students studied colour and figure drawing. He would have liked to have every College art student in his class, painting in glorious colour, and grumbled that if Ruskin kept them too long, pencilling in their light and shade, he would spoil them for colour.

Rossetti's entry into the Working Men's College came about through his relationship with Ruskin, who admired the younger man and wished to help him. 'It seems to me that, of all the painters I know, you on the whole have the greatest genius; and you appear to me also to be—as far as I can make out—a very good sort of person,' wrote Ruskin in 1855 to the handsome young painter. As a practical contribution to help Rossetti's chaotic finances, Ruskin promised to spend a certain sum each year on drawings which Rossetti would bring him. Rossetti's teaching commitments at the College linked the social and art aspirations of the Pre-Raphaelite brotherhood.

Rossetti was a vibrant man, generous with his talents and very popular in the College as a consequence. His students admired him as an artist and liked him as a man. He believed that the world began and ended with art, and when one of his favourite students applied to join the algebra class he lost his temper. 'Give it up!' he urged. 'What good can algebra be for painting?'

The students enjoyed his teaching. He would start by giving general instructions on how to paint a particular subject and then he would sit down and demonstrate. First he pencilled a sketch midway between outline and shadow, then filled a brush with violet carmine and rubbed it on the edge of the paper until only dry colour was left. Next he dragged the brush over the paper to produce some rugged modelling, and repeated the process with other dry colours until a glowing effect was produced. He washed it all together, blending and softening it, and finally, with a flowing brush, he completed a work alive with colour, much to his students' admiration.

With two such powerful prima donnas as Ruskin and Rossetti

in the art department it was fortunate that the third art teacher, Lowes Dickinson, was a calming influence. Ruskin declared that he was teaching art so that working men could learn to see more beauty in life and art than they had done before, and they would enjoy life more fully as a result. Naturally art studies would develop any artistic talent the student might have, but that was never Ruskin's primary aim. Rossetti, on the other hand, had no sympathy with Ruskin's point of view and simply wanted to make everyone artists. That was his way of making sure people enjoyed life more fully. Lowes Dickinson tried to avoid taking sides but he inclined more to the Ruskin view, which came closer to Maurician ideals than Rossetti's.

When Rossetti left in 1858 Ford Madox Brown took over the figure-drawing class,[3] proving more systematic although less charismatic than Rossetti. He did not care for Rossetti's free and inspirational style as a guide to students, and told his classes to be absolutely clear that they wanted to draw before they made any mark on the paper. Unlike his colleagues, Ford Madox Brown found it very helpful to know what his students did for a living and why they joined the classes, and his students grew to like him and to value the invitations to his home and studio where they could see his paintings and those of his Pre-Raphaelite friends.

A few years later Edward Burne-Jones joined the College as assistant to Ford Madox Brown. Burne-Jones was then at the start of his career, a worshipful admirer of Rossetti, whom he had first seen at the College. Like Rossetti, Burne-Jones believed as an act of faith that art was the greatest influence in the world, and that the world was misguided in not acknowledging that truth. Younger than Rossetti or Ford Madox Brown, he was friendly and enthusiastic and carried his romantic democratic ideals into his College life, insisting that the students were his 'brothers in art'.

The high standards of the College art department derived from Ruskin, who brought to his drawing classes the same care and thoughtfulness that he brought to his writing. In fine weather he took week-end sketching parties to the country to draw from nature, and ended the day with tea and talk at his home. It was a side of Ruskin seldom seen in fashionable art circles.

His teaching experience led him to write a handbook of useful hints for the amateur artist, *Elements of Drawing*, published in 1856. It sold rapidly, somewhat to Ruskin's annoyance, for it was used as a popular short-cut to commercial art training, very far from Ruskin's intention, and when it had sold 8,000 copies he decided that enough was enough and allowed the book to go out of print, in spite of a continuing demand. The book was illustrated by Ruskin's own sketches engraved by W. H. Hooper, one of his College students.

Several of his students abandoned their former trades to become copyists and engravers. George Allen became a mezzotint engraver and ended as Ruskin's personal publisher, a responsibility which involved setting up a printing and distributing business in co-operation with Ruskin. An unforeseen product of that successful partnership was the creation of a famous publishing firm.

Such successes, or rather results, of the art teaching were fortuitous. Ruskin was interested in proving that working men could be interested in art and that industry had not entirely quenched the spirit of the Gothic workman, and as he mused and pondered on this demonstration of the tenacity of the artistic impulse he was drawn into speculations upon the nature of society, speculations which culminated in a Ruskinesque brand of Christian Socialism.

Needless to say, the brand was not one which either Hughes or Ludlow would consider authentic. Ludlow had little time for Ruskin and none at all for Rossetti and he tolerated Lowes Dickinson only because he had the wit, or the grace, to revere Maurice. Rossetti apparently was incapable of revering any living man, whilst Ruskin never seemed to grasp what Maurice was saying. Both Hughes and Ludlow consistently underestimated Ruskin and Ruskin's ideas and influence.

What made it particularly irritating for Ludlow and Hughes was that the artists had found their niche in the College whilst Hughes and Ludlow were still at a loss. From being active and indeed essential members of the association movement they had dwindled into teachers without a function at the new College. They needed to regain their self-esteem, but how? They wanted to teach, but where were their students? Hughes offered to take a class in rudimentary law, but not enough students enrolled to justify running the class. Ludlow toiled unseen in the background, supervising the administration and trying to ensure that theology and Bible studies became a fundamental part of College teaching, as Maurice so desperately hoped. It was no easy task for the liberal Maurician view that adult education must be broad, and this actually militated against Bible studies and tended to promote a slackening of religious conviction amongst teachers and students.

The Christian Socialist who surprised everyone was Furnivall. Until that point he had been a junior in the movement, generous with time and money and always ready to help, but never a leading member. The initiative of the Working Men's College might have been tailor-made for him, and it gave him scope for his vitality, his sociability and his passion for the English language and English literature. His English grammar class was always full to bursting and he was at the College five nights a week, no hardship for him as he was unmarried and lived near by in Hatton Garden. Neither Hughes nor Ludlow could spend as much time in the College as Furnivall for they both had household responsibilities and they lived far out in Wimbledon. Maurice dropped into the College most evenings, but he was conspicuously lacking in the easy bonhomie which was one of Furnivall's endearing characteristics, and so it became Furnivall's happy duty to welcome new students and to encourage a friendly atmosphere in the College. The Founders had agreed in their early meetings that the social life of the College ought to be as important as classroom instruction, and Furnivall made this one of his prime tasks. Fifty years later he wrote:

> It was a new and agreeable experience to find oneself trusted and lookt up to by a set of men, many double one's own age, knowing more of practical life, and having different[3] traditions and opinions to mine; and I well recollect the pleasure I used to feel as I walkt about the College rooms, and saw face after face light up as I greeted its owner.

Many teachers followed his example and invited their classes home to tea, an unusual example in those days of middle-class professional men mixing on equal social terms with working men. It was noticeable that Ludlow and Eugène Oswald, a French political refugee who taught French at the College, felt no social embarrassment on this score, their French upbringing having spared them English class prejudice, and invitations to Oswald's

teas were much sought after. The College gave a good impression
to serious working men, with its plain benches, trestle tables and
some good books on the shelves, and the pleasant after-class
conversations over cups of tea and coffee forged permanent friendships which cut across traditional student-teacher lines.

Thomas Shorter, his job as secretary of the Promoters having
ended when the Promoters did, was pleased to become secretary
of the College, and introduced his brother, Henry, as a student.
Like many of the association men, Shorter rather fancied himself
as a writer. He wrote verse of a hortatory nature and published a
collection of English prose in the 1860s, and also edited an
anthology of poetry. He remained secretary until blindness and
incapacity forced him to resign. The College paid him a small
pension and he maintained his link with the College until he died
in 1899. His sister, Emma, used to take him to the College for
the Saturday evening lectures, guiding him to his regular
seat.

Other familiar faces at the College included Walter Cooper
from the tailors' association and William Newton of the
engineers, who brought his brother along to join Furnivall's
class. Then there was Ebenezer Cooke, whose brother had been
in the tailors' association. Cooke was a lithographic draughtsman
who joined Ruskin's class. He was very successful at his craft and
on the way to becoming independent, but the College changed his
life. He fell in love with teaching and became an English pioneer
of Pestalozzian and Froebellian methods of teaching small
children.

The College actually stimulated two new associations, the
Frameworkers and Gilders' Co-operative Society, managed by
Robert Newton, which remained operating until 1891, and the
Working Gilders' Association, with H. R. Jennings as leading
member.

The College attracted a variety of men in a way that the
producer associations had never succeeded in doing. Christian
Socialists joined it, of course, and ex-Chartists, but there were
also members of the Literary and Scientific Institution in John
Street, one of London's main Owenite centres. Those men valued
the education and fellowship at the College and sidestepped
Maurice's Bible classes, tending towards the Positivism of
Auguste Comte, and they followed Frederic Harrison, a leading

English Comtist who became a teacher at the College in 1857, a little to Maurice's dismay. In great contrast to that group was the one introduced by the Rev T. T. Lynch, minister of an Independent Congregationalist church, amongst whom was Robert Curtis, a piano-maker and one of Ruskin's first art students. Curtis was a faithful student at the Bible classes, and he later left the Congregational Church to join the Anglicans. He was a member of the College for many years, acquiring an education as he moved from class to class, and finally emigrated to Australia, where he became a library assistant.

Another prominent student of the early years was William Rossiter, a highly unorthodox Christian. The Founders saw his potential and put him in charge of their Adult School, thus drawing him into professional teaching. He left London to teach in Cornwall, then returned to teach in the pioneer school at Bruce Castle in north London, founded by the Hill family. In the evenings Rossiter taught at the Working Men's College and in 1868, in conjunction with T. H. Huxley, he set up a South London Working Men's College in Blackfriars Road, the building being used by day as a mixed children's school. Rossiter was a science enthusiast and published popular science manuals. Ludlow said of him that he was 'beyond question, one of the eight or ten most remarkable men I have ever met with—and I think I have known not a few'.

A student with a Chartist background was John Roebuck, a woodturner from Leicester who had visited London first for the 1851 Exhibition and been so pleased with what he found that he settled in the capital permanently the following year. He joined Furnivall's first grammar class and later joined the mathematics class taken by Richard Buckley Litchfield, fresh from Trinity College, Cambridge, and recruited for Maurice by the Macmillan brothers. Roebuck and his friend George Tansley became College stalwarts, and although Roebuck took his family to the United States ten years later, he never forgot the pleasures and satisfactions of his College years and kept in touch with his old friends. Tansley was a born student, and he stayed in England, and with the College, until his death, the College forming him and he the College for more than forty-seven years. His contribution to the College was incalculable, especially in the troubled years following Maurice's death, and in the view of several of the Founders

the Working Men's College justified its existence by the effect it
had on George Tansley, if by nothing else.

Once people had recovered from their surprise at the success of
the College a demand arose for a similar institution for women.
Maurice was always sympathetic towards better educational
facilities for girls and women and a few classes for women were
started, but only in a minor way. In 1864 a women's college was
set up but it never had the drive and verve of the men's college.

The men's college went from strength to strength and famous
personalities were pleased to give occasional lectures. Whatever
ideas the Founders had had in the beginning about what working
men should be taught, it was now evident that in adult education
the curriculum was dictated by demand.[4] Tom Hughes racked
his brains to find some subject which he could teach and which
the students wanted to learn. At last he approached Maurice with
a new idea. 'Round shoulders, narrow chests, stiff limbs were, I
submitted, as bad as defective grammar and arithmetic.' It was his
excuse for starting a weekly boxing class, to the amusement and
admiration of his friends. He had skill and experience on his side
and could usually count on winning, even against heavier and
rougher opponents. Jim Donovan, one of the students, stood by
with advice to novices: 'Mind you don't hit Hughes on the nose
by accident. If you do, you'll catch it!'

Hughes found his role in the boxing class, which led him into
the social life of the College. That began after class, that is, after
ten o'clock, and Wednesdays became famous for the 'Smoking
concerts' run by Hughes, Furnivall and Litchfield. The latter
taught singing as well as mathematics, and his choir, which
included women, was in great demand. There was no social or
political significance in the favourite songs. Jim Fisher was noted
for his lusty rendering of 'Come cheer up, my lads, 'tis to glory
we steer'; Litchfield sang 'Leather Bottle' and Hughes brought
the house down with 'Little Billee' and 'Three Sailors of Bristol
City'. Thomas Shorter insisted on reading, with feeling, choice
extracts from Macaulay's verse, and Tansley recited some of
Tennyson's poems, The concerts always ended with 'Brush-
maker Hurst' belting out 'Tight Little Island', and the entire
audience joined in the chorus. Poor Hurst was the victim of his
own standards of professional perfection, for he made such
exceedingly good brushes that they never wore out. Hughes used

to joke ruefully that he owed his increasing baldness to Hurst's tough hair brushes.

But when all was said and done, it was really Furnivall who gave the College its heart of friendship. Kindly, honest, blundering, tactless, a stranger to fatigue, he throve in the hive of activity which he constructed. He organized long walks for the weekends, the working-class equivalent of Leslie Stephen's 'Sunday tramps'.

When folks have a whole day in the open, with 'pitches' on the grass, discussing all possible subjects, and hearing about one another's lives, they get really intimate. And when you've had a hard spell against wind and tide, or a 40-mile walk, with men who put their backs and legs into their work, you get to respect them.

he said.

Some College outings were less strenuous. There was a Saturday in the summer of 1856 when the College was invited to 'The Firs', Wimbledon, for cricket, games, dinner and plenty of good talk. Goderich brought specimens from his collection of butterflies and insects, there was a cricket match, and food and drink was provided in a big tent. Some College wag found a juicy caterpillar which was passed amid great hilarity down the length of the table for Furnivall, the diehard vegetarian. 'A judicious compromise between animal and vegetable edibles,' he was informed.

1856 was the happy summer when Hughes, along with his industrious friend Tom Taylor, journalist, dramatist, civil servant and fisherman, joined Kingsley in Snowdonia for a madcap fishing holiday. They stayed at a little Welsh inn high up in the mountains and wrote humorous verse in the evenings, each claiming in mock alarm to be the victim of the mad excesses of the other two. Declared Tom Taylor:

I write cheerful letters home not to alarm my wife, but in truth I go in fear of my life between this Socialist lawyer and this Socialist parson—two unnatural varieties of the genus professional man, each caring more for his neighbour than himself, or his cloth, and thus departing from the wholesome rules of his craft.

Wrote Hughes in the inn's guest book:

> I came to Pen-y-gwrd a larking with my betters
> A mad wag and a mad poet, both of them men of letters.

Kingsley had already laid claim to the title 'mad poet' by his comic rhymed invitation to Hughes which inaugurated the expedition, a confidential, Philistine effusion which allowed the two old friends to enjoy a private joke against the unfortunate Ruskin:

> Leave to mournful Ruskin
> Popish Apennines
> Dirty Stones of Venice
> And his Gas-lamps Seven;
> We've the stones of Snowdon
> And the lamps of Heaven.

The weather was atrocious, the trio were continually soaked through and Mrs Owen at the inn kept drying out their wet clothes. But the fishing was reasonable, the inn delightful and the company superb. Kingsley amused himself by composing an ode to the cold north-easterly wind, a Berseker wind if there ever was one, and used the inn and the mountains as background material for his next book, a contemporary novel for Macmillans to be entitled *Two Years Ago*.

The public might be forgiven for thinking that writing had become the main occupation of the erstwhile Promoters. Maurice was always engaged on some literary task and his weighty *Moral and Metaphysical Philosophy* had just appeared. It attracted a very hostile review from the *Westminster* whose critic said the book read as if Maurice had finished it in a hurry and had not done much research. In fact, Maurice had spent three years on the section referred to, working in the British Museum Library or the Bodleian, and was considerably aggrieved by the tone of the review. 'If you knew what a thin-skinned animal I am,' he wrote plaintively to Kingsley, in response to the Rector's note of congratulation, 'and how these things make me smart, you would understand better how much I value your soothing plaisters.' More 'soothing plaisters' came from Ludlow, who was at that time having Maurice's Lincoln's Inn sermons collected and privately printed for subscribers. It was a business enterprise which Ludlow continued for the next three years, another small example of the unsung work which Ludlow did behind the scenes.

That year, 1856, Maurice moved into a bigger house at 5 Russell Square. The Prophet had managed to outgrow his youthful shyness, at least to the extent of inviting friends and admirers to breakfast, and there were often house guests in the Maurice home.

Maurice began his day early, at five-thirty, starting it as he ended it, with a cold bath, presumably as much to mortify the flesh as to cleanse it, for he could be heard giving an agonized sigh as he lowered himself into the water. By seven-thirty he was ready to conduct a small party of family and friends to Lincoln's Inn chapel for the day's service and by nine o'clock the party was usually home for breakfast. If Maurice had no urgent appointments, he and his companions would linger over the meal talking on general topics, with perhaps a special emphasis upon literature and politics. After the guests had gone, Maurice would get down to work, dictating his latest articles or chapters to his wife.

He used to pace up and down the room as he spoke, clutching a small pillow tightly to his chest, a practice begun at Cambridge, where his friends used to swear that his black, horse-hair pillow was so well trained that it would follow him round like a dog. He had it in his Guy's Hospital days and Anna Maurice called it his 'black wife'. A pillow seemed to give him confidence to think and talk freely, and sometimes he was so carried away by his train of thought that he needed some violent physical action, and he would rush over to the fireplace and poke furiously at the innocent embers, then walk briskly away, only to return minutes later and repeat the operation, having forgotten he had just performed it.

Maurice and Ludlow shared a mixture of gratification and disappointment about the College, pleasure at its success but disappointment that religion did not mean much to the students. Take, for instance, the long, fierce arguments about the proper use of Sundays. Sunday was the working man's only free day—should he go with Furnivall for a country hike or stay at home and go to church, as Maurice preferred? One evening a deputation of College students waited on Maurice, asking for guidance in the matter. He hated above all things to give firm directives but could not refuse the students, so in the end he said that each man should be absolutely honest with himself and then do what seemed to him right. Maurice realized that his reply would only encourage those who already wanted a secular Sunday to think he agreed with them, whereas of course he did not, but on the other hand he did not think he had the moral right to force his views on other people. Ludlow's instincts were much more authoritarian and he would have given a more forthright answer.

During the Long Vacation of 1856, with the College closed as well as the courts, Tom Hughes had some time on his hands so he devoted it to his children. His eldest son, Maurice (named after the Prophet, naturally, as was Kingsley's son, and Daniel Macmillan's son), was due to enter the enclosed school world of Rugby in the autumn. Hughes had loved every minute of his schooldays and hoped his son would do the same. He began jotting down some memories, and before long his notes took the shape of a boys' novel, not a didactic concoction like *Sandford and Merton* but a wholesome and realistic story. Just as Kingsley had written *The Heroes*, which were the Greek myths retold, for his children, so Hughes began to write *Tom Brown's Schooldays* for his boy. He was rather self-conscious, feeling that he lacked the literary gifts of Kingsley or the intellectual depth of Ludlow or the unparalleled talent of Maurice, but he had a father's love and he wrote the book for his son.

Several chapters were indeed completed when one evening, as he and Ludlow were talking in their library, the conversation happened to turn on children's books and Hughes confessed shyly that he was writing one. A day or two later he showed Ludlow the manuscript and Ludlow immediately saw that it was something special. It was original, it had life and conviction, and if Hughes managed to finish it, it would be a little masterpiece, he thought. Ludlow was frankly astonished. Who would have thought that the man whom the Christian Socialists had all laughed at as a mere cricketer years ago in Little Ormond Yard was capable of this? 'Tom, this must be published,' he insisted, and Hughes wrote to Alexander Macmillan explaining that the book was almost finished and only needed 'a kick in the breach that some cove's saying he would publish would give me to finish it'. Macmillan came to London to discuss the project over dinner, took the manuscript away with him, and had hardly finished reading it before he was writing and promising to publish it.

Publication initiated a close personal and business relationship between the two men, ending only at Alexander Macmillan's death. When Daniel Macmillan died suddenly, his brother turned naturally to his friend, Tom Hughes, to write a biography. *Tom Brown's Schooldays* would give Hughes a second career, a literary one, in addition to the legal profession, and in addition also to his evenings at the College, and to his continuing work for the co-operative movement. The Macmillans published all his books, which sold well, although none of the later ones would burst upon an unsuspecting public with the appealing panache of the first.

There came a moment, however, when it almost seemed that Hughes would never finish the book, for the country was swept by a scarlet fever epidemic in the winter and all the Hughes children went down with the disease. Evie, their eldest daughter, looked to be recovering, then had an unexpected relapse and died in her father's arms. Fanny Hughes collapsed and Hughes needed all his simple Christian faith to see him through the ordeal. He poured out his heart to Goderich, who had recently lived through a similar bereavement and been helped at that time by Hughes's honest piety. Now it was Goderich's turn to help his old friend with sympathy and encouragement.

Indeed, Hughes lost all heart to finish his boys' story but, encouraged by Ludlow, he steeled himself to continue. It was noticeable, thought Ludlow, that the later section of the book did not show the carefree spirit which had sent Hughes bowling merrily from one incident to the next in the earlier part, and the last chapter showed a depth of feeling which was attributable to Evie's death.

The book appeared in April 1857 under the pen-name of 'An Old Boy', for Hughes was afraid it would be a flop and do him no good at the Bar. It was, however, an instant success and after the second edition Hughes was proud to put his name on it. It went through five editions in seven months and made Hughes richer by over a thousand pounds.

For the majority of the British population, 1857 was not the year of *Tom Brown's Schooldays* but the year of the Indian Mutiny, and the Christian Socialists all had something to say about that. Maurice declared that all decent-minded professional and middle-class people ought to assume responsibility for the Mutiny. If they had kept a better watch on the British administration in India they could have foreseen the problems, and by petitioning or demonstrating could have forced Westminster to make timely reforms which would have prevented the Mutiny. The young soldiers sent out to India were, said Maurice, 'suffering for us'.

The Mutiny had an intemperate effect upon Kingsley. The war with China, which had not long ended, hardly a creditable incident in British foreign policy, had given Kingsley some strange and morbid satisfaction which he explained on the ground that it had showed Christian white men embattled against heathen yellow men, a racist and anti-colour sentiment which became even more marked when the Indian Mutiny broke out. Kingsley had, he declared, been anticipating some kind of national disaster ever since the Crimean peace treaty had been signed in Paris, and he was sure that the Mutiny was that disaster.

He had developed a strong interest in military matters since his Crimean pamphlet had brought his name to the army as a sympathetic parson. Officers from Sandhurst College regularly attended the Sunday services in Eversley Church, bringing a splash of colour with their dress uniforms. Kingsley began to identify strongly with the Army as news of the Mutiny reached Eversley, and he slept badly because of nightmares filled with revolting details of sexual outrage perpetrated by brown heathen Indians upon white Christian wives and children, very like his own family. The Mutiny began to obsess him, much to his alarm, and he tried to push it aside by taking on more work. He promised John Parker to write an article on sanitary reform for *Fraser's*: 'I will throw my whole soul into it, please God, and forget India in cholera.'

Ludlow paid a visit to the Rectory and the friends discussed India. Ludlow was amazed by the extent of Kingsley's ignorance of Indian history and realized that his friend was probably typical of the educated British public. He had taken it for granted that Kingsley would know as much as he did about India, and would undoubtedly share his liberal views about Indians. Nothing was further from the truth, and the more the couple talked, the more they disagreed. It was like their old disagreements over Rajah Brooke and the Dyaks.

Ludlow did not think to make allowances for Kingsley, and did not think it significant that his own family connections with India, and his uncle's prominent position in the British India Society gave Ludlow a special interest and knowledge. He left Eversley regretting that he and Kingsley were growing further apart on a number of subjects.

The Mutiny gave Ludlow an opportunity to play a new role in the College, for several students, knowing his family background, asked him to lecture on Indian life and history, and he was delighted to comply. He took great care over preparation for the lectures, which were very well attended.

Ludlow displayed an unsuspected streak of romance when it came to the exotic backgrounds and customs of that distant land. He described the Indian village system in detail and with approval—did he see some resemblance to agricultural co-operatives? He deplored the British taxation system which had broken up the villages; he sighed over the decline of village craft industries—where was the fine muslin which could pass through a wedding ring? Sacrificed to Lancashire? He criticized the government schools which taught Indian children material skills but at the neglect of their spiritual needs. He was sympathetic to Muslims and Hindus alike, and supported the princes in their traditional laws which permitted them to adopt sons to inherit their estates. Dalhousie's 'doctrine of lapse' was monstrously unjust, he commented.

His conclusions were more Christian than Socialist, suggesting that God had sent the British into India so that Christians would one day rule that country, for he appeared to think that by the time India had been granted self-rule the Indian Christians, even if they were in the minority, would form the government. Because truly religious Christians were tolerant towards other religions, said Ludlow, no conflicts could arise over race, colour or religion. And it would be, he continued, warming to his theme, a mature English working class which, after attaining full citizenship in England, would develop a universal social consciousness which would extend to India. The English working class would demand self-government for the Indian working class and thus guarantee a Utopian future for that country. One day, he said, almost carried away, there might even be a working man as Governor-General of India!

Had he really possessed the gift of prophecy he might have said that one day a Christian Socialist would be Viceroy of India, for Goderich, after he had become Lord Ripon, became Viceroy. Whether he would have still called himself a Christian Socialist is another matter.

Ludlow's lectures were published by Macmillan under the title, *British India, its Races and its History*, and sold out the edition of two thousand copies. To Ludlow's intense disappointment, Macmillans declined to reprint. The book was, he was told, too bellicose, too fiercely partisan, too passionate. It was as though he and Kingsley had exchanged personalities. Why not, suggested the Macmillan brothers soothingly, write something in the same fiery, exciting style, but on the Middle Ages? A writer could be safely partisan about the Middle Ages.

Unfortunately, Ludlow's literary style had run away with him in the case of India because it was one of the few subjects which roused him to emotional heights. It was no use offering him the Middle Ages. With other subjects he reverted to his normal, controlled style.

Nevertheless India and the Mutiny had a tonic effect upon him, reviving him as much as it depressed Kingsley. Ludlow decided that he had spent two years mourning Mansfield and it was time to put the past behind him. Maria Forbes might marry him one day, but then again she might not. He had, most importantly, learned to face the fact that Maurice, with all his gifts, would never lead a political movement to cover the face of England with producer co-operatives.

It was time for Ludlow to start work again.

Divergences

1858, Orsini bomb crisis; 1860, Free
trade treaty with France; 1860, success
of Garibaldi in southern Italy; 1861, out-
break of U.S. Civil War; 1861, the *Trent*
affair; 1862 the *Alabama* affair.

For ten productive years the band of brothers had been an
identifiable group spreading their ideas and testing their visions,
undeterred by failures, which they explained away by saying that
either the timing or the form of their experiments had been
wrong. It was now time for the Christian Socialists to start
broadening the scope of their activities and it was left to the individual to choose the activity which seemed most suitable or
most effective.

Ludlow and Hughes turned to the trade-union movement and
to the 'New Model Unions' of the skilled workers. Robert
Applegarth, one of the new breed of union leaders, was friendly
with Ludlow and kept him supplied with material for articles and
speeches in which Ludlow put the case for organized labour. By
so doing, Ludlow hoped to win middle-class Radicals, men like
W. E. Forster, who was already friendly with the Christian
Socialists. A lesser known and more technical contribution by
Ludlow to the unions was in the field of protective legislation,
and he and Hughes sat on a sub-committee set up by the newly
formed National Society for the Promotion of Social Science to
examine trade-union activities. In the course of that work they
came into contact with some of the Positivists, two of whom,
Frederic Harrison and Godfrey Lushington, became good friends
of Ludlow, and these two men not only helped the unions with
legal advice but for a while also taught at the Working Men's
College.

Godfrey Lushington and his twin brother, Vernon, were pro-
ducts of Rugby and Cambridge and had first encountered
Christian Socialist ideas in the Macmillan bookshop in Cambridge. Several young men of their type progressed through
Christian Socialism to Positivism, and Ludlow was alternately
pleased and frustrated in his dealings with the Positivists. He
regretted their negative side. They took no interest in co-operatives, whether producer or consumer; they did not place much
store in democracy and they saw nothing wrong in the division
of labour into employers and workers. Positivists were, Ludlow
concluded, good men who were trying to construct a moral
doctrine upon scientific principles, with the result that their so-
called 'religion', in the final analysis, was cold. It did not suit
Ludlow, but then, nothing much did, and he remained in the
shelter of the comfortably vague Anglican Church, calling himself a dissenter within the Church.

The publication of Darwin's book on the theory of evolution
worried many conventional Anglicans but not the Christian
Socialists, who were not fundamentalists and could easily fit the
Origin of Species into their religious portfolio. Maurice and
Kingsley welcomed Darwin most heartily as a liberating force
whose ideas should help remove the superstitious notion that
God was some kind of master-magician.

Most of the Christian Socialists kept more or less to a
Maurician path with the notable exception of Furnivall, who was
as much transformed by his success at the College as Ludlow
was by his passion for India. Furnivall flaunted his independence
in the matter of the Sunday excursions, despite clear indications
that Maurice wished they could take place on any day except
Sunday. For a while this disagreement was sedately contained
within the College, but it spread to the world outside through
one of Furnivall's articles in the *People*, the organ of the Sunday
League of which Furnivall was a prominent member. Although
unsigned, the article was easily identifiable by its jocular style
and contents, being a light-hearted account of a meeting of
Working Men's College students when a letter from Maurice
was read out in which he appeared to be apologizing for not
having spent more time on class preparation. To anyone who
knew him, that was simply Maurice at his familiar trick of
assuming blame for any failure, great or small, deserved or un-

deserved. The case happened to concern the small numbers at his Bible classes.

To outsiders who knew nothing of Maurice's little ways the incident seemed ludicrous and there was a good deal of sniggering among Sunday League members. Who ever heard of a college principal apologizing for inadequate preparation! And was it true, by the way, that it was not Maurice but Ludlow who had got the Working Men's College going? So Furnivall alleged.

To do him justice, Furnivall maintained until his dying day that it was Ludlow who held the Christian Socialists together and who later organized the College, and there was truth in that statement, but it was also undeniable, in spite of Furnivall, that without Maurice the Christian Socialists would have drifted apart, that without Maurice Ludlow could not have accomplished what he did and that without Maurice the College would never have started in the first place. Furnivall's article annoyed both Maurice and Ludlow and was one of the steps in Furnivall's march towards the Positivists.

He began to clamour for a whole battery of new 'rights'—the right to organize Sunday outings on which working men and women could appreciate the beauties of nature according to Ruskin's precepts; the right to introduce scientific changes into a moral code which had progressively less of religion and more of humanism; and the right to speak one's mind in a bold and democratic manner. He was provoked by Mansel's Bampton Lectures given in 1858; he was stimulated by Herbert Spencer; he was made reflective by T. H. Huxley. When Huxley invented the term 'agnostic' around 1869, Furnivall seized upon it as the very word to describe himself.

In 1858, however, he was demonstrating his new-found independence of spirit by organizing numerous College socials, outings and expeditions. Octavia Hill joined one of his Sunday outings and enjoyed it tremendously, especially the infectious community singing in the dark walking home, but she worried about going out on the Sabbath and asked Maurice for guidance. Although he did not expressly forbid any outings, she could sense his unhappiness about them and decided, sadly, to refuse further invitations.

Frederic Harrison, now teaching at the College, had no such qualms and encouraged Furnivall. He took a party of College members to Switzerland and urged Furnivall to take a similar party to France. Ruskin also approved the plan, so in September Furnivall, with Thomas Shorter and five other companions, sailed to Le Havre. Furnivall made a special visit to Fourniville, believing it to be the birthplace of his family, but found nothing to support that theory. He soon forgot his minor disappointment in the great fun of being abroad. He loved the foreignness of France and its lack of class barriers. The College party was out to enjoy itself and did not disdain simple pleasures. At Mont St Michel they all danced barefoot on the sands.

> Our walk was most enjoyable, paddling barefoot across the sands, and crossing the river 4 or 5 times, the water above your loins, with a soft wind blowing, and the sun out, we were as jolly as we could possibly be, and danced about like wild Indians. I wish one could always go without trousers and boots,

wrote Furnivall when he was home.

During the following year the Orsini bomb incident in Paris led to a national reaction against Napoleon III and the Christian Socialists, who had made heroes of men like Mazzini and Garibaldi and who favoured the cause of Italian unification, gladly shared the national mood when a demand arose for a rifleman volunteer movement. The Working Men's College formed its own College corps, with Maurice as chaplain and Hughes as commander. The College man who emerged was not Hughes, but a quietly spoken student called Philip Read, who had been a professional soldier. He organized and trained the corps until it gained an enviable reputation as one of the best and smartest in London. Ludlow favoured the volunteer movement, expecting it to be the beginning of a democratic conscript army, and he enlisted too, not in the College corps, which was inconvenient for him, but in his local unit in Wimbledon.

Only one prominent Christian Socialist remained aloof from the volunteer movement and that was Neale, still grieving over the demise of the co-operatives and trying to make good the money he had lost in them. The sum, declared Hughes proudly, was £60,000; no, no, only £40,000, retorted Neale with a nervous look at his wife, and even that had been loaned at five

per cent, he added. Loaned or not, it was all lost now and
Neale's marriage, never much of a success, failed with the co-
operatives. Neale had to sell his Mayfair house, full of happy
memories of work done by the builders' co-operative and rent a
small house in West Hampstead. The family surmised that he
had temporarily borrowed clients' money to finance the co-
operatives and therefore had to realize his assets very fast in
order to replace the money, but that was pure conjecture and his
business affairs were never questioned. Neale's real drawback, as
a business man, was to be too trusting, not to be an opportunist.

The College did not appear to have any place for him, but
Neale was quite content to accept that fact, and pleased to return
to the general co-operative movement, where he spent most of
his spare time giving free legal advice to co-operators. He used
to write a column called 'Legal Questions Answered' in his own
Co-operative Commercial Circular and when that paper ceased
publication he wrote a similar column in the *Cooperator*.
Hughes and Ludlow were also on call as free lawyers for co-
operators.

The best-known Christian Socialist, Charles Kingsley, was
also drifting away from the group, and had been for some time.
He was in one of his regular sloughs of despondency and only
slightly heartened by being appointed a royal chaplain at Queen
Victoria's express demand. He had won her heart because the
Prince Consort admired the Rector's passion for sanitary reform.
He was in London less and less, but spoke as a star guest at the
inaugural meeting of the Ladies' Sanitary Association, with Lord
Shaftesbury as chairman. It was held in Willis's Rooms and
Octavia Hill was in the audience, just one of the many who were
inspired by Kingsley as he addressed the kind of audience with
which he could establish instant rapport—earnest, middle-class
ladies eager to use their leisure time usefully and productively.
'What,' demanded Kingsley, dark eyes flashing, 'so terrible as
war? I will tell you what is ten times and ten thousand times
more terrible than war, and this is—outraged Nature.' The
lesson, he explained in his scientific way, was that the laws of
Nature must be understood and obeyed in order to avoid pesti-
lence and disasters. The lecture, under the arresting title of 'The
Massacre of the Innocents', later appeared in a collection of
lectures.

He could rise to an occasion like that one, but he was really at a very low ebb. His former pupil and admirer, John Martineau, who was now reading for the Bar in London and spending all his free time at the Working Men's College, tried to explain to friends that Kingsley looked as busy and sociable as before but that his creative spark had dried up.

There had been some changes in the Kingsley family which had shaken the Rector. For a start, his scapegrace young brother, Henry, who had been packed off to Australia several years before and not heard of since, had unexpectedly returned, no longer a bad penny but with his salad days behind him, and a brown paper parcel in his trunk which held the manuscript of the First Great Australian Novel. Kingsley read his brother's novel with surprise and a little jealousy as he discovered that Henry's book possessed a creative originality which Kingsley, for all his passionate social beliefs and all his poetic gifts, could never match. His novels were written from the pulpit but Henry's novel was written from life.

Who would have thought that young Henry had it in him, or dear old Tom with his boys' story for that matter? Kingsley gloomily resolved to give up fiction and stick to sermons, lectures and poetry. That would please Maurice and Ludlow, if nobody else.

His general feeling of depression and inadequacy deepened as his father lay dying. Kingsley had never been close to his father, had blamed old Mr Kingsley for not appreciating his wife more, but now that the Rector had to observe his father's terminal illness he was consumed with remorse. Surely he should have tried harder to establish a common feeling with his father? Now it was too late to start. Except for the deaths of two brothers long before, there had been no serious bereavement in the Kingsley family and the Rector, who dealt with death professionally every day, could not face it when it became personal. It was 'an ugly damnable solecism,' he wrote bitterly to Maurice. He composed a very careful letter to his son, Maurice, who was at boarding school. 'You must always think of him lovingly, and remember this about him, Maurice, and copy it—that he was a *gentleman* and never did in his life, or even thoughts, a mean or false thing. . . .'

He turned to heavy physical work as an antidote to his

emotional malaise and worked with his assistants constructing an addition to Eversley churchyard. To the sorrowing horror of the Kingsleys the very first burial in the new churchyard was that of Fanny's sister, Charlotte Froude, who died in Devonshire leaving a distracted husband and three small children. Eversley villagers waited knowingly for another fatality, telling each other that death came in threes, and sure enough within weeks there was a third, Kingsley's friend from Cambridge, 'Little John' Parker, son of the publisher. The whole year seemed redolent of death, two of the older generation of the Grenfell clan dying too.

In the public sector, however, things began to look up for the Christian Socialists with the Prime Minister showing favour to Kingsley and Maurice. The Rector was offered the post of Regius Professor of History at Cambridge and Maurice was offered the incumbency of St Peter's, Vere Street, a living in the gift of the Crown.

Kingsley was delighted with his appointment, at his own university, and where the Prince Consort was Chancellor. The money was tempting and the lure of the title 'Professor' quite irresistible. He could engage a curate to mind Eversley for the months when he would be absent, and there would be considerable preparation needed for his lectures, but he never really considered saying no.

It was not quite so easy for Maurice, because when news of his appointment became known his long-time press adversary, the *Record*, solicited clerical protests against him for submission to the Bishop of London. Hearing of that campaign, Maurice said he would refuse the appointment, but Ludlow and his friends had already foreseen Maurice's reaction, and to forestall it Ludlow organized a counter-campaign in favour of the Prophet, naturally without Maurice's knowledge. Signatures were obtained privately and later through the columns of *The Times* and included a glittering array of professional men, including Gladstone and Tennyson, about a hundred working men of different trades and three women representing a large general group.

Maurice guessed who had organized it and wrote to Ludlow:

And now what am I to say about the address, in which I can almost see you were a principal mover? I can only say that it was just like you to have thought of it; and that the words,

exaggerated as they are, have been a greater comfort and
encouragement to me, than I can express.

The criticisms of his opponents were swamped by a chorus of
approval from his supporters and he gladly accepted the
appointment.

He was also just then in demand as a speaker on how to form
Working Men's Colleges, a subject which attracted considerable
attention. One was started at Cambridge, with Fenton Hort and
others as prime movers; another at Oxford where individuals
worked in collaboration with the city council; and more at
Manchester, Salford, Ancoats, Halifax, Birkenhead and Glasgow,
among other places.

Another subject which was increasingly discussed in England
was the American anti-slavery movement, and a number of
abolitionists visited England on lecture tours. The most famous
was Harriet Beecher Stowe, who took several days off so that she
could stay at Eversley Rectory, where the meeting between her
and Kingsley took on the aspect of a mutual admiration society.
Kingsley tended to have that effect on lady novelists. Frederika
Bremer, an honoured Norwegian author, had become one of his
fans after visiting the rectory.

All the Christian Socialists were in favour of abolition on moral
grounds, and indeed Maurice had been so enraged by the policy
of the State of Maryland towards its black population in the late
1850s that he had withdrawn the money he had invested in
Maryland State funds, a principled act which happened to be
sound business, for when civil war broke out in America in 1861
the Maryland shares became worthless.

The Christian Socialist who became most involved in the Civil
War, as a strong supporter of the North, was Hughes, who had
become increasingly involved with American friends and
American literature since the 1850s. His most valued friend in
America was the poet, James Russell Lowell, whom Hughes had
admired since 1850 when Ludlow showed Hughes the *Biglow
Papers*. Many Americans visited 'The Firs' from time to time, to
see Hughes or Ludlow, or both of them, and Hughes was greatly
taken with the unaffected manners of most Americans.

In 1859 Nicholas Trübner, the publisher, asked Hughes to
edit the first English edition of the *Biglow Papers*, an enterprise

Tom Hughes

which began a long and happy friendship between Hughes as editor and Lowell as author. Miraculously, thought the modest Hughes, Lowell actually liked *Tom Brown's Schooldays* and a landscape painting by Stillman showed Lowell under a tree, with a copy of *Tom Brown's Schooldays* in his hand. The two men had something else in common: each had recently lost a son, in Hughes's case it was Maurice, for whom the Rugby story had been written.

So Hughes made a new friend and Lowell's books joined the select company of volumes by Arnold, Maurice, Kingsley, Carlyle and Emerson in Hughes's 'small, prophetic bookcase', books which he could rely on to give him strength as well as pleasure.

Soon after Maurice Hughes died, Hughes's father, the model for Squire Brown, died. Fanny Hughes blamed herself, quite unreasonably, for Maurice's death and 'The Firs' held such sad memories that the Hughes left Wimbledon and took a house in Park Street, Mayfair. Hughes overcame his grief better than his wife did, for he had plenty to occupy his time, work in the law, and voluntary work outside, and both of them had more London social engagements and invitations to country houses than they could possibly accept. It was one of Hughes's contradictions that he enjoyed a high-powered social life in tandem with his Radical activities, in striking contrast to Ludlow who had no time for dinner parties, and in any case was not as amusing and interesting a dinner guest as Tom Hughes.

When the American Civil War broke out Hughes knew exactly where his loyalties lay, and he and Ludlow were among the first in England to come out for the North. Ludlow wrote an article for the June 1861 edition of *Macmillan's* declaring that the North was bound to win. The issue of slavery was vital, he argued, but so was the need to preserve the unity of the American republic and to make sure that Americans were Americans first, and members of States second. Hughes followed those sentiments up in his article in the September issue of the same magazine when he wrote: 'If the North is beaten, it will be a misfortune such as has not come upon the world since Christendom arose.' Maurice was not so dogmatic. He disliked American materialism, seen most clearly in the North, and many of his acquaintances, including Gladstone, were impressed by Lord Acton's arguments supporting the Southern case. He could not, however, stomach slavery.

As for Kingsley, his lectures at Cambridge on American history suggested that he favoured the South, if anything. The war did not absorb him to the extent that it did Hughes and Ludlow because he had a new project, arising from a government report on child employment whose scope had been enlarged at the instigation of Lord Shaftesbury to include chimney sweeps. Kingsley's warm and sentimental heart was wrung by the revelations within its covers, and he did not really need the excuse that his youngest child, Grenville, should have 'his' book in order to write the *Water Babies*. That was a story which Kingsley could not wait to write. He could not keep pace with the ideas, pleas, descriptions and diatribes, not to mention the poems, which flowed from his pen. Gone was all his staleness and frustration. He was a new man because inspiration had returned.

Another Christian Socialist who paid scant heed to the American war because he had other things on his mind was Furnivall, who had just met Eleanor Nickel Dalziel, sister of a student teacher at the Working Men's College, W. A. Dalziel, an engraver and illustrator and a good friend of Furnivall. The romance seemed an auspicious one, allowing Furnivall to live up to his precepts of ignoring class distinctions, and the pair were married at Hampstead Registry Office in 1862. Each partner, unhappily, began with expectations which were never fulfilled. Eleanor Dalziel saw her husband as a gentleman, with a moneyed background, as a leading figure in the College, as a young man who lived, however impecuniously, in an impressively book-lined home. When his father, the successful surgeon, died Furnivall would surely inherit some money. In worldly terms, then, she might be said to be making a good match. As for Furnivall, he hoped to see her blossom under his guidance into a working-class Princess Ida, translating a Tennysonian idyll into real life. Since they had met through the Working Men's College, Furnivall certainly thought his wife would understand and tolerate all his extra activities at the College and elsewhere, more activities, as it happened, than the new Mrs Furnivall had anticipated, for his commitments had become quite extensive.

In 1860 he had formed a Working Men's Rowing Club, with himself as president, returning to a love of river sports which he had had since boyhood. It cost two shillings to join and another ten shillings down, or one shilling a month, for the year's subscription to the club. Furnivall in fact considered that sculling was superior to rowing and in his Oxford days he invented a type of outrigger canoe. Like Hughes with his boxing class at the College, Furnivall worked hard to make the College rowing club a success. By 1865 the club had done well enough to have forty members and to own a four-oared boat. Then it began to flag, and died, to be resurrected later as a new club.

The history of the College rowing clubs showed considerable ups and downs, all with the similar pattern of brief lives, deaths, and successors. They were usually called 'Maurice Rowing Clubs' in a vain attempt to disguise their working-class origins, for such was the snobbish attitude of the organizers of Thames rowing clubs that they operated an unofficial boycott of working men's clubs on the river simply by refusing to allow them to race against other clubs. Social discrimination of that kind drove Furnivall frantic, and he fought that discrimination until the end of the century seeking to get the iniquitous ruling reversed, but without success. The last of the Maurice Rowing Clubs came to an end in 1894, Furnivall having remained president until 1893.

The river club which he founded later at Hammersmith to give healthy recreation to working-class girls, especially the waitresses at the ABC tea shop in New Oxford Street, where he held tea parties every afternoon after his work in the British Museum Library, outlived him and indeed survives to this day.

During the 1860s Furnivall happened upon another interest, one very much to his liking, and that was literary work of an increasingly specialized nature. Unlike the other Christian Socialists, who were writing regularly and profitably, Furnivall made hardly any money from his literary work and research, and even after he had acquired an international reputation his income from writing was minute. A close friend of his later years estimated it was unlikely to have been in total more than five hundred pounds. It was essential for him to continue his conveyancing job, boring though it was.

His interest in scholarly studies had begun in desultory fashion in 1847 when he joined the Philological Society, and became a little more definite in 1853 when he was made one of that society's two joint secretaries. Philology was a popular subject among the Christian Socialists. Maurice enjoyed teaching social history by tracing the development of families of words. His friend, R. C. Trench, was a keen supporter of the society, and indeed it was Trench who in 1858 said that the Society had a moral duty to compile a supplement to the existing dictionaries of Johnson and Richardson. Fired with enthusiasm Herbert Coleridge, grandson of Samuel Taylor Coleridge and a minor poet himself, offered to start the undertaking and Furnivall was unwillingly dragooned into assisting, on the ground that as one of the secretaries of the Society he could not well refuse.

Clearly the young Mrs Furnivall was not going to enjoy her husband's exclusive company and he did not cut down on his work outside the home just because he had become a married man. The first years of their marriage were happy enough and a daughter, Ena, was born. Old Mr Furnivall died in 1865 and his son duly inherited his share of the family fortune, which he deposited, safely as he thought, in the well-known banking firm of Overend and Gurney. When that company went bankrupt shortly afterwards, Furnivall lost all his money and would have been destitute had not two of his rich friends, Lord Aldenham and Henry Huth, purchased Furnivall's personal estate and given it back to him.

Those financial problems produced tensions and anxieties which neither of the Furnivalls could cope with very well, and then their daughter died, a commonplace of Victorian family life but always a fresh tragedy for the parents. Sorrow over their daughter drew them together for a time, and in 1867 a son was born, Percy, who would grow up to inherit traits from his grandfather and from his father, becoming a surgeon by profession and a sportsman by inclination. At one time Percy Furnivall held a world championship as a tricyclist. Meanwhile the arrival of the new baby took up more of Mrs Furnivall's time, although it did not keep her husband at home more often, for by that time he was absorbed in his literary researches.

He had in fact stumbled into them as part of the work for the great Dictionary, the responsibility for which he had unwillingly assumed after Herbert Coleridge's death in 1861. Trench, now in Ireland as Archbishop of Dublin, approached the Oxford University Press with a view to their publishing either an enormous new Dictonary or a small, concise one, the latter being one of Furnivall's despairing ideas to make the task more manageable. The other members of the Philological Society did not seem to grasp what a mammoth and tedious job it was to collect words and trace their first usage.[1]

The problem of finding material for the Dictionary had first directed Furnivall's attention to Early and Middle English literature, a treasure-house of material and a happy hunting-ground for word collectors. In 1862 he published a volume of Early English poems under the aegis of the Philological Society, and then the *Seynt Graal* and *Handlyng Synne* published by the Roxburghe Club. He decided that the readership of the Roxburghe Club was too limited and decided to start a new society himself which would bring the wonderful heritage of English literature to as many readers as possible. Such was the genesis of the Early English Text Society, founded in 1864 with seventy-five subscribers at first, including Ruskin and Tennyson, and its first publication was Furnivall's short metrical *Life of Arthur*.

The new society flourished from its first days and became a model for others, abroad as well as in England. The societies formed bonds between scholars all over the world, and Furnivall's societies were especially helpful because they laid down guidelines for new types of literary research. Furnivall himself became recognized as the instigator and chief organizer and gained a reputation abroad as a literary scholar of an unconventional kind, who would co-operate generously with scholars and students, known or unknown. Co-operation was part of his character and beliefs, and he felt he was continuing to live according to his democratic ideals and visions through his literary researches. It would be difficult to find a man who was less of a social or intellectual snob than Furnivall, and the success he had achieved in the Working Men's College was destined to be repeated in the literary societies.

Also repeated, of course, were some lamentable failures and some even more lamentable personality clashes. The dispute he had with Maurice over the use of Sunday and over the participation or otherwise of students in the College Council was mirrored in the outrageous vendetta he carried on with the poet, Algernon Swinburne.

Eager to press forward into the broad pastures of English literature, and greatly encouraged by his first society, Furnivall embarked upon a plethora of literary societies, beginning in 1868 with the Chaucer Society. He had loved Chaucer since he was a boy, and found him a man after his own heart; sympathetic, witty, genial and fond of nature. The aim of the Chaucer Society was, declared Furnivall, 'to do honour to Chaucer and to let the lovers and students of him see how far the best unprinted manuscripts of his work differ from the printed text'. The society owed its foundation to a suggestion by Henry Bradshaw, but it was Furnivall who supplied the heart and sinews. In 1868 he began work on his great six-text edition of the *Canterbury Tales*, which occupied him for eight years, and was illustrated with attractive coloured woodcuts executed by W. H. Hooper, who had engraved Ruskin's sketches in his *Elements of Drawing*. Hooper was not the only College student to help Furnivall in his literary work. His brother-in-law, W. A. Dalziel, was secretary of the Early English Text Society.

In this way Furnivall was diverging from the main Christian Socialist road and finding interesting byways. So, too, was Ruskin, always a law unto himself, as he began to publish his social criticisms and ideas which horrified his father and startled the public which knew him as an art critic. His articles, first written in the form of letters, were collected in book form under the title of *Unto This Last*, a volume destined to have a good deal of influence on the self-educated, thoughtful working man.[2] Ludlow skimmed through the book and grumbled to Hughes that Ruskin had no right to think he was a 'Christian Socialist'. That title was the preserve of followers of F. D. Maurice. It did not occur to Ludlow that Ruskin's book and its successors would be printed and reprinted and find responsive readers, doing as much or more for the causes Ludlow held dear as Maurice's books.

If Furnivall and Ruskin were striding along paths which Ludlow considered inappropriate, so too was Charles Kingsley. The *Water Babies* had been a huge popular success, taken to the public's heart as *Tom Brown's Schooldays* had been, and indeed Little Tom, the chimney sweep, would endure as a children's character longer than Tom Brown. The Queen showed Kingsley favour, too, when she invited him and his wife to the wedding of the Prince of Wales, Kingsley's former student at Cambridge, to Princess Alexandra in Windsor Chapel. Ten years ago who would have believed such a thing possible? To make his cup of satisfaction complete, Kingsley learned that his name was being put forward for the Oxford honorary degree of D.C.L.

Kingsley, alas, was not the only man to hear about it. Dr Pusey, a power in Oxford circles, also heard and saw a chance to hit at Kingsley, and through Kingsley to hit at the man Pusey really disliked, F. D. Maurice. Pusey had attacked Kingsley ever since *Hypatia* appeared, saying it was an immoral book, and he now put it around that he would create a scandal if Kingsley's name stood. Scandal was the last thing that Kingsley ever invited, so with hurt dignity he wrote to the authorities at Oxford and requested his name be withdrawn. It was a grave disappointment but he swallowed his pride and began to spend time instead at his son's school, Wellington College. Its headmaster, Dr Benson, a future Archbishop of Canterbury, greatly enjoyed Kingsley's company and conversation, the Rector lectured the boys on science and natural history, and he helped them start a natural history museum.

Those activities led him back to his old hobbies of natural history and geology. As far back as 1855 he and Sir John Lubbock, a supporter of the Working Men's College, had stumbled upon the fossilized remains of a musk-ox in a gravel pit of the Thames near Maidenhead. The discovery suggested strongly that the old river deposits had been laid down in Arctic conditions, an exciting conclusion to reach in those pioneer days of geology. Kingsley had kept up his amateur geological studies, and frequently wrote and lectured on the subject, so he was gratified at being made a fellow of the Geological Society in 1863. It was hardly on a par with being made an Oxford doctor, but it was certainly not to be sneezed at, and at least he had been proposed by Sir Charles Bunbury and seconded by Sir Charles Lyell, men of eminence in their field as Dr Pusey was in his.

Also in 1863 was a new venture, which promised well, and recalled old days for the Christian Socialists. This was a new weekly periodical, which Macmillans would publish, to be called the *Reader*. It was not exactly a revival of the real Christian Socialist periodicals since it was intended to cover general contemporary progress, but its editor and contributors sounded like a roll-call for the *Christian Socialist*. Ludlow would be editor, and among those who promised to write were Kingsley, Furnivall,

Maurice, Neale, Hughes, Lowes Dickinson, Llewelyn Davies and John Westlake.

The magazine was launched but soon became too much for Ludlow, who was expected to be business and production manager as well as editor, and who at the same time had to see that his law work did not suffer. He had to resign and David Masson, who edited *Macmillan's*, and was a personal friend, took the paper over. Kingsley liked Masson but much regretted Ludlow's resignation:

> I could have worked with you (*entre nous*) with a very different feeling from what I should have to Masson [he wrote Ludlow]. He is a good fellow; but you—you are one of the dearest friends I have, a man whom I know I can say anything to, even if we differ—

The *Reader* was never really successful although it limped along for some years. Hughes remained associated with it and Huxley became its general scientific adviser. When Masson left, Hughes was asked to recommend a new editor and his choice fell upon an amateur astronomer and journalist, Norman Lockyer, whom Hughes had first met in Wimbledon. Lockyer tended to specialize in scientific articles, and when Macmillans at last sold the *Reader* he persuaded Alexander Macmillan to back a new scientific magazine. This was called *Nature*, and unlike the *Reader*, which gradually sank into oblivion, *Nature* survived to be a permanent success.

Separation

1863, Bismarck and the Schleswig–Holstein dispute; 1864, Danish war; 1865, Death of Palmerston; 1866, Austro–Prussian War; 1866, Gladstone's Reform Bill

Maurice was very well known among certain sections of the population and frequently asked to pronounce upon current topics. He avoided any overt political stand and would make involved statements based upon moral principles as he interpreted them, so that his opinions were not always easy to follow. There was, for example, the affair of Bishop Colenso and his book on Bible history. Colenso belonged to Maurice's small army of younger disciples, and it took moral courage on Maurice's part to denounce his friend's book but denounce it he did, adding that it was really so misconceived that the Bishop should resign. And since Maurice did not approve of anyone suggesting a course of action which he was not prepared to take himself, he immediately said he would resign from St Peter's, Vere Street, displaying a Maurician purity of conduct which nobody but himself ever adopted. His friends should have been used to that, but they were dismayed none the less and entreated him to change his mind. Even the Bishop of London joined in the chorus.

Finally he agreed to withdraw his resignation and had to tell his congregation: 'I cannot call it eating the leek, except that being a Welshman by origin I am bound to like leeks. But it was a humiliation, however much I might rejoice to feel myself once again the minister of a most kind and friendly people,' he told his younger son, then a student at Oxford. His elder son, having finished with university, was an Army officer in India. Like Kingsley, Maurice considered the Army an honourable profession and was proud of his son. (His grandson also became a soldier, General Maurice, of Maurice Debate fame in World War I.)

Maurice tried to avoid being asked to pronounce about the American Civil War, which was often discussed publicly and privately, but he was slowly coming round to Ludlow and Hughes in their support for the North. Hughes had made his pro-Northern opinions first widely known in January 1863 when he spoke at a packed meeting in Exeter Hall, and he became a propagandist for the Northern government, speaking all over the country to audiences which resembled those which had heard him when he lectured on co-operatives. The north of England, the working class and the social reformers tended to side with the North; the government and the landed gentry felt more sympathy with the South.

The American Minister (it was before the United States had an ambassador in Britain) reported perceptiently that the men and women of the provinces who flocked to Hughes's meetings were the same kind who, a generation or two earlier, had combined to force the British Government to abolish slavery. Trade-union leaders organized meetings to support the Northern government and once again Hughes found himself sitting next to Holyoake on public platforms.

Despite his lack of eloquence and wit, Hughes had a happy blend of ringing sincerity and honest indignation, and his reputation as a public figure grew in America as it did in England. He was one of the first to call for an Anglo-American *entente*, if not a definite alliance. More than one observer considered Hughes to be Parliamentary material, although when Holyoake hinted at it in 1862 Hughes grinned sheepishly and pooh-poohed the notion.

The Civil War did not affect Kingsley as much as it did his old friends. One reason was his accidental involvement in 1864 in the celebrated battle with Father John Henry Newman, a duel which arose from Kingsley's carelessness and not from his choice. It began when he wrote a review of Froude's latest volume on Tudor England, a book which dealt with Protestant and Catholic antagonism. Kingsley, the arch Protestant, had not forgotten the High Church Dr Pusey's malice over the Oxford degree. Kingsley was also opposed to Pope Pius IX's illiberal policies, and indeed to the Roman Catholic Church in general as a social institution. The Pope had been hostile to Garibaldi and Mazzini and he denounced new scientific theories and discoveries.

At a deeper level Kingsley had an intense dislike of the orthodox Catholic view that celibacy was a more exalted spiritual state than wedded bliss.

So the Rector's review, published in *Macmillan's*, began normally enough but then went further than necessary by including a gratuitous sneer at Newman, apparently tossed in as an afterthought. 'Truth, for its own sake, had never been a virtue with the Roman clergy,' wrote Kingsley, speaking there of the sixteenth century, and in the next breath he jumped ahead to the nineteenth.

> Father Newman informs us that it need not, and on the whole ought not to be; that cunning is the weapon which heaven has given to the saints wherewith to withstand the brute male force of the wicked world which marries and is given in marriage.

That was the self-confident voice of the heterosexual male, contemptuous of the man who bore the title 'Father' but had no flesh-and-blood children of his own; it was also the voice of the Puritan reformer with flaming sword who regarded the Catholic priests of the nineteenth century as heirs of Machiavelli and the Borgias. Alas for Kingsley, it was not in his nature, as it was in Maurice's, to give Newman credit for following *his* truth implicitly, no matter where it led him. Kingsley assumed that Newman would condone deception.

The article appeared at the right time for Newman and the wrong one for Kingsley. Newman was at a crossroads. Twenty years ago he had thrown over a promising career in the Anglican Church because he felt it the right thing to do, and he had been condemned to live in the wilderness as a result. He desperately needed a chance to explain to an uncaring world, and to his countrymen in particular, exactly why he had become a Roman Catholic, but in his wildest dreams he could not have hoped that an opportunity would present itself in the shape of England's most famous and militant Protestant. It seemed as though Providence were leading Kingsley like a lamb to the slaughter and Newman was waiting with his sacrificial knife.

First Newman demanded a public apology for the misquotation Kingsley had made in the review, and for the implied insult deriving from it. Kingsley looked up his references, discovered he had indeed made a mistake, and gave what he deemed a sufficient apology. Newman fiercely insisted on something more, which puzzled Kingsley, who thought that he had apologised for his carelessness, as any gentleman should, and that Newman ought to be satisfied by it.

Kingsley's friends understood the situation far better than he ever did, and hoped he could be rescued somehow.

> I would have given much that Kingsley had not got into this dispute with Newman. In spite of all apparent evidence, I do believe that Newman loves truth in his heart of hearts, and more now than when he was an Anglican.

wrote Maurice to Dean Stanley, expressing his anxiety. Newman's subtle arguments and unerring sarcasm in the press were quite beyond Kingsley's comprehension, and the public quarrel amused sophisticated and literary-minded liberals whose religious beliefs had broadened so much that they were almost invisible to the untutored eye. Most spectators imagined that Kingsley and Newman disliked one another, and R. H. Hutton, whose article in the *Spectator* helped to precipitate the affair into a doctrinal *cause célèbre* went on record as saying that he believed a repulsion did exist between them. If so, it was more a repulsion based on what the other man personified than a personal antipathy.

Kingsley simply could not fathom why Newman kept scoring pedantic debating points against him instead of answering the wider questions, which Kingsley thought were more important, concerning the record of the Roman Catholic Church on social problems. 1864, after all, was the year which would see the publication of the Syllabus of Errors.

If the Rector could not see his exposed position in the protracted debate with Newman, his family and friends certainly could and they packed him off to France with Froude, who was planning to continue to Spain and carry out some historical research in that country. With luck, hoped Kingsley's supporters, the hubbub would have subsided by the time he returned. Kingsley began the trip in great spirits, for it was only his second time abroad, but the familiar lassitude and depression soon returned. He could not keep up with the energetic Froude, who went on to Spain alone. Kingsley missed his wife, and he had been strangely intimidated by the awesome sight of the Pyrenees. Man was puny, after all, he reflected, overtaken by melancholy. He could not wait to be home.

Whilst Kingsley was in France trying to gain strength, the good Father had remained in England toiling night and day on his autobiography, *Apologia pro Vita Sua*, which was first printed in sections under the title of 'General Answer to Mr Kingsley'. The fair-minded British public gave the book a very sympathetic reception and Alexander Macmillan sent Kingsley a copy, with a note saying that the Rector might find it 'soothing'. Kingsley raced through the book, found nothing in it to make him change his mind, and replied to Macmillan that he found it impossible to understand a man who had to believe in the infallibility of one Church. (The doctrine itself was not formally adopted until later, but there was sufficient evidence in 1864 to suggest that it would become an article of faith fairly soon. When in fact it did, Ludlow took exactly the same position as Kingsley.)

So there the matter stood. The thin-skinned Rector of Eversley had been taught a lesson, first on a small scale by Dr Pusey and then on a much grander one by Father Newman. The altercation gave Newman the chance to explain himself. When the dust had all settled and people could review the arguments calmly most Protestants continued to believe that there was a good deal of truth in what Kingsley had said. Subsequent editions of Newman's book omitted the sections about Kingsley, and Newman felt so comforted by writing it, and by its success, that he called it a 'wonderful deliverance'.

Neither man bore a lasting grudge against the other. The squire of Eversley, Sir William Cope, a great admirer of Newman, tried to get Kingsley to see his opponent in a better light and in 1868 gave him a collection of Newman's poetry which included the *Dream of Gerontius*. That poem impressed Kingsley deeply, and he commented that one had to admire and

be thankful for any man, even Newman, who could teach the irreverent and trivial younger generation to acknowledge universal truths like the soul's deepest longing to see God.

As for Newman, when Kingsley died in 1875 he ordered
masses to be said for the Rector.[1]

Scarred in 1864 by the Newman clash, Kingsley vowed to
live a private life and he busied himself with parochial and family
concerns. His brother, Henry, married Sarah Haselwood, an
intelligent and vivacious governess saddled with a demanding
mother, a change of status which meant that the newly-weds
took a cottage a few miles away, at Wargrave, on the Thames,
and old Mrs Kingsley came to live permanently at the Rectory.

His Cambridge history lectures were published as a book, *The
Roman and the Teuton*, receiving the habitual quota of derision
and dislike reserved for Christian Socialist authors. Kingsley was
generous in forgiving and did not understand how other people
could perpetuate grudges, and why reviewers seemed to enjoy
raking over his past actions and opinions, condemning him repeatedly for his same early 'crimes'. His Christian Socialism was
mentioned only to be sneered at, as were the presumed attitudes
of the so-called 'muscular Christians', a term which he found
especially offensive. What was even more wounding, the reviewers dismissed the historical content of his lectures, which
had cost him hours of anxious research and consideration, as the
ravings of a sensation-loving novelist!

Maurice shook his head at the review in the *Saturday Review*
and at the one in the *Spectator*. He wrote to Dean Stanley saying
how much he had enjoyed Kingsley's book. It was 'most delightful and instructive, expecially good for the Cambridge men'.

The liberal dons at Cambridge, who almost without exception
supported the North in the Civil War, had classified Kingsley as a
reactionary, and they were now disconcerted because he joined
them in fighting hard for the establishment of a lectureship in
American History, with Harvard University supplying the
lecturers. The campaign failed because the deeply prejudiced and
conservative elements at Cambridge, England, were alarmed in
case a link with Cambridge, Massachussetts, would permit radicalism and 'self-conceit' to permeate the English colleges. Once
again, Kingsley had made himself conspicuous in a minority
cause.

His students had none of their dons' reservations about their famous professor and his lecture halls were always full, as was the University church when he delivered the university sermons in the summer of 1865. His favourite sermon was devoted to his hero David, the very model of a warrior, poet and king. Still, Kingsley's career at Cambridge was not exactly triumphant and in that respect was in sharp contrast to the career of his fishing mate, Hughes. In the year when Kingsley's greatest achievement was to deliver the university sermons at Cambridge, Hughes was offering himself to the voters of Lambeth as a candidate for the House of Commons.

It was all Holyoake's doing. He had not forgotten that when Hughes turned down the idea of a parliamentary career some years before, he had not dismissed the suggestion outright. So Hughes was approached again and assured that Lambeth, with a strong working-class core of voters, would provide an organizing committee, a rota of loyal canvassers and would pay all his expenses. Without that last assurance Hughes could not possibly have afforded to stand, and this time he agreed.

Nobody, except Holyoake and the Lambeth committee, expected Hughes would win because the sitting members, Frederick Doulton and James Clark Lawrence, were important local employers who would naturally exert economic pressure on the voters. The political pundits, however, underestimated the sturdy resolution of the labour leaders who had worked so long with Hughes and who respected his fighting qualities. They rallied their Lambeth supporters, and when the votes were in Hughes headed the list with 6,143; Doulton came second with 5,897; Lawrence polled just over 4,000 and an unknown Conservative had under 500 votes.

The election had been followed with utmost interest by members of the Working Men's College and when Hughes was elected, Ludlow organized a College social in his honour. Maurice, the chief speaker, was for once at a loss. Where could one find the words good enough for their old friend? he asked.

Thomas Hughes, M.P., was an independent in the Commons as he was anywhere else and took his stand on each issue as it cropped up, never following any given or even predictable line. In the following year he was joined in the Commons by two friends, Henry Fawcett, the blind Radical (husband of Millicent Fawcett, the campaigner for women's rights), and John Stuart Mill.

Hughes was a leading supporter of Parliamentary reform but disliked some of the methods used by other supporters. He complained that the huge meeting held in July 1867 outside Hyde Park had been needlessly provocative and, although he remained a member of the Reform League, he refused thereafter to speak publicly for the League. When Disraeli and the Conservatives introduced the Reform Bill that year Hughes voted with them, hoping that the enfranchisement of the town workers would lead to a new political party of practical and pragmatic reformers, men in fact like himself. His kindly and paternalistic supporter for under-dogs, of whatever colour, brought him into the Governor Eyre controversy, an affair which split the Christian Socialist group down the middle. Ludlow stood with Hughes; Kingsley was ranged on the other side.

Governor Eyre of Jamaica had made his reputation years before by explorations in Australia. In 1859 he was sent to Jamaica, first as temporary governor, and then his appointment was made permanent. Jamaica was a poverty-stricken island, with economic and racial unrest, like the neighbouring island of Haiti. The American Civil War and the slavery question added to its tensions.

Eyre was a narrow-minded Anglican, quite determined to keep Jamaica under control, and he blamed George William Gordon, a black Baptist leader, for most of the Jamaican discontent. When a black rebellion broke out on Haiti, Eyre took a strong line in Jamaica, believing that the meetings of Jamaican blacks in support of their brothers in Haiti were really secret preparations for a mass uprising. To forestall such an eventuality, Eyre ordered suppression, and blacks were shot or hanged, their houses were set on fire and Gordon himself was arrested on a flimsy charge of sedition, found guilty and summarily executed.

The governor congratulated himself. 'So widespread a rebellion and one so effectually put down is not, I believe, to be met with in history,' he reported confidently to London. Queen Victoria disagreed, and so did her Colonial Secretary, Edward Cardwell, who recommended Eyre's suspension pending a commission to ascertain the facts. In April 1866 the commission reported that Eyre had been too severe and that Gordon had been unjustly sentenced.

At that information John Stuart Mill rose in the Commons to denounce Eyre. The government dismissed the Governor and withheld his pension by way of punishment. Mill was not appeased by that gesture, and formed the Jamaica Committee, enrolling Hughes, Ludlow, Huxley and Herbert Spencer, among others, pressing for Eyre to be tried for murder. That was going too far, exclaimed Eyre's supporters, and they formed a counter-committee which boasted among others Carlyle, Tennyson and Ruskin. Henry Kingsley, who had hero-worshipped Eyre in Australia, was an active member of this committee and roped in his brother, Charles, whose celebrated name gave the committee a good deal of publicity.

Ludlow was so outraged at what he judged to be a final betrayal of principle on Kingsley's part that he wrote at once to his old friend, saying that their paths had diverged so sharply that it was useless ever to correspond again. Kingsley read his comrade's angry letter with sadness but understanding—it was 'Old Gruff' at his most stiff-necked. He replied with simple dignity that he would always remember and value their past association.

Hughes could see both sides of the Kingsley/Ludlow breach and he sympathized more with Ludlow than with Kingsley, but managed to stay on friendly terms with the latter all the same. Some of the youthful fun and warmth disappeared from his relationship with Kingsley, but that was as much due to the passage of years and pressure of work as to the Governor Eyre disagreement. Afterwards Ludlow regretted having yielded to his impulse to break with Kingsley but he was too proud to say so, and they did not meet again until Maurice's funeral in 1872 when the shared emotion of that day united them as nothing else could have done.

It was one of the disadvantages of Ludlow's virtuous adherence to principle that he would rush into dogmatic opposition, even to old friends. He had been equally stiff-necked in the College Council fighting Furnivall over the question of winter dances. Those dances had developed from Furnivall's summer Sunday excursions and although they were held in the Salters' Hall, and not in the Working Men's College building, they were patronized by College students, and by the friends, sisters and sweethearts of College members. To all intents and purposes they *were* College dances, as Litchfield pointed out sourly at Council meetings.

Many of the girls belonged to his singing class, which irritated him still more. Dances, he insisted, led working men to spend more than they could afford. 'As a rule, *dancing* men are certainly not *working* men,' he wrote in the College journal, continuing the controversy. It went without saying that the College would attract more students if it ran dances. '. . . a casino will fill any night better than a classroom,' he remarked, but that was *not* the purpose of the College.

Furnivall never saw anything wrong in harmless recreation and he retorted that the men and women who went to his dances were sober, decent folk with plenty of common sense, not ragged fools who needed to be told what to do and what not to do. Litchfield flinched and so did Ludlow. Was that another of Furnivall's veiled jibes against Maurice? wondered Ludlow. Was Furnivall reopening the earlier struggle against the Prophet?

Ludlow joined Litchfield. The purpose of the College, he asserted, was to give the manual working men of London an education to help them overcome some of the evils against which the masses of the English people were fighting. His impassioned arguments were like hammer blows against gnats, but Ludlow and Litchfield were deadly serious and they contested the 'Heads versus Heels' debate until Furnivall was isolated in a minority of one on the College Council.

Litchfield's criticisms did not stop at dances but extended to the College Volunteer corps. He believed, probably correctly, that some students joined the College not from love of learning but from a desire to join its smart Volunteer corps. Like Ludlow, Litchfield was sorry that the Volunteer movement had not become a genuine people's militia. Anyone could see, he grumbled, that the College corps was much too dandified to stand alongside a real College hero like Garibaldi—(the College had raised £7.50 in a shilling subscription to help the Italian patriot and his Red Shirts)—and the College should seriously consider severing its connection with the Volunteer movement.

At that point Maurice intervened. He said that the College existed to serve the students and so had to take heed of student demand in work and in leisure. If the Volunteer movement were a true expression of popular feeling in the country, and it would be hard to deny it, then the College could not, and indeed should not, stand aloof, nor should Council members try to stop working men from sharing in what was, after all, a national enterprise.

The dances were stopped: the Volunteer corps continued.

In 1866 Maurice was appointed, to his surprise but also to his joy, as Professor of Moral Philosophy at Cambridge, a move which made it inevitable that this time he must resign from St Peter's, Vere St.

The circumstances of his election as professor were interesting because they showed that he, like Kingsley, could not shake off the stigma of the Christian Socialist background. Seven Cambridge professors, including Kingsley, had the right to vote, and when Maurice's name was first put forward as a candidate Kingsley was delighted, feeling that Maurice's election to a Cambridge professorship would prove once and for all how wrong King's College had been to dismiss him.

Maurice was in two minds about allowing himself to be considered in case his association with Cambridge, whether successful or not, might harm the university, and the history of the past fifteen years gave him cause for this anxiety. Another candidate was Fenton Hort, but the instant that he heard Maurice was even being considered he withdrew his name and canvassed strongly for the Prophet. Nobody disputed that Maurice's intellectual stature and his imposing list of publications put him head and shoulders above everyone else, yet the outcome remained a matter of doubt until the last moment. It was, everyone agreed, a matter of 'moral courage'. To be identified publicly as a man who voted for Maurice was to risk putting one's head on the block and to invite scorn and reproach from the religious and political press. Yet vote for Maurice they did, the professorial seven, and boasted about it afterwards.

Maurice was thrilled. Cambridge had certainly changed for the better since his student days, he decided, and when he took up his duties there he noted approvingly that tutors and established professors went out of their way to welcome newcomers. It did not seem to occur to him that Frederick Denison Maurice was not an average newcomer!

The change meant also that Maurice had a perfect excuse to resign the principalship of the Working Men's College, for he would not be in London very often. Secretly he still blamed himself for the failure of his religious and Bible classes at the College. As soon as word got round that he intended to resign he was besieged by teachers and students begging him to continue and very reluctantly he agreed, but only if a Vice-Principal were appointed for the administrative work. A College teacher, J. S. Brewer, who was also a teacher from King's College, was appointed Vice-Principal, a thankless appointment, for whilst Maurice lived no one else could be more than a shadow in the bright glow of the Master, and Brewer was well aware of that fact. His position was unenviable but he did his best.

The success of the Working Men's College created certain difficulties, rather as the passing of Slaney's Act had created difficulties for the Promoters. The College had about five hundred students, which meant it could no longer be run on the haphazard and amateur basis which served well enough when the College was not much more than a family concern of the Christian Socialists. It had soon outgrown the cramped Red Lion Square quarters and moved to 45 Great Ormond Street, which premises were purchased for £1,500, Maurice giving £500 and the rest being raised on a loan basis. By 1866 this loan was down to £400 but the College planned to expand and Council decided to appeal for more funds.

Hughes approached the Privy Council for a grant but after that body looked at the expressed aims of the College—to provide a liberal education for artisans at hours and prices they could manage—it decided that the College was outside the normal run of educational establishments and ineligible for State help. The Founders accordingly began to solicit money from private individuals. The Prince of Wales donated twenty-five guineas and John Stuart Mill and Samuel Smiles each stumped up a fiver, but the bulk of the money came in dribs and drabs from teachers, students and friends, in other words, from the College.

It registered itself as a company, and those members involved in its management realized they could not postpone for ever the day when they would have to revise the College terms of reference and agree upon a constitution. At that point the real division inside the College over the question as to how far it should be democratic and self-governing, with students elected to the governing Council, would show itself. Ludlow and Furnivall stood shoulder to shoulder in support of democracy, Litchfield and George Tansley opposed it on the grounds of efficiency. Council certainly needed pruning, for by definition all teachers, past or present, were members of Council, a situation which resembled the old Council of Promoters.

With a characteristic flair for compromise, the College simply shelved the problem. It would have to be solved, but not just yet. The Christian Socialists had followed Maurice far too long to make fundamental changes in an organization so intimately connected with him unless they had first obtained his sanction, and Maurice, as he had frequently shown, had no faith in democracy for democracy's sake.

Gradually he was detaching himself from the Working Men's College. He spent a little time assessing the work of the Christian Socialists and defended his choice of the name as 'a desirable defiance of two kinds of popular prejudice, and was worth all the obloquy and ridicule which it incurred'. He told Ludlow that they *had* been right in saying that co-operation as applied to trade needed a Christian foundation, otherwise they might have become 'the victims of clever sharpers like Lechevalier', but Maurice admitted that he had always thought it likely that the group would disagree among themselves and end up as anything but co-operators. So when King's College dismissed him and his name was dishonoured, he felt entirely free to find something better suited to his talents than forming producer associations, and he had found it in the Working Men's College.[2]

Naturally the College could not dream of letting its Prophet's elevation pass without some celebration, and a social was held on 8 December 1866, its spirit strongly recalling the socials and Festivals of association days. Maurice was visibly moved when friend after friend, of every age and class, stood up to testify to the value to him of Maurice's friendship. Tom Hughes made a joke of it, saying that if he had ever differed from Maurice, even over how to make boots—(that produced guffaws, for most of those present remembered how Maurice and Hughes had once disagreed over policies to be adopted by the Bootmakers' Association)—then, in the end, events proved that Maurice was right and he wrong. Many students thanked Maurice for what he had done for the College, and especially coming out to the College night after night, at his age, in all weathers.

It was, however, Ludlow who brought the tears to Maurice's eyes in a speech which was like himself; brave, honest and proud and at the same time, deeply personal. He had never known a

J. M. Ludlow

father, said Ludlow, and Maurice had taken that place, and through his long and intimate knowledge of Maurice's life he, Ludlow, had come to feel a reverence for him. He now asked Maurice's forgiveness for any words or acts which in the past had pained him—'and to offer him the apologies of a man not much wont to bend the knee to any human authority'.

It was handsomely said and handsomely received. Next morning Maurice wrote to thank him again. 'It was far more than I would well bear to hear all that was said about me by others, but yours was quite overpowering.'

The change in direction of Maurice's activities marked the end of an era for the Christian Socialists. They were no more eager young men, hoping Maurice would decide where to channel their energetic idealism. They had become mature men in mid-career, prepared to take action as they saw fit. Had Maurice accepted the role of leader they would have remained his faithful cohorts, but his refusal forced them to decide for themselves. They could not entirely throw off his influence, and however dissimilar they might seem as individuals, a closer examination would reveal them as men marked by the ideas and examples of Maurice.

Individual Paths

1867, Second Reform Act; 1868, Glad-
stone's first ministry; 1870, Forster's
Education Act; First Irish Land Act; Civil
Service reforms, Army reforms; 1870,
Franco-Prussian War; 1871, Kaiser
William I. 1871, Trade union reforms;
1872, *Alabama* arbitration, Secret Ballot
Act.

For a few years, therefore, both Kingsley and Maurice were
teaching at Cambridge and Kingsley often listened to one of
Maurice's lectures, speechless with admiration at the depth and
sincerity of his dear Master's words. Fenton Hort, who had
become a country parson and an ecclesiastical historian, also
attended some of Maurice's lectures but did not share Kingsley's
emotional reaction. He thought it a great pity that relatively few
students went to Maurice whilst Kingsley, a worthy man but a
lightweight compared to Maurice, always had crowded classes.

Kingsley had just published a new historical novel, *Hereward
the Wake*, a catchy title which bestowed a popular sobriquet on
Hereward Leofriccson, the last of the English, as Kingsley
declared patriotically, or the first of the literary Vikings, as critic
Andrew Lang would suggest. Hereward was another of
Kingsley's Berseker heroes, following the Goths in *Hypatia*.
Mindful of the bad reviews for his Cambridge lectures, Kingsley
had researched his latest story very carefully, proving it by the
liberal use of footnotes. It was a fairly mature novel with less
philosophizing and preaching than his earlier books contained,
and with many loving portraits of the English landscape. The
book sold well and, like the *Water Babies*, was destined to live as a
children's classic.

The Rector's elder son, Maurice, was studying at the university, thus fulfilling a favourite dream of Kingsley, that the two of them should be at Cambridge together, although it had to be admitted that Maurice was no scholar. Like his uncles George and Henry, Maurice was better suited for an adventurous outdoor life, and his brother, Grenville, was of a similar temperament. Neither of the boys ever considered being a social reformer. That did not disappoint their father, for he followed the Christian Socialist idea that all children should be taught the fundamental virtues and decencies and after that they should be free to choose their own way in life. So Maurice left Cambridge in 1868 to work on a farm in South America, and his departure eased his father's financial burden, so that he decided to resign the professorship. Kingsley had not enjoyed his Cambridge teaching as much as he had anticipated. The waspish dons had been gratuitously unkind and Kingsley had fussed greatly over the preparation of his lectures, whilst the salary was not great enough to outweigh the drawbacks.

When the students heard that 1869 would be Professor Kingsley's last year they flocked in even greater numbers to his lectures. He hoped to make his final year important and sought to master Comtism, hoping to talk about it to his students and perhaps save them from adopting it as a form of belief. He was in demand as an outside lecturer, too, and spoke on education for the Social Science Association in Bristol. Maurice gave him a long list of points to bear in mind for his lecture. Examinations had a bad effect on young people, said Maurice, especially on girls, assuming they were admitted 'as of course they should be, to all the privileges of the other sex. You must be aware of all the degrading talk, about what will pay in an examination, which is heard at the Universities.' Maurice had no time for crammers and was unhappy that at Cambridge, of all places, he rarely found anybody prepared to take the time to talk to him about the iniquities of the examination system.

Education was a general subject for debate following the 1867 parliamentary reform act which had made State educational provision virtually essential, and as the Liberals had won the recent election and Gladstone was Prime Minister, Christian Socialist hopes for the new government were high. Gladstone showed his favour towards the Christian Socialists by having Kingsley appointed a canon of Chester, much to Queen Victoria's pleasure. She had tried to get Disraeli to give similar preferment to Kingsley, but the Tory leader had refused, saying that association with a Christian Socialist would tarnish the Conservative Party image. Clearly Mr Gladstone was made of sterner stuff.

There were three other canons, so Kingsley's duties covered only three months of the year, which meant that Kingsley would keep his Eversley living with the assistance of a curate to cover his absences. The canonry was a sign of public honour as well as preferment and Kingsley, prematurely old at fifty, was well satisfied. His father had reached the summit of his clerical career at the same age. There was a batch of young supporters who asserted loudly that their hero should have been given something better but, as it turned out, Chester suited Kingsley marvellously well, and in no time at all he made a place for himself in adult education in the city as well as in the cathedral. He did not abandon his other interests and joined John Stuart Mill in demanding women's suffrage, although he was soon frightened away by the movement's militant wing. Women should be feminine like his Fanny, he pleaded, not masculine viragos! He returned to education and enjoyed his role as public educator. His sermons and lectures were printed and sold in their thousands and his striking phrases were borrowed by other speakers. We should not, he said, tolerate bad social conditions which wasted a percentage of the population like 'human soot'. We should not be afraid to feel a 'divine discontent' at bad conditions.

In contrast to Kingsley, who was branching out, Maurice had reached an age when it was sensible to contract his activities. His habit of assuming endless tasks gave many people the impression that he had the constitution of an ox, but his wife and his doctor knew better. Time and again Maurice tried to cut down his work load but he was incapable of saying 'no' when asked to take on some fresh responsibility. But by 1870 he knew he had to start somewhere and he resigned from St Peter's, Vere Street. His congregation was saddened by the news. Not every member had understood Maurice's thought processes but every one felt he was a very special person. Maurice was surprised by the response to his resignation. 'I have had such loving and kind friends there that I feel much the parting,' he wrote to a friend. 'But I believe at present Cambridge is the place for me. There also I have met with toleration and affection such as I could not have dreamed of.'

His farewell sermon filled the church and more than three hundred took communion.

Like Kingsley, Maurice also supported Mill and women's suffrage, but he warned Mill that he would not agree to make public speeches. Somewhat late in life, Maurice had come to the conclusion that he was a totally ineffective public speaker whose utterances were almost guaranteed to be misunderstood and held against him. The term 'Broad Church' had been lately coined by his friend, Dean Stanley, and to Maurice's annoyance many of his admirers assigned him to that camp, confident that this would please him. Instead he complained that he had spent most of his life warning people that it was dangerous to divide human beings into sects, and yet there they were, still at it!

His son Edmund was in Prussia in the summer of 1870, studying and travelling, and wrote to his father praising the Protestant German State which showed so much vigour and vitality. Maurice did not feel so sure about Prussia, and his fears were realized when the Franco-Prussian War broke out. He was quite prepared to see France chastized, and Napoleon III, but he feared that Germany's 'moral tone' would be spoiled by victory and that Prussia would go on to conquer an empire. He could not condone an empire gained through blood, although he excused the British Empire, which he regarded as a development of overseas trading.

In spite of his resolutions to do less work, he was pressured into serving on the Royal Commission on the Contagious Diseases Act, and for six months in 1870 he travelled every week to London to sit on the commission. Then he accepted the tiny living of St Edward's, Cambridge, which entailed few duties and carried no income. He said he liked it because he could preach, he could visit parishioners and he could teach little children. Maurice was not really cut out to be that kind of parson, however much he might have wished it, and his other duties meant that he needed a curate in any case. At one time his curate was Edward Carpenter, an exceptional young man of liberal opinions who was at least a century in advance of his time in social, sexual and artistic matters. Carpenter was the wrong generation and the wrong type to be attracted to Maurice or to appreciate him at anything like his true value. His relationship with Maurice was short and he felt obscurely that Maurice was an unusual person, but that was as far as it went.

Another Christian Socialist on a new path was Ludlow, whose self-appointed position as Maurice's faithful assistant and expositor was virtually ended. His interests began to spread outside the British Isles. He noted with great approval a rising tide of republicanism in Paris. He was pleased to be on the winning side for once, as in the American Civil War, and he took a fresh interest in India, declaring it should be administered on democratic lines with one man, one vote, and not split on national divisions. He had supported the 1867 reform act, and as Radicalism was becoming almost fashionable in some English circles, Ludlow no longer felt himself an outcast.

Finally, and most important of all, his new path was dictated by his changed marital status, for in 1867 Maria Forbes suddenly said she would marry him in spite of her elderly father's opposition. Ludlow's mother died in 1868 and he married his cousin the following year. He was a prim bachelor of forty-seven who had spent his life and income promoting social reform: she was a conventional Victorian spinster of forty-six who had spent most of her life caring for sick relatives. She shared none of her husband's social and political views, was Tory, High Church Anglican and given to hypochondria and spending the afternoons on a sofa. Any prettiness she had possessed as a girl had long since faded. Yet Ludlow felt blessed above men for the gift of such a bride with his hopes of nearly a quarter of a century fulfilled at last. He made his last important sacrifice for her, renouncing his past volunteer social work in order to adopt a new career, that of professional civil servant, which would give him a salary adequate to maintain a wife.

One of his last 'Christian Socialist' achievements before his marriage was to collaborate with Lloyd Jones on a very readable book called *The Progress of the Working Class, 1832–1867*, making the point that the condition of the working class had improved in that period partly through working-class campaigns and partly through legislation like the legalization of savings banks, friendly societies, co-operative associations and partnerships in industry. By 1867 there existed several facilities for adult education and the working man had taken full advantage of them. Trade unions had become mature and responsible and now deserved the protection of new laws. It was a pity, Ludlow thought, that Christianity had made only slight progress among the working class, but he blamed that on parsons who spent more time lecturing their congregations than establishing a fellowship with them.

The first volume of Marx's *Capital* appeared in England at about the same time and there could hardly be two books more different. Marx judged the English working class to be at about the same level as Engels had described twenty years earlier. Ludlow's and Lloyd Jones's book insisted that the conditions of the working class had improved, and would improve, and that the remedy for a better society was class co-operation and not class warfare.

Ludlow enjoyed writing the book, which had the added pleasure that it took him temporarily back into the co-operative movement, rejoining Hughes and Neale. The book was translated into German, where it came to the notice of Lujo Brentano, a young German Catholic who was in England in 1867 studying co-operative partnerships. After reading the book, he called in Ludlow to talk about co-operatives, and Ludlow suggested to him that the British working man was more interested in trade unions than in partnerships or co-operatives, an important point which Brentano had not appreciated. He thereupon changed his line of research and began to study the trade union movement instead, and wrote a book which was published in 1872 and was one of the first serious European studies of trade unionism. Brentano was deeply respectful of Ludlow and his attitude strikingly resembled that of the young Ludlow towards Maurice.

The Franco-Prussian War of 1870–1 shattered many international friendships. The Christian Socialists began by rejoicing at the downfall of Napoleon III, but they later became afraid that the embryonic French Republic, the hope of democracy, would be killed by the relentless Prussian military juggernaut. One of Ludlow's good friends, a French refugee named Martin Nadaud, went to France to offer his services to Gambetta. What would happen to him and to others like him, if the Prussians over-ran France, the Christian Socialists wondered.

What alarmed them thrilled young Brentano, much to Ludlow's grave dismay. Brentano was suffering from 'a fit of German chauvinism', he complained, and it prevented him from seeing that Bismarck was posing a threat to the rights of individuals and of nations. So 'Old Gruff' ticked Brentano off much as he had ticked Kingsley off over Governor Eyre. The more Ludlow thought about it, the more Francophile he became. How could Brentano approve of the annexation of Alsace and Lorraine, he asked his friend. England must support the new French Republic which was the hope of the working class, and Prussia was revealing herself as a bogeyman.

Ludlow's opinion was not shared by the bulk of Radical and Liberal opinion which favoured neutrality, a policy dictated by Britain's military weakness as much as anything. When the Paris Commune was formed in 1871 Ludlow hesitated to support it, wondering if it would harm the infant Republic and worried in case its establishment whilst foreign troops were still on French soil did not smack of treason. On that point he parted company with his Positivist friends who were strongly in favour of the Commune. But when the Commune was defeated by the regular French army and appalling vengeance exacted upon the Communards, Ludlow's sympathies swung back. 'I am haunted by the butcheries carried on in Paris in the name of Order, Religion and Property,' he wrote in an article, and he worked with Eugène Oswald in collecting signatures for a petition to Thiers, President of France, to commute the sentence of deportation on Elisée Réclus, geographer and co-operator, to the lesser one of exile.

Another Christian Socialist who was taking a new path was Thomas Hughes, questioning his suitability as an M.P. after two years in the House of Commons. It was one of his weaknesses that he always spread himself too thinly and supported too many causes at once. Nor could he bring himself to join political alliances. John Leech drew a cartoon of Hughes as a prize-fighter flexing his muscles before going into the ring, and this amused Ludlow. It hit off his friend very neatly, he thought: did Hughes have enough muscle for the Parliamentary arena? More to the point, if Hughes lacked the muscle now, was he willing to work at it and acquire the strength to be a power in the Commons?

The answer seemed to be 'no'. Hughes was almost fifty, with a large family which claimed his time and income. He was an experienced part-time author and enjoyed a busy social life which was surprisingly aristocratic and completely separate from his trade union and co-operative activities. His stint in the Commons had reinforced his private conviction that trade union and co-operative activity would help the working class a good deal more than Parliamentary debates and fresh laws. As the new decade opened, Hughes began to look across the Atlantic to American affairs, especially after his 'impossible dream', a trip to the United States, had unexpectedly materialised in the form of an invitation from his hero, James Russell Lowell. 'Come early and come often, as they say to the voters in New York,' wrote Lowell lightheartedly, and Hughes, in company with a young barrister called Rawlins who taught at the Working Men's College, sailed during the 1870 Parliamentary summer recess for Canada, en route for Boston, to stay with Lowell, and a lecture tour of the States afterwards.

Hughes had an infinite capacity for enjoying himself, and he made the most of his holiday from the time he set foot on board ship. He surveyed his middle-class fellow passengers and decided he preferred the company of the immigrants travelling steerage. When he arrived in Canada he was rather embarrassed to find that his fame had preceded him and he was lionized as a celebrity. On the train to Boston, and Lowell's house, he began to have misgivings, like a nervous schoolboy outside the headmaster's study. Lowell had been a hero for many years—would the reality be an anti-climax? To make matters worse, when they reached Lowell's home they found they were not expected so soon because Hughes's last letter had been delayed in the post!

Happily that discomfiture lasted only a moment as Lowell appeared, welcomed them warmly and sat down with them on the verandah to sip sherry and munch biscuits. They all talked far into the night and admired Lowell's famous garden elms, gleaming in the moonlight. Hughes described it rather naïvely in a letter to his wife saying that he went to bed that night as happy 'as the Queen of Sheba when she realized that Solomon was far better and bigger than all the accounts she had heard of him in her own land'.

In the following days, Lowell introduced Hughes to the most interesting people in Boston and in Cambridge, and when Hughes had to start on his lecture tour, he declared that if ever he had to leave England he would come to live in a quiet, book-

lined house in Boston bordering the Common. Lowell was sorry
to see his friend depart—'it was saying goodbye to sunshine,' he
said.

In New York Hughes was able to see John Roebuck, whom
he had last met at the Working Men's College, and he also
visited Cooper Union, which he called a fine American equivalent to the Working Men's College. His American hosts had no
trouble in liking Hughes, who had the gift of easy sociability,
and nothing was too good for the author of *Tom Brown's
Schooldays*. He was even given free railway passes so that he
could afford a journey through the West. At the end of his tour
he returned to Boston, where he was booked for a final lecture.
Lowell was rather nervous in case Hughes was not a good
enough speaker for the sophisticated Bostonians, and he took the
precaution of packing the hall with reliable Harvard students
who were instructed to cheer Hughes on if the audience
appeared unresponsive. That turned out to be quite unnecessary.
Hughes's sincerity shone through everything he said, and won
his listeners, which was something of an achievement, given
that relations between Britain and the United States were
decidedly cool at that time because of the *Alabama* dispute.
When Hughes prophesied that if ever Britain needed to borrow
money he believed that America would guarantee the debt,
there was loud and sustained applause.

That American visit was an important event in Hughes's life.
He made many good friends there and returned home to take on
the task of unofficial ambassador and public relations man,
explaining America to the British. In December 1870 he formed
an Anglo-American Association, and he took great interest in
the Anglo-American *Alabama* arbitration proceedings of 1871,
recommending to the Americans his friend Lord Ripon (as Lord
Goderich had now become),[1] whom Hughes described as a
liberal-minded peer whom the Americans could safely trust.

Hughes believed that Canada and America offered admirable
opportunities for a free life and he approved of young people
leaving overcrowded England. It was all right for middle-aged
folk to stay in their own country, but if their children wished to
emigrate, they should be encouraged to do so. His oldest son,
Jim, emigrated to Canada, and then went to America, before
deciding in the end to return to England, but Hughes's

youngest son emigrated to America, and his elderly mother spent the last years of her life there, in the pioneer settlement of Rugby which her son was instrumental in setting up. The direct descendants of the archetypal Englishman, Tom Hughes, are American.

This American interest brought far more satisfaction to Hughes than his evenings in the House of Commons, or his work for the unions. He was disappointed that the new trade unions seemed to limit their aims to getting more money for members, instead of combining the two ideals of co-operation and more pay. Was he witnessing the triumph of Comtism over Christianity for the hearts and minds of the British labour movement, as Ludlow had foreseen? He told Ripon that he was shocked that trade unionists were not even ashamed of being selfish. It was the disillusioned cry of Squire Brown's little boy who expected everybody, no matter what their economic background, to have instinctively at heart the good Dr Arnold's moral principles.

Hughes was an official trade-union arbitrator and believed that he had always obtained good agreements for the unions. So why were they not satisfied? In 1871, following one of a series of complaints from the unions, he was stung to reply to them that in the two years of his arbitration work he had got their wages increased by fifteen per cent. 'You come here like spoiled children, and won't listen to me because I have only given you an advance of five per cent when you asked for ten per cent.'

Certainly Hughes was always a 'doer', as he called himself, and there was plenty of evidence to show that he was a beginner. Was he also a finisher? Just as he was becoming deeply involved in American issues, and less involved in his British trade-union work, a new debate arose to claim his time and his loyalty. It concerned his much-loved Anglican Church, now the target for considerable abuse following the Education Act of 1870, introduced by Hughes's friend the Quaker W. E. Forster, in Gladstone's ministry. That Act supported Church of England influence in elementary schools, thus infuriating Nonconformists and secularists alike. Those unexpected groups joined forces and determined to carry their fight against the Established Church to Parliament if necessary.

To forestall the worst of such attacks a number of Anglicans, including Llewelyn Davies and Tom Hughes, had formed the Church Reform Union in 1870. It was not a purely Christian Socialist initiative, but covered a very broad spectrum and included several prominent Tories. The result was that when Hughes stumped the country, campaigning for the new Church reform, he had the exceedingly unpleasant experience of being heckled at public meetings by the very same kind of people whom he had spent most of his life trying to help. If that were not enough, he found that he had also become the target of abuse from a new pressure group made up of shopkeeping interests, which identified Hughes as a prime enemy because of his years of association with the co-operative movement.

No wonder that he often felt those days as if he could do nothing right. Nobody was grateful to him any more. Nobody even listened to him any more. What had happened to the ideals of the 1850s? he lamented. Where were the giants to encourage and inspire ordinary men and women? And who was there who would, or who could, ever take the place of Frederick Denison Maurice?

That last sorrowful remark was echoed, silently or aloud, in many hearts, for Maurice died in 1872 at Easter, the season of death in the Maurice family.[2] Most of his friends and acquaintances were taken by surprise by his death, although close observers could have noticed him growing gradually weaker, like a fading sunset, in the past year or two. Perhaps his admirers could not bear to think that even he was subject to the laws of mortality.

If his friends had not been aware that his life was slowly ebbing away, Maurice himself had been, and he spent a good deal of time in his last months remembering the past with his son, Frederick, who would become his biographer. Looking back, it seemed to Maurice that he had always been far too quick to defend his views in public debate, a habit which had provoked unreasonable hostility to him personally and, what was worse, to the ideas he believed in. Had those causes and ideas been harmed by his conduct? Would it have been better if he had not been so combative, or if, having once become notorious, he had refused to be associated with the causes he loved?

'I have laid a great many addled eggs in my time,' he told his son sadly:

but I think I see a connection through the whole of my life that I have only lately begun to realise: the desire for Unity and the search after Unity both in the nation and the Church has haunted me all my days.

He remained true to this yearning for unity, to his hatred of schism, and to his mistrust of regulations, what he called his 'systemphobia'.

When he went in the spring of 1871 to speak at the Working Men's College he knew, as his hearers did not, that he would probably never speak there again. Under Hughes and Brewer the College was doing fine work in its own way, but the religious education which meant everything to Maurice was still failing to appeal to the students. It was significant that a new boys' school being set up as an adjunct to the College had no religious instruction class. Maurice noted that with regret, but kept his feelings private, for he believed it was his fault for not having been more successful as a teacher of religious studies, and it would not be right to reproach other teachers or the students for what, at bottom, was his responsibility.

Llewelyn Davies had sent him details of the Church Reform Union when it was formed, begging him to join, but Maurice refused. 'I fear that I am becoming less and less fit for associations,' he said.

He did not find it so easy to refuse requests for additional preaching, although he knew he was not really strong enough for more work. Take the Cambridge Preachership at Whitehall. In 1871 the Bishop of London asked him to take on the preachership for the year and Maurice at first refused on the grounds of ill-health. The Bishop persisted and at last said simply: 'Many will come to hear you who will not go to hear anyone else.' That was incontrovertible and Maurice felt he had no moral right to refuse, even if it used up the last ounces of his strength.

At least, he told himself, he could reserve Christmas for the family. He loved the company of children and young people and to his great happiness he had recently become a grandfather. It was his last Christmas.

During the cold months of the new year he grew frailer and frailer and an intense spirituality infused his face, so that a man who had always been handsome now possessed an other-worldly beauty. At the beginning of March 1872 he was so ill that his wife sent for his London doctor and told the family. When weeks slipped by without any improvement in his condition, Maurice decided he ought to resign his living of St Edwards and he dictated a letter to that effect. His wife gave him the letter and he just managed to find the strength to sign his name. That was on the Saturday following Good Friday.

He still did not realize how ill he was, and whispered to his wife that if he got better he would take up hospital work again, his illness having given him fresh insights into the needs of the sick. Then he became deeply depressed, a return to the morbid self-reproaches which had afflicted him when he was younger. He had wasted his life, he kept saying, and the doctor and Georgina Maurice tried to comfort him, knowing, as he did not, that he was dying.

On Easter Sunday he asked if his sons had been sent for. Georgina Maurice hesitated, not wishing to distress him further. Maurice guessed what her hesitation meant. 'I am not such a coward that I cannot bear the truth,' he gasped. 'I am not going to *Death*, I am going into *Life*!' She told him she had telegraphed the boys to come home. Then Maurice looked at the doctor. 'I know you think I am very ill—is it days or is it hours?' he asked. 'Not *days*, dear Mr Maurice,' murmured the doctor and, when Maurice understood, he asked for the communion to be administered as quickly as possible.

Another thought struck him. They had engaged a barber to come in on Monday to shave him, and now it looked as if he would be breaking that appointment. The least he could do was to apologize to the man. 'You *will* explain to the barber why I can't see him,' he begged his wife.

It was his last intelligible request. He spoke again, but indistinctly, then gathered all his strength, blessed his family in clear tones and in an instant he was dead.

Widening Circles

1874, Disraeli Prime Minister; 1875, Public Health Act; Purchase of Suez Canal shares; 1879, Afghan War, Zulu War, Irish Home Rule Party; 1883, Fabian Society; 1884, Third Reform Act, Social Democratic Federation, Russian encroachment in Afghanistan.

Dean Stanley offered to have Maurice buried in Westminster Abbey, but the family knew that Maurice would not have wanted such ostentation and arranged for him to be buried in the family vault in Highgate Cemetery with his mother, father and sisters. Although the funeral was kept very quiet, the lanes round the cemetery were thronged with people climbing the hill to pay their last respects to a unique individual, eloquent testimony to the power Maurice exerted over so many different characters. The Christian Socialists were there in force and Kingsley and Ludlow hurried to shake hands, burying their old division in their common loss. Working-class men whom they had known twenty years before and not seen since came up to speak to them. Everybody shared in the deep emotion evoked by the simple ceremony.

Once the man of controversy was safely gone, a small section of the population suddenly burst into eulogies. Nothing like it had been seen since the old Duke died, remarked some of Maurice's friends, and the remarkable intensity of feeling among those who had known him was in great contrast to the utter ignorance about him shown by the majority of the population. Someone offered a portrait of Maurice to the Royal Academy, only to find that nobody on the Council of that body had ever heard of him.

Now that the Master was not available to listen patiently to problems and to suggest solutions, the Mauricians had to make their own decisions. At a Working Men's College council meeting in May Ludlow called for a new constitution which would allow the older students to share in the general running of the College, except for the educational direction. Such a constitution would be a pioneer approach to adult education. Debates, researches and recommendations over Ludlow's demand occupied most of the following year with Ludlow and Furnivall as allies on one side, and Litchfield and Tansley arrayed on the other. It was a tense battle, won by Litchfield.

As a result, the College liquidated itself and in November 1874 the new College was incorporated under the Companies Act of 1862, its expressed aims being unchanged, to bring a liberal education to the working classes, fees and hours to be such that artisans could attend the classes.

The College was divided into Corporation and Council, and although students were invited to sit on the Council, authority remained almost totally vested in the teachers and Founders, an outcome which led to the resignation of some of the more democratically-minded old-timers, including Brewer, Cave Thomas (who was then in charge of the art department), Henry Rawlins and Eugene Oswald. Litchfield took these resignations in his stride and pressed for the appointment of a new Principal and Vice-Principal. John Martineau suggested Dean Stanley as Principal and Professor Flower of the Royal College of Surgeons as Vice-Principal.

Furnivall decided that the situation demanded a speedy resolution and he took it upon himself to approach Stanley independently, instead of following College protocol and waiting for Council to consider the candidature. It was an action which annoyed Litchfield deeply. At the best of times he and Furnivall were like oil and water, and the College was too small an institution to hold the two of them in comfort. The storm aroused by Furnivall's initiative led to a flare-up between the two men and Furnivall left the College, and turned to his literary endeavours, returning only after Litchfield had left. The Council compromised by making the offices of Principal and Vice-Principal tenable for a year only at a time, renewable by the Council, and Ludlow begged Hughes to stand as Principal, if only to unite the College. He did not have to spell it out to Hughes that they should both try to see that Litchfield was not left a completely free hand in the College.

Hughes held back, saying that he was not a big enough man to replace Maurice, and in any case he had no spare time. In the end his good nature proved stronger than his doubts, and he took the job on, remaining Principal until he lost all his money in the Rugby, Tennessee venture and had through financial necessity to become a circuit judge in Chester. Hughes was not really happy as Principal and was frequently in a minority of one over various questions, one particular issue being the admission of women. He was not to know that it would take until 1966 for that to happen in the College.

He began to see why Maurice had repeatedly tried to resign and found himself acting in a similar way, but was always talked round finally. He stayed, he told everyone, only for love of his 'old Master' and for the many members, teachers and students who had died meanwhile. Hughes found it some slight consolation that Llewelyn Davies was elected Chairman of the Council.

These College rearrangements allowed Ludlow to make a graceful departure. He had become a professional civil servant, a change which had not been accomplished without difficulty. When John Tidd Pratt, the first Registrar of Friendly Societies, died in 1870 his natural successor was obviously Ludlow, in view of the latter's experience in that field, and Hughes submitted his friend's name to the Home Secretary, in the belief that that Minister appointed the Registrar. As it happened, it was the Chancellor of the Exchequer who had that responsibility and in 1870 the Chancellor was Lord Sherbrooke, the former Robert Lowe, who had no liking at all for Ludlow. He had suffered in the past from harsh criticisms from Ludlow and his Radical friends and now he was determined not to appoint Ludlow.

Nevertheless Ludlow had influential friends who urged his appointment and Sherbrooke could not ignore them, so he fell back on the well-tried governmental formula of appointing a Royal Commission to examine the whole field of Friendly Societies. In the meantime the post of Registrar would remain vacant and he hoped that by the time the Commission had completed its task Ludlow would have found other employment.

Alas for the Chancellor's best-laid plan. The Commission's

chairman, Sir Stafford Northcote, thought highly of Ludlow, who accepted the post of paid secretary to the commission. Recommendations which Northcote and Ludlow agreed upon were later accepted without question by the rest of the Commission, and the Fourth Report of the Commission, published in 1874, was Ludlow's work. The Conservative victory of 1875 had the indirect result of making Northcote Chancellor, and in his new role he instructed Ludlow to draft the Friendly Society Bill which was to incorporate the findings of the Northcote Commission. Ludlow's first draft demanded a unified law covering all working-class voluntary associations, but that was going a little too far for the new government, so only the clauses relating to Friendly Societies were passed. After that, Ludlow was offered the post of Registrar, which he naturally accepted, holding the position until he retired.

As a senior civil servant he was bound to withdraw from active participation in social reform campaigns although he maintained his interest in them, and through his friendship with Brentano he made contact with a German group called the *Katheder Socialister*, or 'Socialists of the Chair'. Like the English Christian Socialists of an earlier generation, those men believed that a welfare State would keep a socialist revolution at bay. Ludlow became the recipient of their respectful admiration and he enjoyed corresponding with them. He certainly approved the Christian bias to the group. Many of these men were Roman Catholics who either left the Church or joined the Old Catholics after the Vatican formally adopted the doctrine of Papal Infallibility.

The new anti-science and anti-socialist trends in the Roman Catholic Church saddened Ludlow. 'For me, the search for infallibility is the hunt after the rainbow, or rather, it is *the* primary sin,' he declared. His new interest in German politics led to his giving Bismarck the kind of attention and dislike he had once reserved for Napoleon III.

Six years later Bismarck dropped his *Kulturkampf* policy, broke with the Liberals and allied himself with the Conservatives, a change of policy which so alarmed several of the Socialists of the Chair that they abandoned all their political initiatives. It would be an over-simplification to say they were frightened into submission, for in spite of being socialists they shared in the feeling, almost universal in Germany, that Bismarck was irreplaceable as a minister, and they left political directives to him.

Whilst Ludlow was being attracted into quieter and calmer circles, the reverse was happening to Tom Hughes. His support of the Church Reform Union had alienated him from many working-class people, especially co-operators, whose trusted spokesman he had once been, and Hughes was distressed by this. The trade-union movement seemed to be suspicious of him, in spite of his support for Joseph Arch, and for the dockers. He felt resentful that nobody in the movement was grateful for his past work and put it down to a growing materialism. Nor did he have any effective power base in the Commons, and he had once or twice hinted for a legal appointment which would allow him to leave Parliament with dignity.

Nothing came of his hints, and in 1875 he offered himself to the Marylebone Liberals as a candidate in the forthcoming election, not realizing that after espousing so many unpopular causes he had become an embarrassment to them. Encouraged by his Christian Socialist friends he insisted upon being considered. Among his loyal supporters was the Rev W. Fremantle, of Marylebone, who was also a friend and helper of Octavia Hill in her low-rent housing schemes for the needy, in addition to being an active member of the Church Reform Union. Then there was Fremantle's socially committed curate, the Rev Samuel Barnett, another of Octavia's gallant band, who had just married Henrietta Rowland, one of Octavia's favourite assistants. Finally there was the indomitable lady herself, no longer an eager young girl but the battle-scarred heroine of the slum dwellers, and by the same token the *bête noir* of most landlords, J.P.s and publicans. The publicans were already angry with the outgoing Liberals because of their recent restrictive Licensing Act and Hughes and his unconventional admirers were the very last people to win votes from that quarter. Octavia Hill's highly organized canvassing for Hughes hindered rather than helped his cause, partly owing to a mistaken belief that she wanted Hughes adopted and returned as part of a complicated plot to get votes for women. In fact, she did not take much interest in women's suffrage, considering that it distracted her followers from the more practical and useful work of housing reform.

Octavia Hill, from a pencil sketch by Edward Clifford 1877. Clifford subsequently went out to work in Father Damien's leper colony in Africa

A less controversial campaigner for Hughes was his friend, Anthony Trollope, but he was no more successful than the rest because the Marylebone Liberals, whilst liking Hughes as a person, did not have confidence that he would win the seat for them. Accordingly they chose two candidates, one of whom was barely distinguishable from the Conservative candidate. Hughes stood as an unofficial Liberal candidate, and the election which was to bring position and security to Ludlow inflicted a humiliating defeat upon Hughes. When the votes were counted the chief Liberal candidate, elected with one of the Tories, polled 8,251 votes, and the second-string Liberal polled 7,882. Hughes could only muster 294 votes.

At least it solved his problem of how to leave the House of Commons, though he could have wished for a more comfortable method.

The new government set up a Royal Commission to review trade-union laws, the legislation of Gladstone's ministry not having gone far enough, and Hughes and Alexander MacDonald, chairman of the Parliamentary Committee of the T.U.C., both sat on it, much to the disapproval of the T.U.C., which thought the commission should have been boycotted. It felt justified when the commission's main report recommended the retention of the existing trade-union laws, including the hated anti-picketing provisions of the Criminal Law Amendment Act, but Disraeli was hoping to win the loyalty of the newly-enfranchised working-class voters and he over-rode the commission. New acts were passed giving the union the right to peaceful picketing, and placing employers and workmen under the same law in cases of breach of contract.

These laws represented an important advance for the unions, and in their jubilation they were generous enough to thank Hughes for all his past efforts on their behalf, to which he replied that everything he had done was by way of helping in a just cause. He was not the kind of man to expect praise or gratitude, and tried to live according to his conscience. He was not at all sure that he understood the new generation of union leaders. What had happened to the moral basis, to the brotherhood, to the co-operation, he asked himself.

Things did not seem much better when he turned to the co-operative movement. Its ideals seemed to have shrunk in inverse proportion to its growth. Hughes began to sound more and more like Maurice as he warned of the danger of 'trusting in a great system'. The 1875 Co-operative Congress, dominated by J. T. W. Mitchell, the powerful secretary of the C.W.S., initiated the practice of inviting T.U.C. delegates to the Congress, which was reciprocated by co-operators being invited to the annual T.U.C. meetings. Once Hughes would have applauded the innovation but now he was cool—he detected hardly a grain of Christianity in either the T.U.C. or the Co-operative Congress. He did not even have the satisfaction of pointing to successful producer co-operatives since those had not survived the economic depression, and one of his biggest disappointments was the failure of the Cobden Mills, made even more painful when William Nuttall, one of Hughes's chief opponents in the co-operative movement, took control of the mills. He immediately made profits by the simple expedient of making and selling inferior goods. Hughes did not know whether to rage or weep. Had they all forgotten those meetings when the Christian Socialists campaigned for better quality goods, and that particular one when Kingsley drafted the resolution that the co-operatives should produce good quality goods and sell them according to a truthful description of the goods?

Unhappily Kingsley was no longer alive to commiserate with him, or to cheer him up with a new fishing expedition. Hughes had not seen much of him over the past few years, and they had had their disagreements, but after Kingsley died in January 1875 all Hughes could remember were the good old days when they were all young and enthusiastic.

Kingsley seemed to have grown suddenly old once he passed fifty. Everyone remarked upon it when they saw him at Maurice's funeral. The Prophet's death was a deep loss to Kingsley, who had always had a special relationship with Maurice. Ludlow believed that Maurice had a particular warmth for Kingsley, as a father for a favourite son, filling the void left for Maurice by Sterling's death. Nothing could fill for Kingsley the void left by Maurice's passing. In all his doubts and perplexities, and they had been many, Kingsley had always had Maurice to turn to. Now he had only his own resources, and like Maurice, he began to use the Bible as a guide and comforter. He wrote and spoke about Maurice frequently, and in March 1873 he had delivered a special sermon on behalf of a girls' home, addressing a large congregation of old friends from Lincoln's Inn and from St Peter's, Vere Street. They included Octavia Hill, deeply moved by Kingsley's solemn manner and the memories he aroused. The Hill and Maurice families, always close, were now especially linked by the marriage of Octavia's sister, Miranda, to Maurice's son, Edmund.

Kingsley was far from being the wild young fighter of 1848 and 1849 and had become a reflective man, much given to remembrance of things past. This was reflected in his poetry, his conversation, and in his advice to students to read the old, tried authors. He liked his months each year at Chester, where he indulged his love of teaching science and natural history. He was practically idolized there, unquestionably the result of his extra-cathedral duties, for his performance in the pulpit was not very impressive. Henry James, visiting Chester in 1873, paid a special visit to the cathedral to hear Kingsley but was disappointed to find him a 'weak sister'.

It came as a surprise to the Kingsley family when Mr Gladstone in 1873 offered the Rector a canonry at Westminster Abbey, a greater honour than Chester and one which he could hardly refuse. 'I had to take it for my children's sake,' he wrote to a friend in Chester, breaking the news. 'Had I been a bachelor I would never have left Chester.' Appropriate congratulations were sent to Eversley, but the townsfolk were unhappy to lose him. 'All Chester mourns,' wrote one dramatically. Mrs Kingsley, old and frail, was proud that she had lived long enough to see her adored son gain the distinction he deserved.

The honour had come only just in time for he was, said his wife, like a candle spluttering in its socket, and he looked a generation older than Hughes or Ludlow. Kingsley worried more about his wife's health than his own, however, because she had developed a dangerous heart condition. She was five years his senior and Kingsley feared she would die before him, a heartbreaking prospect. He comforted himself with his peculiar belief that happily married couples could be reunited in heaven and continue to enjoy the physical delights of sex. Fanny Kingsley was too weak to accompany her husband during his first tour of duty at Westminster and his capable daughter Rose accompanied him. His name attracted large crowds and he often preached twice on a

Sunday, working himself up into a state of nervous excitement. When his spell of work was ended his doctor insisted that he rested, preferably by taking a long sea voyage.

It was a tempting idea but, for all his fame, the Rector did not have the money to afford a real holiday and so a lecture tour of the United States was arranged, and his convalescence was limited to the sea crossing! He even had to borrow the fare from an old friend, a debt of honour which he repaid meticulously from the proceeds of his first lectures. Like Hughes, Kingsley responded at once to the warmth and hospitality of the American people and his lectures were well attended, although the audiences seemed rather surprised by his mannerisms. They tended to agree with Henry James about his abilities as a lecturer. His accent was too English, they said, and he read his lectures instead of speaking without notes. He was shy to the point of absurdity, they complained:

> . . . he shrinks, covered with confusion, blushes in his arm-chair, and when the time comes, rolls himself off his cushion, seizes his manuscripts as a sheet anchor, fumbles off his last kid glove, straightens himself up, and launches out with a voice that sounds like the wail of miserable sinners in his own Abbey service.

wrote the reporter of the *New York Daily Tribune* of February 1874. In spite of that doleful picture, the people queued to buy tickets for his meetings, and he cut a more dashing figure at informal gatherings.

As a health-building exercise, however, the American tour was an unmitigated disaster and when Kingsley returned to England in the summer he was more of a wreck than ever and preoccupied with thoughts of death. The hot, dry weather brought its customary fever to Eversley and the Rector dragged himself round the parish, lecturing the cottagers about the need for clean water, sitting up by sick-beds and badgering the healthy villagers into obeying the elementary laws of hygiene.

Before he knew it, autumn had returned and with it the date for him to move to Westminster. This time his wife went with him, in spite of having suffered another heart attack. His Abbey congregations were larger than ever and Kingsley rose like an actor to his audiences, giving of his very best, which meant that he returned to his cathedral house drained of strength. All his sermons seemed to dwell upon death and an afterlife, and he continually stressed God's goodness and mercy to sinners as if he himself needed personal reassurance. He had a number of additional duties because Dean Stanley was detained in Paris, but when these had been taken care of he was free to take the family home to Eversley for Christmas. He hoped his wife could withstand the journey, for she had frightened him by succumbing to another attack in London. He was not much stronger than she, and both of them collapsed when they reached Eversley.

Messages of goodwill arrived at the rectory as the public became aware that both the Kingsleys were seriously ill. It was assumed, quite naturally, that Kingsley would recover, but that his wife would die. The Queen wrote, also the Prince of Wales, and the good people of Chester, and the neighbours called with anxious inquiries. The Queen even sent her royal physician to assist the local doctor, as it became clear that it was Kingsley who was going to die first. His widow survived him, although a semi-invalid, by sixteen years.

First Maurice dying in 1872, and then Kingsley in 1875, revived interest in the old Christian Socialist movement and its aims, and their books were reprinted and read by a younger generation, interested in seeing for themselves what relevance there might be in the 1870s. Kingsley's funeral at Eversley created a great stir and resembled Maurice's in that it was notable for the diversity of people who made their appearance. Local gypsies, to whom Kingsley had always been very friendly, stood near the representative of the Prince of Wales. Villagers and country labourers walked soberly by the side of academics. Anglican and Nonconformist ministers walked with colonial governors. There were soldiers from Sandhurst, and huntsmen in pink whose horses and hounds waited restlessly outside the churchyard. There were, of course, the personal friends and relatives.

Dean Stanley had wired to say Kingsley could be buried in the Abbey if the family desired, but Fanny Kingsley's answer had been the same as Georgina Maurice's, and the Rector was buried in Eversley churchyard, where in due course his wife would lie beside him. Stanley helped conduct the funeral and commissioned

Thomas Woolner, a leading sculptor and Pre-Raphaelite, who was associated with the Working Men's College, to make a marble bust of Kingsley. This was later placed near the memorial to Maurice in Westminster Abbey, and thus Stanley ensured that his two friends were suitably commemorated.

At the Co-operative Congress in London held not long afterwards, Tom Hughes paid tribute to 'Parson Lot' and the delegates all stood for a moment's silence.

Who would be next to go? pondered Hughes gloomily, thinking how the ranks of his friends were sadly depleted. How long would Neale last, sixty-five years old, and working full-time as General Secretary of the Central Board of the Co-operative movement, a post which carried a small salary, both merited and needed by the impecunious Neale. Hughes had originally thought that Neale was too old for that job, but events had proved otherwise, and it was obvious that Neale had the stamina, ability and industry of two or three younger men rolled into one.

A good deal of Hughes's depression proceeded from troubles in his family circle. His admired brother, George, had died the same year as Maurice, and Tom never stopped missing him. His brother, Hastings, always an unlucky business man, became bankrupt. Hughes's small investments dropped in value. Fanny Hughes became ill, and even Tom's splendid health was shaken.

Somehow he had to make some more money, and with a guilty sigh he decided he would have to give up voluntary work, at least for a while, and write some saleable books. He composed a memorial account of Maurice in a preface to a reprint of Maurice's, *Friendship of Books*, and wrote a similar preface for Kingsley in a new edition of *Alton Locke*. His tributes were loyal, affectionate and admiring. Maurice, he declared, had done more than any of his contemporaries to show the truth plainly and to destroy groundless fears. Kingsley had always been a true fighter in spite of certain differences with his friends after 1854. True in outline, the accounts contained a few slapdash errors of detail, but that was Hughes's style.

He followed those studies with an assignment very close to his heart, a biography of his brother George. That was an ill-judged project, for nobody except Hughes thought his brother worth memorializing, and his sister, Mrs Jeannie Nassau Senior, who was as staunch and active a Christian Socialist as any of them but considerably less naïve than Hughes, tried to talk him out of it. He persisted with his book, and wrote a kindly, forgiving and incurably optimistic portrait of George Hughes which said more about the author than about the subject.

In 1877 the Hughes family suffered another blow when Jeannie Nassau Senior died, a shock to many outside her personal circle, for she was a valued worker in the voluntary services. She was Octavia Hill's 'dear, dear Janey', a tower of strength and a generous friend in the latter's social work. For Tom Hughes she was not only a dearly loved sister but a colleague who understood what he was trying to do to set right the wrongs of the world. The Maurice family had known and loved her for years, and her death seemed the more unfair because she was only forty-nine and had seemed so fit and well. Indeed, she was about to start on a new career, having been appointed the first woman inspector of work-houses and pauper schools.

In years gone by Hughes would have sought help from Maurice to help him get over his grief, but now he had to rely upon his own simple, gentlemanly Christian faith, like Chaucer's poor knight. His faith did not let him down and he gave a series of lectures on practical religion at the Working Men's College, and later collected them into a book called the *Manliness of Christ*, rightly subtitled 'A layman's faith'. It was a dignified reply to the malicious jokes about the 'muscular Christians', and sold well in Britain, and was published in the States, with good reports, so Lowell wrote to Hughes.

Hughes returned to his work in the co-operative movement, maintaining a sturdy opposition to the Co-operative Wholesale Society by insisting on the need for producer associations as well as the consumer stores, and he joined Neale and Lloyd Jones in a new co-operative propaganda body called the Guild of Co-operation. The Guild linked men of his generation with men of the next like J. J. Dent and the Rev Stewart Headlam. Ludlow was asked to join, but he merely sent ten guineas to become a life member.

Hughes and Neale collaborated to compile a *Manual of Co-operators*, following a directive from the Co-operative Congress, and one of the main themes in the manual, understandably, was that producer co-operatives and a great labour bank would be as important to the sound progress of the co-operative movement as consumer stores. It was the old Christian Socialist credo and annoyed Holyoake intensely. He had certainly worked as long and as hard in the movement as any of them and he complained that Hughes and Neale were trying to introduce religion into what should be kept as a secular movement. At the 1881 Congress, Holyoake tried to stop publication of the *Manual*, but Lloyd Jones rallied a body of support in the hall and the *Manual* was published just as it had been written. Nevertheless the entire episode hurt Hughes deeply.

Neale took a more robust view of the affair than his friend did. Neale's idealism and religion had always been more practical than Hughes's, and he was pleased with the success of the Guild of Co-operation, especially as his son, Henry, was taking an active part in it and proving, to his father's satisfaction at least, that one member of the Neale family did not hold it against him that so much family money had gone down the co-operative drain. Stewart Headlam was proving a fine recruit, receptive to the outlook of the old-time Christian Socialists and full of energy. He went on to be a founder member of the Christian Socialist Guild of St Matthew, and also a member of the Fabian Society.

Neale found it rather more difficult to be optimistic when he reviewed the history of the short-lived Mississippi Valley Trading Company, which had absorbed some of his time and money. He had founded it in 1875 to serve as a medium of exchange of goods between Americans and Britons, a trading venture which resembled the Central Agency in Charlotte Street but was on a more ambitious, transcontinental scale. It had started when Neale made contact with a group of American farmers called the American Patrons of Husbandry, commonly known as the Farmers' Grange. The idea behind Neale's company was that the Grangers would supply their staple goods, mostly farm produce and cotton, and the British would supply manufactured goods. As the Mississippi Company flourished, it would help strengthen the infant American co-operative movement in general, and would also encourage the establishment of new producer co-operatives in Britain. Neale had at last come round to Ludlow's way of thinking about the moral basis of producer co-operatives and his mature vision was of a land covered with co-operatives which would outnumber the non-idealistic consumer stores.

Soon after the formation of the Mississippi Company, Neale

went out to see how it was faring and was disillusioned by what he found. The company was weak, its farmer members were widely scattered and those who grew cotton were not strong enough to break the monopoly of the big cotton merchants in New Orleans. What had seemed a clear, bright vision in England was faint and blurred across the Atlantic. Still, there was no lack of goodwill among the Grangers, who were anxious to carry on and begged Neale to help them. He could not ignore their pleas. Twenty years earlier he would have gladly sunk his money into the company but now his money had gone, and all he could really do was to draw up a model plan of co-operation, based on his experience of English co-operatives, and wish them well.

He returned to England, with the company on his conscience and, being Neale, he could not endure to let the company die, so he found enough money to keep it on its feet for another year or two. After that the inevitable happened and the company stopped trading. It had been, reflected Neale, just another failure.

In that, however, he was mistaken, for although from an English angle it might have been called a failure, it was another story in the American perspective. The Mississippi Valley Trading Company has an honourable, if minor, place in the history of the American co-operative movement. It allowed the Farmers' Grange to continue their fight for co-operative ideals, which were preserved long enough to become incorporated in the aims of early American labour unions. Without the Mississippi Company and without Neale, the history of American agricultural co-operatives might have been different, since the practical details about running co-operatives, following the guidelines indicated by Neale, were adopted by American farmers who did not have much money, and the co-operative movement was strengthened in consequence.

The Mississippi Company represented Neale's last gallant fling for his ideals. The settlement of Rugby, Tennessee, represented Tom Hughes's last adventure, a challenge made on behalf of all the anonymous Tom Browns in the country. His idea was nothing less than to organize, and substantially to finance, a new model agricultural community in the United States where decent young men from the new English public schools could work with their hands and brains, but mostly with their hands. In time the settlement would be self-supporting, of course, but profit was not to predominate. It would have all the virtues of the dear old English village, promised Hughes, thinking nostalgically of his boyhood in Uffington. The Tom Browns of England would find a place and an identity as young Christian men in America, reclaiming and farming the land, and enjoying their recreations on the playing fields of their township or in the unspoiled countryside around it.

The project represented most of Hughes's fantasies and long-ings, the dreams he had learned from Kingsley and Carlyle and the spark ignited by Citizen Cabet. The more he became involved in the plan, the easier it was to convince himself that all would be well. He lectured on the theme in England and in the United States and wrote numerous articles. By a strange coincidence, a group of Boston bankers had been considering a similar kind of settlement and had purchased land in 1878 on the Cumberland Plateau in Eastern Tennessee. The onset of a business depression made them drop the idea. Hughes came to know of it and despatched a certain John Boyle to make a survey. Boyle was a remarkably bad choice, being a smug, aristocratic Englishman who knew nothing whatever of American conditions and dis-dained to ask local farmers about the site. He was an easy prey for Cyrus Clarke, the former agent for the Boston company, who suddenly saw an opportunity to make money. The two groups, Hughes's company and Clarke's American one, amalgamated under the title of The Board of Aid to Land Ownership, Hughes being president. The main impetus and control came from England, where £150,000 was raised to buy 7,000 acres of land. In 1879 the Board was incorporated under the laws of Tennessee and Clarke was confirmed as its purchasing agent.

Hughes refused to see any problem in managing such an enter-prise from across an ocean and refused to listen to Hastings, who told him that Clarke was probably swindling the company by taking an excessive commission on his purchases. Hughes was shocked to find that his brother could accuse a man without any proof, and certainly during the early months of the company's operation Clarke appeared to conduct himself honourably. After-wards he behaved exactly as Hastings had predicted and Hughes had to admit that he had been deceived.

In the early months, however, Hughes refused to see anything but the sunny side of the settlement, and it was one of the happiest days of his life when the little township, which he had named Rugby (tradition said it was on the spur of the moment whilst watching a tennis match there), was ceremonially declared open on 5 October 1880. Hughes embarked upon another extensive lecture tour of the States, praising Rugby to the heavens, and returned to England to repeat the process. He wrote a book, *Rugby, Tennessee*, published by Macmillans, and gave the profits to the settlement. The venture became well known, and although a few journalists expressed doubts as to its eventual success, the majority, especially if they had not actually visited Rugby, took the cheerful Hughes line.

The settlers built a church, and a library, and a tourist hotel. A number of visitors stayed there for a day or two, interested in the pioneer experiment. In May 1881 Rugby's most famous immigrant arrived. Tom Hughes's elderly mother resolved to spend her last years in the colony. The settlers built her a house called Uffington, and her presence among them was seen as a symbol of faith and a herald of good fortune.

It was, in fact, the high point of Rugby's fortunes, and followed by a succession of difficulties, some of them of the settlers' own making, like laziness and inexperience, and others being outside their control, like bad weather, poor soil and even a typhoid epidemic. Their weekly magazine, the *Rugbeian*, took a sour view and commented that the Cumberland mountains had brought forth 'a very ridiculous mouse'. Hughes had to swallow the bitter pill that the public school Tom Browns, 1880 vintage, were simply not pioneer material. They liked living at Rugby, but were inclined to spend more time at games and sports than at the hard work of farming bad land.

It was even more painful when Hughes counted his money losses, something over £7,000, which in terms of the Hughes finances was certainly equivalent to the sums Neale lost in cooperatives. Fanny Hughes, a wonderfully devoted wife, complained hardly at all. Hughes was luckier than Neale in that respect! The Hugheses rented their fashionable London house and moved to smaller and cheaper quarters.

Although the sensible thing would have been for Hughes to break his ties with the Rugby company as quickly as possible, he could no more do it than Neale could have abandoned the Mississippi Valley Trading Company at the most prudent moment. He decided to give it one last chance and campaigned for more funds for the township, explaining to the contributors that Rugby was just going through a bad patch and that more capital would put it on its feet again. The situation resembled that of the co-operatives thirty years earlier, except that now the sums needed were infinitely larger. Ripon, still Hughes's good friend, donated £1,000.

The injection of fresh money did help the colony, but only for a few years. Each year Hughes went to Rugby, mainly to visit his mother, and when she died in 1887 he did not have the same incentive to go there. He secretly hoped that his son George would decide to settle in Rugby and offered him his own plots of land there, but George, like his uncle Hastings, could not see a future in Rugby and went to Texas to raise cattle.

Hughes was disappointed, but he did not believe in putting pressure on his children. The child who carried on her father's tradition was his golden-haired daughter, Mary, usually called May, who found her destiny among the poor of London's East End.[1]

In 1891 the Rugby settlement collapsed for the second and last time. Anyone but Hughes would have regretted the lost years and the lost money, but he insisted doggedly that the colony had sown good seed and its value would be seen in the future. It was the confident line taken against all odds by the Christian Socialists when the producer co-operatives failed in the 1850s.

Hughes's conviction in his middle age that the sturdy English spirit would be best preserved by emigrating to the United States or to Canada, which offered better opportunities for a fuller life, represented one extreme of the Christian Socialist vision. The opposite extreme, that reform, like charity, begins at home and that the sturdy English spirit would be best preserved by digging for its roots in English literature, was represented by Furnivall. He was at least as tenacious and self-sacrificing as Hughes, but whilst Hughes stood for the team spirit, Furnivall stood for freedom of the individual. He had never bothered with the Maurician respect for moderation or sympathized with the need to understand another person's point of view. He was thoroughly undisciplined and rather enjoyed his reputation as a literary and social reforming maverick.

His marriage had become as unsatisfactory as Neale's, but he was not the kind of man to chain himself dourly to an office desk like Neale and plod away at organizational work. Like the others, Furnivall believed in co-operative effort but his practical application of the co-operative principle was unusual, to say the least, when he carried it out in literary research. Like Ruskin and Neale, Furnivall placed his life's mission unhesitatingly ahead of his marriage, and had so much satisfaction from his work that his wife could not fail to see that their marriage was a very poor second best to her husband.

The Furnivalls remained living together in the eyes of the world until their son was adult, and then a discreet separation was arranged. Some onlookers hinted that he grew more than a little fond of one of his lady assistants in the literary societies, but she died and Furnivall plunged into even more work.

There was not much time for grief or wishful thinking in his busy life. His evenings at the Working Men's College were matched by hours at conveyancing work and by further hours grinding away copying manuscripts in the Reading Room of the British Museum, and by weekends on his beloved Thames. His great weakness, which in some respects was also his great strength, was that he was so sure that he was doing valuable work in his way, that he refused to pay any attention to criticism, even constructive criticism. His lack of tact was monumental but never deliberate.[2] He would pass a remark about a colleague which that individual might find deeply wounding, and Furnivall would shake his head in bewilderment. His comment had been well meant, even jovial—what was the fuss about?—life was something of a joke, surely?

In 1873 Furnivall applied for the secretaryship of the Royal Academy. The interesting fact was not that he failed to obtain the post, but that he applied at all, and in making his application he printed a detailed pamphlet listing his activities and giving a most impressive list of names as referees: Tennyson, Kingsley, Hughes, Trench and Alexander Macmillan of the old guard; William Morris, Henry Morley and J. R. Seeley of the new generation; and some very respected foreign scholars, including ten Brink and Prince Louis Buonaparte.

Perhaps it was as well that he did not join the Royal Academy staff since in that same year, 1873, he founded the New Shakspere Society, which was an important step in the studies of

English literature. The Society's aim was 'To do honour to Shakspere, to make out the succession of his plays and thereby the growth of his mind and art; to promote the intelligent study of him, and to print Texts illustrating his work and times.' Furnivall persuaded Robert Browning, whom he admired greatly, to be president, and there were sixty-six figure-head vice-presidents, but the donkey work was carried out by Furnivall as director.

It was a serious and scholarly society whose papers and deliberations formed the basis for Shakespearean studies at British and foreign universities. Furnivall had an obsession with the metrical texts of Shakespeare's plays and was known to go to ludicrous lengths to prove his ideas. Opponents quickly discovered that Furnivall was impatience personified and one disgruntled colleague named him 'Furnivallos Furioso'.

Furioso he could certainly be, as evidenced by the squalid literary brawl with Charles Algernon Swinburne over the Shakespeare studies. Young Swinburne had been singled out, with avuncular approval, by Kingsley and Ludlow, not to mention Ruskin, as a poet of distinction and originality but as far as Furnivall was concerned he was simply a young upstart of dubious sexual proclivities who certainly did not know what he was talking about when it came to the Bard. Their mutual scorn and dislike was well rooted by the time it was aired in the press in 1879 and it did neither of them credit. They enjoyed using childish and outrageous language which resembled school magazine vendettas, except that in this case the protagonists were in deadly earnest, to the sorrow of their friends. As the years went by, the quarrel became consolidated with articles and letters from both sides printed and reprinted. Furnivall always referred to Swinburne's friend, Halliwell-Phillipps, as 'Mr Hell-P.' and he thought it a great joke to call the pair of them 'Pigsbrook & Co.'.

Each side appealed to Browning to intercede in these Shakespearean disputes but he remained prudently aloof, embarrassed by the tone of their quarrel, and Furnivall's ruffianly style so upset some of the distinguished vice-presidents that they resigned in protest. Furnivall shrugged. His dealings with Swinburne were personal and private, he said, and if all that Society members could do, in return for all his years of faithful volunteer work for them, was 'censorious caballing', then let them resign and good riddance!

The quarrel had not been confined to London. The most public repercussions occurred in Stratford-on-Avon on the day Furnivall took a party of members of the Sunday League there for a tour of Shakespeare locations and a lecture on the playwright. Halliwell-Phillipps refused to let the party inside New Place because Furnivall was with the members. That did not however stop Furnivall from setting up a Sunday Shakespeare Society, himself as president, in October 1874 and the activities of that society, together with Furnivall's writings, helped towards the Shakespeare tourist industry in Stratford.

In 1881 Furnivall startled the literary world by starting a Browning Society to pay respect to 'the Gladstone of poetry', and to guide the reading public into an understanding of Browning's poems, quite an ambitious undertaking. Rather ingenuously, Furnivall asked Tennyson if he would be president and seemed surprised when the Poet Laureate refused. Eventually Furnivall was nudged into taking the post in 1887 at Browning's suggestion—'indeed you have all along really ''presided'', and any interloper would cut a poor figure in your visionary stead,' wrote Browning. The society published studies of Browning's poems and arranged for dramatic readings of his plays.

Furnivall became well known in academic and literary circles. He had the kindest heart and took infinite trouble helping young students and friends, and his correspondence was always heavy. Berlin University granted him a doctorate, which made him so proud that he had new letterheads printed up. Much later he was given a doctorate from Oxford University and an honorary fellowship of his own college, Trinity Hall, Cambridge. In 1884 his services to literature were publicly recognized by Gladstone's government and he was granted a civil list pension of £150 a year.

The End of the Group

1886, Gladstone's Irish Home Rule Bill,
'Liberal Unionists' leave party; 1887,
Queen's Jubilee; 1888, Miners' Federa-
tion; 1889, Dockers' strike; 1892, Keir
Hardie, M.P.; 1893, Independent Labour
Party; 1897, Diamond Jubilee; 1899,
Second Boer War; 1900, Labour Repre-
sentation Committee; 1901, Taff Vale
decision, death of Queen Victoria; 1902,
Balfour's Education Act; 1904, *Entente
Cordiale* with France; 1906, Liberal elec-
tion victory, Trade Disputes Act; 1909,
Lloyd George's People's Budget; 1910,
Election fought over budget, Irish Home
Rule and power of House of Lords; 1910,
Death of Edward VII.

Ludlow had joined the civil service just before the extensive
reforms in that profession, and he remained there until retiring
in 1891 at the age of seventy. He was the first to arrive in the
office and the last to leave and ate sandwiches at his desk for
lunch. He continued to believe that self-help organizations were
superior to State ones and was suspicious of Bismarck's State
welfare benefits in the new Germany. He insisted that more
Friendly Societies and co-operative units would be the best way
to help the working class, and that those would make any State
system of comprehensive insurance quite unnecessary. Nevertheless, when he noticed that other countries were adopting
State schemes, for example, Austria and Switzerland, he thought
again and his final report as Registrar hinted at a modification of
his views. He was in a key position to ensure that the law helped
the British co-operative movement and with Neale, whom he
now regarded, in affection and respect, as 'the moral pivot' of

the movement, and with Hughes, he hoped to maintain the old Christian Socialist values there.

Neale had been lucky in finding Edward Owen Greening to help him, a young man of the Lloyd Jones type.[1] The pair of them represented the group which advocated producer co-operatives in contrast to Mitchell and Benjamin Jones of the Co-operative Wholesale Society, who represented the group which supported the consumer stores. On paper the constitution of the C.W.S. was democratic, but since the average member was apathetic in practice Mitchell, as secretary, could be as autocratic as he liked. Neale indeed called his system of management 'Caesarism', a description which did nothing to improve personal relations between the two men.

At the 1880 Co-operative Congress held in Newcastle, a resolution had been passed that wherever possible all co-operators should buy goods produced by co-operatives, but the C.W.S., led by Mitchell, disregarded the resolution, which so irritated Neale and Greening that in 1882 they collaborated with several independent producer associations to form a Co-operative Productive Federation, whose function was to act as an agency for its members. Neale could not help recalling his Central Agency in Charlotte Street thirty years earlier. Hughes agreed wholeheartedly with Neale and Greening, and was so incensed by Mitchell's attitude that he wanted to have the C.W.S. expelled altogether from the co-operative movement.

The rift widened between those on the side of the old Christian Socialists and those on the side of Mitchell, and young men who felt attracted by the idealistic background and aims of the producer associations called for a more positive organization than either the Guild of Co-operators, which was not strong in the north of England, or the new Co-operative Production Federation. Accordingly, the Labour Association was founded in 1884 with Neale, Greening, Hughes and Ludlow as leading members. The short name was Greening's idea, its full legal name being much longer, and evocative of the old Christian Socialist fighters—'The Labour Association for the Promotion of Co-operative Production'. Holyoake at first remained outside the Association, afraid that its establishment might divide the co-operators even more, but two years later he overcame his scruples and joined.

The Labour Association, planned as a national body, had to contend with the unremitting rivalry of a similar organisation, the Co-operative Aid Association, which had been formed as an offshoot of the Southern Section of the Central Board of the co-operative movement. The C.A.A. was virtually run by members of the London branch of the C.W.S., and they believed that Neale's ultimate aim was to absorb the C.A.A. into his larger Labour Association. Feelings between the two organizations ran high, to Neale's disappointment, for the older he grew, the more he wanted to see unity in the movement.

The Guild of Co-operators, in which Henry Neale, now a civil servant at the Admiralty, was a leading member, continued in its modest way to encourage new producer associations. Its most important achievement was the formation of the Co-operative Permanent Building Society. Neale's belief that co-operatives were the practical fulfilment of his utopian vision intensified. He noticed the influence of Henry George, author of *Progress and Poverty*, on a generation of young men who were turning to new forms of social experiment, but he continued to believe that co-operation and profit-sharing was the best solution. He had been greatly impressed by an experimental enterprise in Northern France, the iron foundry of M. Godin, where the workers shared in the profits and lived in a workers' village. The firm was very successful and made singularly beautiful heating stoves. The work scheme was called the Familstère, and it took Neale's fancy. He wrote articles and lectures on its merits, and hoped that English Familstères would be set up and ask the Co-operative Permanent Building Society to finance them.

Idealistic middle-class young men of the 1880s had a greater variety of groups or parties available than had the Christian Socialists in the 1850s. Arnold Toynbee, a young neighbour of Ludlow's in Wimbledon, who often dropped in to chat with the veteran of social causes, decided that settlement work in London's East End was the best thing for him. Maurice would certainly have approved. Toynbee had found himself stimulated by listening to Ruskin at Oxford and by sharing in the Slade Professor's 'gospel of work' in the famous road-digging project. England would never have a sound culture while there were slums, said Ruskin, and Toynbee decided to do something about that. Ruskin, indeed, had already contributed to slum clearance by lending Octavia Hill money for her housing units, and although she was meticulous in giving him a five per cent return on his money, he could have obtained ten per cent anywhere else. Other young men, secular and clerical, followed Toynbee's example. The Rev G. J. Adderley, a High Church priest, had friends and relatives in Mayfair but he chose to labour in Bethnal Green at settlement work. He admired Maurice, was friendly with Keir Hardie and called himself a Christian Socialist.

Ruskin's utopian experiment was the Guild of St George, set up to establish and finance small farms where tenants could work honestly and happily, but the farms were never really successful. One of the branches of the Guild was a museum at Sheffield managed by Henry Swan, an ex-student of Ruskin's from the Working Men's College, and stocked mainly from Ruskin's own collection.

In 1882 Hughes was appointed a county court judge, which was very welcome in view of his parlous financial situation. He moved to Chester to be close to his circuit, and his loyal wife uncomplainingly moved into a succession of rented houses before they had one built overlooking the River Dee, which Hughes nostalgically called Uffington House. When it became known that Hughes was curtailing his co-operative activities because of his new appointment, the co-operators got up a subscription as thanks for his past efforts on their behalf. It was very embarrassing for Hughes, who considered people ought to work without expecting thanks, and he said that he would not accept a subscription unless it was clearly understood that nobody was to contribute more than one penny. Even then he had misgivings, and when the sum raised amounted to fifteen hundred pounds he realized that the limit of one penny could not have been kept! He hesitated about taking it, but he had undoubtedly spent that amount on the movement in his lifetime, and he was indeed very hard up. So he accepted it gracefully and it helped to ease him and his wife into their new life at Chester.

Hughes drifted further and further from the Liberals, especially after Gladstone adopted an Irish Home Rule policy in 1886. Even America began to disappoint him because so many Americans favoured Home Rule, and Hughes began to reconsider his former indiscriminate advice to go West. The States was not a land of milk and honey, he warned prospective immigrants, and hard work was necessary. How he wished that precept had been soundly drummed into the young men going to Rugby! He noticed the young men who in the 1850s might have followed Maurice joining the new doctrinaire groups, and grumbled that they seemed to think society could be made perfect merely by passing new laws. They did not realize that the only way, the Maurician way, was to improve men's hearts and minds first.

Ludlow tended to sympathize with Hughes over Irish Home Rule and the Liberal Party, but as a civil servant he had to remain outside politics. He took a keen interest in European socialism and co-operation, and his friend Brentano had become a respected university professor who made sure that Ludlow was well informed. He met a Danish student, Harold Westergaard, who was studying in England and invited him to stay. Westergaard was an agnostic, but he was so impressed by the atmosphere of family prayers at the Ludlow home that he changed his religious views. In 1886 Westergaard became a professor at the University of Copenhagen, and his social researches were used by the government in its social welfare planning. He was the centre of a circle of socially committed Danes who became interested in Ludlow's Christian Socialism through Westergaard. In his turn, Ludlow was pleased to hear of the establishment of Scandinavian co-operatives and wrote an article about them for *Macmillan's*.

He also helped Westergaard start a Danish journal strongly reminiscent of *Politics for the People* which brought together men and women interested in social work. Westergaard gave a number of lectures to Danish working men on Marxism and Christian Socialism, much to Ludlow's approval, for they sounded to him like the start of a Danish working men's college.

He was also interested in Austrian affairs, having made a new friend in 1883 Dr Baernreither, an Austrian M.P. in Britain on a survey of working-class organisations. Born in 1845, Baernreither was the son of a successful industrialist who had encouraged the young man to be interested in art, social conditions and liberal politics. Baernreither had worked for better working conditions in factories in Bohemia, had a job in the Ministry of Justice, was an expert in international trade and gave a course of lectures at a university. In short, he was the kind of polymath to whom Ludlow could relate with ease and the two men became very friendly.

The Austrian's book, *English Associations of Working Men*, was translated into English and published in 1889 with an introduction by Ludlow. One of Baernreither's chief points was that the dire forecasts about England made by Engels in 1844 had not been fulfilled because the early Christian Socialists had helped form a vanguard of working-class aristocracy which demanded and obtained legislation within a liberal society to safeguard working-class bodies and associations. Baernreither approved of that as an alternative to the Marxist recipe of seizing power by force.

Ludlow's interest in European social development could be carried on by correspondence, which suited him at that time because there was a change in the Ludlow family circumstances. Since 1876 the Ludlows had given a home to the three children of Maria Liot, following the death of her husband, and in 1883 Maria Ludlow's brother, a clergyman, died very suddenly, to be followed almost at once by his wife. This left six young children stranded, and since the comfortably-off Forbes family, High Church and High Tory, showed no signs of coming to the rescue of the unfortunate orphans, Ludlow decided to play the Good Samaritan himself and teach his relatives a lesson. He had room to take two of the children into his home at once and would help financially towards the others. The Liot children, although adult, resented their uncle's benevolence, particularly since he told them they were old enough to fend for themselves, but the Forbes children were grateful and all of them grew to look upon the Ludlow home as their own. They supplied the family which Ludlow and his wife were too old to have, and he enjoyed these responsibilities which he took very seriously.

Ludlow was not the only one in the Christian Socialist group to have unexpected changes in his personal life. Two older members of the Neale family had died without heirs, and the historic Bisham Abbey with its two thousand acres of fertile land descended to Neale in 1885. His younger co-operative associates assumed that he would use that windfall as an excuse to retire. After all, he was seventy-five and had worked excessively hard all his life. They were mistaken.

Edward Vansittart Neale

His inheritance made little difference to the 'Grand Old Man', as his admirers called him, borrowing the Gladstonian title. In the week he lived a frugal bachelor existence in Manchester, buying a pennyworth of radishes for tea on the way home, the latter being some cheap lodgings. At the weekend he travelled third class on the train to Marlow, working on his papers, and managed the rather awkward last trip from Marlow to Bisham. In addition to the routine duties of a general secretary, Neale was expected, because of his legal experience and knowledge of languages, to serve as translator and legal consultant as well and to produce translations of international reports practically overnight. He always managed to produce those documents on demand, so a feeling grew that there was nothing unusual in the general secretary's coping with such tasks.

Whenever the subject of retirement was broached Neale would answer that he was thinking about it. He did not want to leave the scene whilst there was apparently a rekindling of co-operative activity on the Continent, especially in France and Italy, and he was continually worried about the struggle with Mitchell and the C.W.S. Members of the Labour Association looked to him for a lead, so did supporters from the Working Men's College and from Toynbee Hall, and Hughes kept hinting that Neale should take a more positive stand against Mitchell. In the summer of 1887 he held a successful garden party at Bisham Abbey for the co-operators, and later that year there were celebrations, resembling the old Association Festivals, at the Hebden Bridge Fustian Manufacturing Society, a profit-sharing co-operative which Neale regarded highly. During the Hebden Bridge celebrations a new steam engine was named and christened, and later bore the proud plaque—'Started by E. V. Neale, Esq., M. A.; July 30th, 1887; named "Thomas Hughes" by the Most Noble the Marquis of Ripon, K. G., October 15th, 1887.'

Ripon was proud to be commemorated with his old friends. He had come a long way since the Hull campaign with Citizen Bezer, as far as India in fact, where he was sent out in 1880 as Viceroy by Gladstone's government, with instructions to reverse Lord Lytton's policy in Afghanistan. His appointment as Viceroy was a controversial one because in 1874, after much solitary deliberation, he had joined the Roman Catholic Church. He had spoken to nobody about his religious anxieties, so the conversion was something of a bombshell. He had to resign as Grand Master of the English Freemasons, and he was the first Roman Catholic to become Viceroy of India.

He had been a singularly liberal-minded Viceroy, taking a pro-Indian stand on matters of civil rights, with the result that he was rapidly as popular with the Indian community as he was resented by the English and European ones. When his term of office ended in November 1884 he was given an unprecedented number of grateful addresses from Indian groups, and considered that was a sufficient vindication of his policies.

In 1886 he was appointed First Lord of the Admiralty, and he was to hold important offices in all future Liberal administrations until 1908, the year before his death. He never lost his interest in the co-operative movement, joining Hughes and Neale in supporting the producer co-operatives, and he served as President of the Guild of Co-operators.

It was ironical that after forty years Neale had come round to Ludlow's position about the moral basis of co-operation, and that he was destined to meet the same fate as Ludlow had in that earlier period. The vast majority of the members of the co-operative movement were quite ready to leave their leaders to make the decisions, and the empire-building C.W.S. grew stronger day by day. Neale refused to take that lying down and became increasingly fervent in his old-fashioned, conservative brand of 'social socialism', as he termed it. He mistrusted the bureaucrats in his beloved co-operative movement and was hurt by the indifference with which members listened to Mitchell and Benjamin Jones belittling the work of the Christian Socialists in the movement's younger days. His own work was enormously appreciated, but that was a personal tribute to an industrious general secretary. It did not extend to approval of the producer co-operatives he had striven so hard to promote.

In March 1890 he slipped in the street after leaving his Manchester office, injuring himself so badly that the doctor made him stay indoors for a fortnight before allowing him to return to Bisham Abbey. The fall was aggravated by a severe hernia condition which he had been suffering from for some time, but had kept secret from his friends and colleagues. He was up and about, hobbling on crutches round the Abbey for his eightieth birthday, and coping with a mountain of work and correspondence just as if he were at the office. He attended the Co-operative Congress in Glasgow, at which he had persuaded his old friend, the Earl of Rosebery, to act as president. But the fall had shaken him and later that year he announced his retirement. He was formally re-appointed for one more year, to give the movement time to find a successor and to plan the next Congress at which he would receive his testimonials.

Although frequently in pain, Neale continued to work as hard as possible, quoting Kingsley's favourite dictum that it was better to wear out than rust out. His last Congress was held at Lincoln in May, when the weather turned unseasonably cold and blustery, so that Neale and Holyoake joked together that they had to keep themselves warm by sharing a bottle of wine. The Congress was a sentimental occasion. Neale was given a gold watch and chain, and a photograph album of leading co-operators and, best of all, a scholarship was funded at Oriel College in his name. Mrs Neale was presented with an oil painting of her husband. All the speeches honouring Neale were warm and sincere, but none of them indicated that his policies would be continued after his departure.

He retired officially in September 1891 but still continued to campaign for producer co-operatives and to act as unpaid legal adviser for the Labour Association and the Guild of Co-operators. He wrote articles supporting the use of peaceful, not violent, means to achieve social change, and he parted company with the Fabians over their faith in democracy, which he considered largely irrelevant. He also disagreed with the Fabian trust in high-minded bureaucrats. Younger members of the co-operative movement, however, turned more and more to Fabian socialism as expounded by Beatrice and Sidney Webb, with its insistence that the only realistic policy in the movement was to support the domination of consumer stores over producers.

Hughes could sympathize with Neale, but he had now retired to the sidelines of the movement, calling himself a 'Bystander'. Greening, younger and more active, was still at Neale's side and assisted him in a new project, the International Alliance, which was intended to include co-operators from Europe, especially the French, in a society which strongly resembled the Christian Socialist Society of Promoters. Neale wrote two new pamphlets, one of them an up-dated version of the *Manual for Co-operators*, bearing Hughes's name with his on the title page, and the other being a final statement of his political beliefs, *Thoughts on Social Problems and their Solution.*

One of Neale's last official acts, and a sad one, was to move at a meeting of the Guild of Co-operators in 1892 that it should break its connection with the Central Board of the Co-operative movement. The breach was inevitable, given the hostility of the C.W.S. towards the Guild, but it was an unhappy proof of the destructive power of factions, as Maurice would have said. Neale had always tried to prevent it, and now, regrettably, it had come about, and he, of all men, had to propose the divisive action. Maurice was much in his thoughts when shortly afterwards he lectured on Robert Owen to a private circle called 'F.D.M.' in memory of the Prophet.

That talk was his last engagement. In September he became so ill that his family took him to London for an operation, but he was not strong enough to withstand surgery and died peacefully a few days later. He had concealed his infirmities so successfully that his friends were startled by his death. The flags flew over the Co-operative buildings in Manchester for five days in tribute and all shades of co-operators gathered at Bisham Church for the funeral. Everyone was eager to praise him, even his old enemies. Hughes and Ludlow wrote commemorative articles and Benjamin Jones said that Neale was as near perfect as one could expect in an imperfect world! Admirers asked the Dean of Westminster to allow a plaque to Neale in the Abbey, but the Dean refused, and they applied with success to the Dean of St Paul's. On 3 March 1894 a marble tablet was unveiled to Neale's memory in the cathedral crypt.

Without Neale to back him up, Greening was no match for Mitchell and Jones, and Hughes, even as a 'Bystander', was so intemperate in his opposition to the C.W.S. that he was a counter-productive force. Holyoake had agreed with Neale on the need for unity but he lacked the skill, or the youthful energy, to achieve it. By the end of the century the idealism which the Christian Socialists had patiently tried to foster and preserve down the years had all but vanished.

Hughes remained in great demand as a writer and lecturer on the co-operative movement and on Christian Socialist personalities, so much so that he often wondered if the public were not in danger of being bored by him. He had become totally disillusioned with politics and declared that political success was meaningless unless it were accompanied by unity, by brotherhood and by belief in God. He passed those strong convictions on to his daughter, May, who in the next century would live in London's East End and champion the downtrodden and the down-and-outs. She would ally herself with all shades of opinion on the left, and would work and live for others there until the blitz of World War II.

In his last years, Tom Hughes came to enjoy his work as a county court judge, and he reserved his hopes for the new breed of socialist parsons who were carrying the work of the old Christian Socialists forward. Indeed it was true that there appeared to be more rebellious, socialist-minded clergymen around in the 1890s than had been the case in the 1850s, and social as well as religious problems were often discussed at church sessions. Clergymen as individuals were more free to join political groups than heretofore, especially if they were willing to risk their clerical careers. In 1894 there were no less than twenty-five clergymen in the Fabian Society, whilst about a hundred had joined Stewart Headlam's Guild of St Matthew, founded in 1877 when he was a parish priest in Bethnal Green.

Headlam ran into the kind of antagonism which Maurice had incurred, and he was suspected of all sorts of dubious opinions because of his socialism and because of his friendships with writers, actors and ballet dancers. His Guild of St Matthew had originated as a simple parish guild started as a means of helping the slum youngsters of Bethnal Green. It outgrew those bounds and by the 1890s, with Headlam as permanent Warden, it could boast more than three hundred and fifty members, lay members outnumbering the clergy by more than two to one. The published aims of the Guild showed clearly its descent from Maurice and from Kingsley. Headlam was a product of Maurice in more ways than one, for he had been educated at Eton, where he was taught by William Johnson Cory, poet and Christian Socialist,[2] and at Cambridge when Maurice was a professor there. He never met Maurice but he was profoundly influenced by the whole Maurician attitude to Church and society.

Headlam's first curacy was in Drury Lane, where he met actors and dancers, and he came in contact with the poor in Bethnal

Green where he went as an ordained priest. He began lectures and classes in the parish as part of his pastoral work, but his theatrical bent so alarmed his clerical superiors that they dismissed him. Nevertheless Headlam continued to live in Bethnal Green and run his Guild from that locality.

The Guild, and Headlam, were often in the news. Headlam offered to go surety for Oscar Wilde when he was arrested, a charitable action which led to several resignations from the Guild, not that those dismayed Headlam. Bernard Shaw was a friend and fellow Fabian who frequently spoke at Guild meetings and it was rumoured that Headlam was the model for Morell in *Candida*, written in 1895. Shaw said that the character also contained traces of Stopford A. Brooke, another Fabian who had been interested in Maurice's ideas, and of Canon Shuttleworth, a great friend of Headlam's,[3] and of Fleming Williams. Headlam did not desert Wilde when the writer was in Reading Gaol and, with a friend, met Wilde upon his release and hid him from the journalists for the few hours necessary before Wilde could catch the boat train for France. Many years later Shaw revealed casually that Headlam's marriage had broken down because Mrs Headlam was a lesbian, and it is possible that Headlam's experience with his wife made him more understanding of Wilde's problems.

The success of the Guild of St Matthew as a social pressure group forced the Church of England to set up a broader rival organization, the Christian Social Union, founded in 1889 by Charles Gore and Henry Scott Holland. Ludlow liked the general ideas behind the C.S.U., of which he heard a good deal because Gore's parents were friends and neighbours in Wimbledon, and from 1891 to 1903 Ludlow served on the London branch committee. Hughes also approved of the C.S.U., although he complained that its organisers should have had the moral courage to call it the Christian Social*ist* Union. Both the Guild and the C.S.U. attracted High Church clergymen who in Maurice's day would not have joined the Christian Socialists, nor indeed have been welcomed there, but in the 1890s it was clear that through their settlement, educational and social work, they were a unifying force in the true Maurician tradition. Significantly the C.S.U. founded a hostel in Hoxton called the Maurice Hostel, and Ludlow, once the arch-Puritan, was now happy to work with a High Churchman like Percy Dearmer.

Ludlow's pension was only one-third of his salary so that he was not very well off, and from time to time he had to sell books and papers from his specialized library. When Hughes died of pneumonia in 1896, Ludlow was the last well-known Christian Socialist engaged in social work. The most famous of them was of course Ruskin, who was not, strictly speaking, one of the group but a law unto himself, and only indirectly connected with them.[4] For the last twenty years he had alternated between periods of health and periods of depression and mental instability, but from his home at Brantwood,[5] overlooking Lake Coniston, he continued to write and correspond with friends, and there were times when the old dazzling charm of conversation and manner returned to remind his companions that Ruskin was a genius. His eightieth birthday was nationally celebrated with addresses and congratulations by leading men in art and literature, and when he died of influenza in January 1900 there was a flood of addresses and memorials. His influence was deep and inspiring in a variety of ways.

Gerald Massey, the people's poet of the 1850s, had moved on to quite different spheres. After a fairly successful career as a general lecturer and writer on social and artistic subjects, he had been drawn almost exclusively into spiritualism and telepathy, and for the last thirty years of his life those subjects had obsessed him. His final thesis was that the ancient Egyptians had been spiritualists and telepaths, and his last literary work, in support of that idea, running to twelve volumes, was published by Fisher Unwin in September 1907, one month before Massey died. He was gratified to have lived to see his *magnum opus* in print—'in despite of many hindrances from straightened circumstances, chronic ailments and the deepening shadows of encroaching age', he wrote. He devalued all his former social work and was convinced that he would attain immortality through his books on spiritualism.

So it was Ludlow who assumed the role of the elder statesman of the Christian Socialists, the prophetic survivor of the battles of the 1850s, and a man still untamed despite his long grey beard. He had never given up his love for France and he was now following the Dreyfus case. He helped Eugène Oswald collect over six hundred signatures in support of Dreyfus, and it was presented to the French authorities in 1899. The *Entente*

Cordiale between France and Britain pleased him greatly, and he remarked that it was a sign that even the Kaiser could be an instrument for good! He read accounts of the Russian revolutionaries and considered the implications of the Russian revolution of 1905, which he disliked because of its class nature. Russia needed a national revolution, he said, and national revolutions did not start with a general strike of the workers. He was sure that another, and more serious, revolution was bound to come in Russia and he felt nervous about the ultimate values which would emerge from it. Russian revolutionaries, he said, showed an amazing mixture of motives and emotions and it might well be that Russia would throw up the 'devil's socialism' instead of 'God's socialism' of the Christian associations.

He started on his autobiography, which set him pondering, as he surveyed his long and industrious life, as to why he seemed to have achieved relatively little. Perhaps he was 'one of God's odd job men', he decided, an able person who could have been a first-rate lawyer, or critic, or economist or even business man, but instead he had turned his hand to what was needed at some given time. As for his politics, he thought now that he had been a new Radical and an old Conservative at the same time.

He and his wife were in their late eighties, living a quiet Darby and Joan existence, the devotion of their later years proving the success of their marriage. Ludlow's deepest fear was that he would die first and leave his wife alone, but as it happened she died in 1910 and he died a year later.

Ludlow outlived Furnivall by one year, to everyone's surprise, for the active and athletic Dr Furnivall had seemed well-nigh indestructible. The literary societies, the Working Men's College and his sculling clubs had been his life. In 1910, at the age of eighty-six, he had sculled fourteen miles on the Thames, but that was his last river feat. His strength failed him suddenly and his son, the surgeon, told him that the diagnosis was cancer of the intestine and that he had possibly a year to live. Fortunately, in view of the pain, the sentence was reduced to six months. Furnivall took the news with characteristic stoicism, telling his friends at society meetings or informing them by postcard. As had been the case with Neale, Furnivall's friends and colleagues could not accustom themselves to the prospect of his death, for he had been part of their lives for so many years.

He was always an outsize character, doing what he thought right without regard for the consequences. His presence on the Thames used to horrify the snobbish boating fraternity, partly because of his working-class companions and partly because of his shocking behaviour, especially in the locks. Even when he was last in the lock he would stand at the front of his large boat, boathook at the ready, manoeuvring it among the smaller, frailer craft already packed in, until his boat was at the front, ready for a dramatic exit. 'Never! never! must it be said that the Doctor's boat was not first out of the lock!' wrote Jessie Currie, a young artist who lived in the same house as Furnivall in Primrose Hill.

He was deaf to expostulations, threats, warnings, jeers, everything! until he stood triumphant with the bow of the boat wedged against the middle of the slimy oozing gates, waiting for the first opening movements, when he would shout 'Now'. Woe betide the unhappy individual amongst us who bungled his or her sculls in the rowlocks, as we prepared to dash out into the river again.

He was as well known in Hammersmith and West London as he was in Bloomsbury or Primrose Hill, and neither rain nor fog stopped him from his Sunday river excursions. The Hammersmith Sculling Club for Girls and Men was his favourite institution, and when his friends asked him, at the end, whether he would like to be commemorated by a scholarship to a university he answered simply: 'I want the Club'. After his death, his friends solicited donations and gave the profits of a book about him to buy the freehold of the Clubhouse, thus ensuring its continued existence.

Furnivall loved children and had a disconcerting habit of leaving his friends in the street whilst he disappeared into a sweet-shop to buy boiled sweets, usually acid drops, so that he had a supply to give to any child they might pass on the way. He used to dress up as Father Christmas in Hammersmith and hand out toys to the children, and he used the excuse of his birthdays to organise treats for the elderly poor of Hammersmith or for the deprived children of that area.

He was famous in the Working Men's College, having

returned there after Litchfield retired, and the numerous College Clubs owed much to his vitality. His interests were manifold: cricket, chess and debating; cycling, rowing and sculling; Shakespeare readings; excursions to Snowdonia and North Devon, and generally speaking, promotion of the commonroom life of the College.

The 1880s and 1890s showed a growth in the College student body with numbers remaining fairly constant at around eight hundred. College members were more interested in politics than they had been in Maurice's day, and they joined the new Socialist groups like H. M. Hyndman's Social Democratic Federation, William Morris's Socialist League or the Fabian Society. Furnivall was one of the few of the older generation of College men to join the Fabians. Sidney Webb taught political economy for a year or so at the College and sat briefly on its Executive Committee. His students were inspired to start an Economic Club, pursuing that subject outside classroom hours, and Frank Galton, a silver crest engraver who was the prime mover in founding the Economic Club, went on to become secretary to the Webbs. Later he became secretary of the London Reform Union for ten years, and from 1920 to 1939 he was general secretary of the Fabian Society. The interest in economics and social studies which the early Christian Socialists had failed to arouse became very strong in the 1890s and Tom Mann, famous for the dockers' strike, gave four lectures on social problems at the College.

The turn of the century marked a period of national expansion in adult education, and in 1903 Albert Mansbridge founded the Association to Promote the Higher Education of Working Men, soon shortened to the Workers' Educational Association. Mansbridge admitted that he owed a debt to Maurice and to Toynbee in his work with the W.E.A. Like Maurice, Mansbridge thought that education should be a thing of the spirit which would promote better understanding between social classes, and he hoped that the W.E.A. would be a kind of university for its members. The Christian Social Union strongly supported the W.E.A., whose branches and membership grew in a way which the Working Men's College movement had never done. A number of Working Men's Colleges had been set up, but only a handful survived, and of those the London Working Men's College was the only one to continue in the Maurician spirit and

with the self-governing and independent element which had been
its vital feature since its inception.

It was, of course, no accident that the burgeoning W.E.A.
coincided with a general upsurge in the labour movement and
with the start of the Labour Party, so the times were altogether
more propitious for the W.E.A. than they had been for the Working Men's Colleges. It was felt in the London College that they
had to move with the times and expand, and an appeal was
launched for a Building and Maintenance Fund to enlarge its
premises in Great Ormond Street. Everyone connected with the
College, past or present, joined in, including its recently retired
Principal, Sir John Lubbock, irreverently dubbed St Lubbock in
the College because he invented Bank Holidays, and its existing
Principal, Professor A. V. Dicey, a leading legal luminary. The
College also received bequests from past students but the real surprise present came indirectly through the generosity of the
American millionaire, W. W. Astor, who gave a munificent
donation to the Children's Hospital, adjacent to the College. That
gift enabled the hospital to make an offer for the College building,
which in turn permitted the College to commission an architect
to design a new college and to start negotiations to buy a site in
Crowndale Road, St Pancras.

Only when all of those proceedings were in train did the
College discover, typically, that its Constitution was not worded
so as to give its Corporation the legal power to sell the Great
Ormond Street site, so a special Petition had to be drawn up and
presented to the High Court to amend the College Constitution in
order to legalize the position.

On 16 July 1904, almost fifty years to the day since the
College first opened its doors in Red Lion Square, the foundation
stone of the new building was laid by the Prince of Wales, accompanied by the Princess.[6] It was a brilliant summer's afternoon
and a guard of honour was drawn up consisting of the 1st Volunteer battalion of the Royal Fusiliers, representing that Middlesex
battalion to which the College Volunteer corps had been attached.
On the platform sat St Pancras dignitaries with College members,
among them four of the original Founders—Lowes Dickinson,
Professor Westlake, Ludlow and Furnivall. Llewelyn Davies was
alive but not well enough to attend. Maurice's eldest son, Sir
Frederick Maurice, represented his dead father and Fanny

Hughes was there, representing her dead husband.

The building was completed by October 1905 in time for the Michaelmas term. Some of the College members at once complained that they missed the cosy atmosphere of the house in Great Ormond Street, although the architect had tried to incorporate memories by bringing fireplaces, pictures, books and furniture from the old building. Very soon the students and teachers found their places and Furnivall claimed one particular seat in the new commonroom, by the window opposite the door so that he could see everyone coming in.

He was still wonderfully young and adaptable in spirit despite his age, and he enjoyed repeating his provocative but deeply-held maxims on all occasions, appropriate or inappropriate. One of his favourites was: 'The three great curses of England are drink, gambling and the House of Lords!' He was a teetotaller as well as a vegetarian and had not tasted alcohol since he was fourteen. He called everybody 'My boy', no matter what their age, and he radiated cheerfulness, so much so that G. P. Gooch christened him 'the Grand Old Optimist'.

He was a lifelong champion of the working man, declaring that his place was wherever his abilities should take him. And of course women should have the vote, seeing that they bore their share of life's responsibilities. He had a fine speaking voice and great charm, with a fund of stories and recollections which almost spanned the century. He would talk about his adult experiences and struggles in the social reform movements and then recall how, as a boy, he had seen the old Duke of Wellington drive through Egham, bolt upright on his seat.

Naturally he was a famous personality in the London rowing and sculling world and was largely responsible for the foundation of the National Amateur Rowing Association in 1890. The Lea Branch of that association honoured Furnivall in 1909, on his eighty-fifth birthday, by dedicating its President Challenge Cup to him. It was Furnivall's great regret that university men who were ready to help in settlement work or would volunteer to teach for a spell at the Working Men's College seemed to forget democracy when they reached the Thames and were reluctant to join him in his struggle to overcome class distinctions on the river.

His strength and vivacity did not desert him until his last year, when he seemed to crumple. In the fastness of his scriptorium at

Oxford Dr Murray received a postcard from Furnivall announcing his illness. It gave Murray a pang. They had never been intimates in spite of being lifetime colleagues on the Dictionary. Furnivall wrote that he had hoped to see the completion of the Dictionary but it was not to be. 'Quite upset', Murray replied saying he would arrange for Furnivall to see the gigantic 'TAKE', just completed. At least Furnivall died in the secure knowledge that the Dictionary would be finished and that others would see it.

He died in July 1910 and was cremated at Golders Green. His friend, John Munro, found a quotation from Zenophon on Furnivall's study table, recently copied out, and he felt it summed up the doctor's life. 'There is no ignorance more shameful than to admit as true that which one does not understand; and there is no advantage so great as that of being set free from error. Socrates.'

It was a quotation which any one of the Christian Socialists might have endorsed.

Chapter notes

Chapter 1

1. Stephen Mayor's *The Churches and the Labour Movement*, London, 1967, devotes chapter 4 to Christian Socialism. He thinks that Maurice felt a sense of sin because the Anglican Church to which he belonged had been so remote from the needs and ambitions of the working class.

    Maurice himself said in a letter to Fenton Hort in November 1849: 'When I began in earnest to seek God for myself, the feeling that I needed a deliverer from an overwhelming weight of selfishness was the predominant one in my mind.' The Webbs rightly said in their history of trade unionism that the Christian Socialists displayed 'an almost apostolic fervour'. Their influence was seen in social reforms in the latter half of the nineteenth century.

    John Saville's article on 'The Christian Socialists of 1848' stops before the formation of the Working Men's College and the subsequent activities of members of the group. The criticism that the Christian Socialists actually prolonged poverty and suffering because by distracting the working class they inhibited them from seizing political power is impossible to prove or disprove. Lord Altringham, in *Two Anglican Essays*, London 1958, describes Maurice's preference for a society with defined orders and a monarch, and agrees that in that sense Maurice's Christian Socialism was 'the prophylactic for revolution', but he attributes the limited growth of an anti-religious workers' movement comparable to the Continental anti-clerical movements to the Nonconformist Churches rather than to the Christian Socialist group. Those Churches had strong links with the working class and provided satisfying outlets for responsible young men brought up in the chapel tradition of self-government. Those men might well prefer chapel work to trade union, co-operative or political activities exclusively. With the influx of Irish workers there was also an increase in membership of the Roman Catholic Church in England, which then provided another religious restraint on any rise of anticlericalism.

Chapter 2

1. Alec R. Vidler, *F. D. Maurice and Company*, London, 1966, suggests that the influence of Coleridge on early nineteenth-century minds could be compared to the influence of Martin Buber on early twentieth-century minds. Coleridge's ideas were a romantic and liberating reaction to the philosophers of the eighteenth-century Enlightenment. He felt the Bible had to be true because it had such a profound influence upon him.

    Maurice was impressed by Coleridge's idea that society was a unified and organic whole, whose laws and institutions should cater for man's spiritual as well as material needs. The country would be guided and led by a wide grouping which would include not only ministers of religion but also professional men and members of the liberal arts—these he called a 'clerisy'.

2. Southey was a liberal-minded man who found Oxford too traditional for his taste. He said he learned nothing there except how to swim and row. Coleridge thought that Southey at Oxford was like a 'nightingale among owls'.

3. The best source for the life of F. D. Maurice is still the two volumes of his *Life and Letters*, written by his son, Frederick Maurice, London, 1884.

Chapter 3

1. Torben Christensen's *Origin and History of Christian Socialism, 1848–1854*, Aarhus, 1962, is the best account of the movement during those six years, and it is also particularly illuminating about Maurice and Ludlow in the period preceding 1848, as well as afterwards. The fact that a Danish professor has written such a sympathetic and detailed account is not as surprising as it might seem once one remembers that towards the end of his life Ludlow was a

close friend and adviser of Harold Westergaard, who became an expert on social welfare planning and a professor in the University of Copenhagen.

Readers wishing to know more about Ludlow are referred to N. C. Masterman's biography, *John Malcolm Ludlow*, Cambridge, 1963.

2. Ludlow's Puritan ancestor was one of the regicides.
3. Ludlow graduated bachelier ès lettres of the University of Paris in July 1837 and was called to the Bar at Lincoln's Inn in November 1843.
4. Charles Henry Bellenden Ker was interesting in other respects, in addition to being a successful Whig lawyer. He overcame the disadvantage of having a famous father, supported the spread of popular education, wrote articles and designed woodcuts for the *Penny Magazine*; was a founder member of the Arundel Society; had a notable collection of orchids and wrote for the *Gardener's Chronicle*, and retired to Cannes in 1860.

Chapter 4

1. Richard Chenevix Trench, 1807 to 1886, was an Irishman educated in England who went to Trinity College, Cambridge. He belonged to the Apostles' Club and was a friend of Maurice and Sterling. His great love was literature, especially Spanish literature, and he went with General Torrijos and the Spanish liberals on the ill-fated attempt to get the King of Spain to grant a liberal constitution. Sterling had also planned to go, but he got married instead. Trench returned to England, disillusioned with politics, and decided on a career in the Anglican Church. He was a keen philologist and largely responsible for the inception of the *Oxford English Dictionary*.
2. Ludlow's article in the *Economic Review*, vol. IV, January 1894, 'Some of the Christian Socialists of 1848 and the Following Years', gives a lively account of the less famous of the young men. Several were dedicated to spelling reform—notably Furnivall, who to the end of his life would write 'lookt' for 'looked'—and their addiction to phonetics, coupled with their other quirks, gained them the name of the 'Fonetic Nuts'.

Chapter 5

1. Holyoake said of Lloyd Jones that he 'had the repute of having the best voice of any of the social lecturers, and that readiness of speech which is the common endowment of Irishmen'. Lloyd Jones was of Welsh extraction but was born in Ireland, where his grandfather had settled.

2. Although the two intellectual leaders of the Christian Socialists were Maurice and Ludlow, it was Kingsley who had the greatest influence upon young people. Kegan Paul said that he had 'a sunny joyousness, an abounding vitality, and a contagious energy which were most attractive'. He first met Kingsley in the spring of 1849, on a visit which was meant to last a day or two at the rectory, but which lengthened into weeks. He had a habit of saying quite outrageous things, to shock his hearers, and when he began by saying: 'I've *always* thought . . .' it was a sign to his intimate friends that what he really meant was: 'It's just occurred to me . . .' Kegan Paul, *Memories*.

Chapter 6

1. Walsh died prematurely. Had he lived, the bias towards public health and sanitary reform among the Christian Socialists would have been stronger. He was an active member of the Council of the Metropolitan Sanitary Association.

2. Fenton Hort was clearly fascinated by the Christian Socialists as individuals but frightened by the word 'Socialist'. Also it would have been difficult for him to have joined in their endeavours since he did not live or work in London. He remained always a devoted Maurician.

3. Charles Sully finally returned to England, not wishing his children to grow up in the United States. Ludlow found him a job as manager of a slate quarry in North Wales, and Sully became very friendly with Kingsley, under whose guidance he became a Christian.

Chapter 7

1. Edward Vansittart Neale introduced his cousin, Augustus A. Vansittart, of whom Ludlow said it was 'a great misfortune for

Augustus Vansittart to have been born rich'. He had excellent abilities, but was lazy and indecisive. He had a sense of humour and
enjoyed collecting schoolboy howlers. He was Treasurer of the
Society of Promoters.

2. E. V. Neale has never really had the recognition he deserves for his
   work in the co-operative movement. Philip N. Backstrom in *Christian Socialism and Co-operation in Victorian England*, Croom
   Helm, London, 1974, redresses the balance and provides an
   interesting portrait of the man and his work.

3. Charles E. Raven's book, *Christian Socialism 1848–1854*, London
   1968 (a reprint of the 1920 edition) is still a useful and sympathetic
   account of the group, and represents the first twentieth-century
   attempt to do justice to the Christian Socialists.

Chapter 8

1. The *Christian Socialist* runs to approximately 100,000 words, and
   although it contains a certain amount of repetition, nothing else
   quite gives that flavour and inside atmosphere of the associates, and
   their aims, friends and activities.

2. The 'earnest German student' was Victor Aimé Huber, who visited
   England in 1824, 1844, 1847 and 1854, meeting the Christian
   Socialists on the last occasion. He wrote an account of his meetings
   with them. He took a keen interest in the co-operative movement in
   Germany.

3. A. H. Louis was studying law when Ludlow met him. He eventually
   went to Australia and thence to the United States, where he became
   something of a rolling stone. He certainly never fulfilled the promise
   which Ludlow saw in him.

Chapter 9

1. Mansfield had a busy mind which was always active. As a result of
   reading a casual article about a balloon machine in Paris, he had
   visited that city in September 1850, looked into the problems, and
   returned to spend the next few months writing a long book—480
   pages—on the theoretical and practical problems of aerial naviga-
   tion. The book was an excellent example of Mansfield's innovative

imagination. He hoped, he said, that it would benefit humanity but it was to 'deliver my brain of a burden which came upon it uninvited, and which will not quit it at my bidding without receiving leave to rush into the press'. He was never content to be merely a research student, but always wanted the discoveries of science used for the advantage of mankind. Part I of his book dealt with problems of air travel and Part II with possible solutions; shape—the cigar-shape of a javelin; gas—how to produce large quantities of cheap hydrogen; propulsion—a fan-blast or centrifugal wheel.

Nor did he forget his social views. 'We are never likely to get the best of anything till co-operative experiment by picked men for the social purpose of public benefit is substituted for the competitive adventure of rival producers for private advantage.' (p.451)

His book was too much in advance of its time to be published when written, but after interest in balloon travel was aroused in the Franco-Prussian War, his brother and Ludlow prepared the manuscript for the press and it was published by Macmillan in 1877.

2. Mansfield was interested in Paraguay because there had been a revolution and the country had gained its independence from a dictator. A British embassy was set up, and Mansfield was one of the first Europeans to go there. When he returned to England, with notes for a book on that country, he first of all wrote up his 'Theory of Salts' lectures for a book.

Chapter 10

1. Maurice had frequently discussed with friends and correspondents what he thought was the meaning of the word 'eternal' in the phrase 'eternal death'. He made it quite clear always that he did not see 'eternal' as meaning 'something of very long duration' and thought the word had nothing at all to do with time. It was connected with an individual's relationship with God. The ideas in his latest collection of Essays, therefore, were certainly not new to anyone who had been following Maurice's books and articles.

Chapter 11

1. Goderich was on holiday at Pau in the Pyrenees when the College

was launched, but he sent a cheque for £25.00 with a request that he should be listed as an original member.

2. Furnivall became acquainted with the Ruskins in 1849 and thereafter regarded his friendship with John Ruskin very highly. Ruskin had been married to Effie Gray in Perth on the very Chartist day when Ludlow and Kingsley first met.

Chapter 12

1. When he heard of Hare's death, and the bequest of the library books, Fenton Hort wrote to the Rev Gerald Blunt: 'One hardly knew how one loved him till he was gone'.

2. Fenton Hort had a preview of Kingsley's *Westward Ho!* because Macmillan sent him galley sheets. He approved wholeheartedly of the new novel—'I hardly know a more *wholesome* book for anyone to read,' he told Blunt. Kingsley had recovered all 'his old energy and geniality, tempered with thorough restraint and real *Christian* wisdom'.

   He took a close interest in Kingsley's and Maurice's published works because both those men had the habit of sending Fenton Hort their manuscripts or proofs for his careful advice and correction.

3. Ruskin said of Rossetti, in *Praeterita*, that he 'was the only one of our modern painters who taught disciples for love of them'. About Ford Madox Brown, Ruskin said that he was 'an entirely worthy fellow'. Of himself, Ruskin said at his Inaugural Address at the Cambridge School of Art, 1858: 'I am never satisfied that I have handled a subject properly until I have contradicted myself at least three times.'

4. In 1855 Fenton Hort, with other Cambridge men, and assisted by Maurice, tried to set up a Working Men's College in Cambridge. It was aimed at giving a broader and more liberal education for adults than did the Mechanics' Institutes, and its list of tutors, founders and wellwishers was very impressive. It did not last however, more because of lack of students than lack of tutors.

   There was a similar attempt at Oxford, where a similar College was set up, working with the city council. Again, however, it did not last very long.

Chapter 13

1. In 1862 Furnivall spurred on the members of the Philological
    Society who were helping with the word-finding and text-copying for
    the Dictionary project: 'We have set ourselves to form a National
    Portrait Gallery, not only of the worthies, but of all the members of
    the race of English words which is to form the dominant speech of
    the world. . . . Fling our doors wide! all, all, not one, but all, must
    enter.'

2. Ruskin's *Unto This Last* sold 100,000 copies by 1910, was pirated
    in the States, and translated into French, German and Italian. A
    young lawyer in South Africa named Gandhi read the book and said
    it marked a turning-point in his life. He translated it into Gujurati,
    entitling his translation 'The Welfare of All'. The book was full of
    telling phrases, such as, 'There is no wealth but life', 'People are a
    nation's capital'. Ruskin applied ethical and practical considerations
    to economics, and thought that the future would bring abundance to
    mankind. 'Luxury is indeed possible in the future—innocent and
    exquisite; luxury for all, and by the help of all.'

    His Utopian visions were of a green and pleasant land, like
    Blake's *Jerusalem*.

Chapter 14

1. An interesting study of the Kingsley/Newman affair, taking
    Kingsley's side, is C. Egner's *Apologia pro Charles Kingsley*,
    London, 1969.

2. College journals; committee minutes; letters; J. F. C. Harrison's *A
    History of the Working Men's College, 1854–1954*, London, 1954;
    and *The Working Men's College 1854–1904*, ed. Llewelyn Davies,
    London, 1904, are the chief sources for details about the Working
    Men's College, London.

Chapter 15

1. Ripon did indeed serve on the arbitration committee which adjudged
    the *Alabama* claim.

2. At the beginning of 1872 Fenton Hort was made a Fellow of
    Emmanuel and in March that year was delighted to move to 6 St
    Peter's Terrace, Cambridge, only three doors away from where the
    Maurices were living. He was looking forward greatly to being a
    neighbour of Maurice. Unhappily Maurice, seriously ill, was taken
    to London the very day the Horts moved back to Cambridge, and he
    died in London. The Sunday after Maurice's funeral, Fenton Hort
    preached a memorial service in St Edward's Church, Cambridge.

Chapter 16

1. Mary Hughes was a leap-year baby born on 29 February 1860
    when the family was rich enough to live at 80 Park Street, Mayfair.
    She adored her father and grew up with a strong sense of duty and
    social service. In 1883 she went to act as housekeeper for her uncle,
    the Rev John Hughes, Vicar of Longcot in Berkshire, where she
    met Octavia Hill's friend, Emma Cons. When he died, her uncle left
    her enough money to live on, so she went to London to live and
    work in the East End parish of her brother-in-law, the Rev Earnest
    Carter, and her sister, Lillian Carter. The Carters went down in the
    Titanic in 1912, and she was deeply upset. Friends noticed a change
    in her. She sacrificed herself increasingly for the poor, living on
    scraps of food, never bothering about her dress.

    Nevertheless she became a famous and important figure in Bow,
    the 'Angel' of the district. She marched with the unemployed, she
    sat on councils and committees; she kept an open dosshouse for
    waifs and strays; she co-operated with Father Groser, and with
    George Lansbury, and she was not afraid to march with the
    Communists if she approved their cause. She died, still at work, in
    1941.

2. Some people felt that Furnivall was so tactless as to be a real
    mischief-maker. Dr James Murray was warned in 1873 that
    Furnivall was 'a regular sieve'. Professor Freeman once said to
    Murray: 'Put Furnivall in an asylum and I will join the Early
    English Text Society at once!'

Chapter 17

1. Lloyd Jones remained a loyal supporter of the co-operative move-

ment. He gained his living as a successful professional journalist and was, said Ludlow, 'a diligent haunter of book-stalls and second-hand bookshops'. Like Ludlow, he was forced from time to time to sell some books when money ran short. In his later years Lloyd Jones acquired such a soldierly air that he was frequently mistaken for a retired army officer. He died at seventy-five, still in harness, out canvassing in the north of England for a Parliamentary candidate.

2. William Johnson Cory was best known as the author of *Heraclitus*.

3. Irreverent young friends called Shuttleworth and Headlam 'Shuttlecock and Headlong' in tribute to their dash and energy.

4. James Clark Sherburne's *John Ruskin or the Ambiguities of Abundance*, Harvard, 1972, is very interesting in considering Ruskin's ideas by the side of those of the Christian Socialists.

5. Brantwood was a rambling cottage which already had literary and progressive associations when Ruskin purchased it. In 1852 it was the home of William Linton, poet, engraver, publisher and democrat, who let it to Gerald Massey between 1858 and 1864. Ruskin paid Linton £1500 for it in 1871.

6. On the College centenary in 1954 there was a visit by Queen Elizabeth II. In 1972, the anniversary of Maurice's death, the occasion was marked not only by 'his' College but also by Lincoln's Inn, King's College and Queen's College, in London, as well as by other remembrances elsewhere.

Select Bibliography

ADDERLEY, JAMES G., *In Slums and Society*, London, 1916

BUBER, MARTIN, *Paths to Utopia*, London, 1949

BRIGGS, ASA, *Chartist Studies*, London, 1978

BROSE, OLIVE, *Frederick Denison Maurice. Rebellious Conformist*, Ohio, 1971

COLLINGWOOD, W. G., *Life of John Ruskin*, London, 1900

COLLOMS, BRENDA, *Charles Kingsley*, London, 1975

COOPER, THOMAS, *Life of Thomas Cooper*, London, 1872

COOPER, THOMAS, *The Purgatory of Suicides*, London, 1847

DEARMER, PERCY, Fabian Tracts No. 133, *Socialism and Christianity*, London, 1907

FESTSCHRIFT FOR FREDERICK JAMES FURNIVALL on his 75th Birthday, London, 1900

FURNIVALL, FREDERICK JAMES, *A Volume of Personal Record*, Oxford, 1911

GAMMAGE, R. C., *History of the Chartist Movement, 1837–1854*, London, 1976

GRAVES, CHARLES L., *Life and Letters of Alexander Macmillan*, London, 1910

GREENING, O. E., *The Co-operative Traveller Abroad*, London, 1888

HARRISON, AUSTIN, *Frederic Harrison: Thoughts and Memories*, London, 1927

HARRISON, FREDERIC, *John Ruskin*, London, 1913

HEADLAM, STEWART, Fabian Tracts No. 42, *Christian Socialism*, London, 1892

HEARNSHAW, F. J. C., *The Centenary History of King's College, London*, London, 1929

HOBHOUSE, ROSA, *Mary Hughes*, London, 1949

HOLYOAKE, GEORGE JACOB, *History of Co-operation in England*, London, 1908

HOLYOAKE, GEORGE JACOB, *Sixty Years of an Agitator's Life*, London, 1892

INGLIS, K. S., *Churches and the Working Classes in Victorian England*, London, 1963

JONES, BENJAMIN, *Co-operative Production*, Oxford, 1894

JONES, PETER D'A., *The Christian Socialist Revival, 1877–1914*, Princeton, 1968

KENDALL, GUY, *Charles Kingsley and His Ideas*, London, 1947

LECHEVALIER, J. L. ST. ANDRÉ, *Five Years in the Land of Refuge*, London, 1854

LITCHFIELD, RICHARD BUCKLEY, *A Memoir*, Cambridge, 1910

MARTIN, HUGH, *Christian Social Reformers of the Nineteenth Century*, London, 1927

MASSEY, GERALD, *The Ballad of Babe Christabel and other Poems*, London, 1854

MASSEY, GERALD, *Poetical Works*, London, 1861

MASTERMAN, C. F. G., *Leaders of the Church. Frederick Denison Maurice*, London, 1907

MAURICE, EDMUND, *The Life of Octavia Hill*, London, 1913

PAUL, C. KEGAN, *Biographical Sketches*, London, 1883

REARDON, B. M. G., *From Coleridge to Gore. A Century of Religious Thought in Britain*, London, 1971

REDFERN, PERCY, *The Story of the C.W.S., 1863–1913*, Manchester, n.d.

ROSENBERG, JOHN D., *The Darkening Glass*, London, 1963

RUSKIN, JOHN, *The Diaries of John Ruskin*, ed. Evans, J. and Whitehouse, J. H., Oxford, 1958

SMITH, WARREN SYLVESTER, *The London Heretics*, London, 1967

WOLF, LUCIEN, *The Life of the First Marquess of Ripon*, London, 1921

Index